School Reform in a Global Society

School Reform in a Global Society

William E. Segall

ROWMAN & LITTLEFIELD PUBLISHERS, INC.
Lanham • Boulder • New York • Toronto • Oxford

ROWMAN & LITTLEFIELD PUBLISHERS, INC.

Published in the United States of America
by Rowman & Littlefield Publishers, Inc.
A wholly owned subsidary of The Rowman & Littlefield Publishing Group, Inc.
4501 Forbes Boulevard, Suite 200, Lanham, Maryland 20706
www.rowmanlittlefield.com

PO Box 317
Oxford
OX2 9RU, UK

British Library Cataloguing in Publication Information Available

Library of Congress Cataloging-in-Publication Data

Segall, William E. (William Edwin), 1938–
   School reform in a global society / William E. Segall.
     p. cm.
   Includes bibliographical references and index.
   ISBN-13: 978-0-7425-2460-6 (cloth : alk. paper)
   ISBN-10: 0-7425-2460-4 (cloth : alk. paper)
   ISBN-13: 978-0-7425-2461-3 (pbk. : alk. paper))
   ISBN-10: 0-7425-2461-2 (pbk. : alk. paper)
 1. Educational change—Social aspects—United States. 2. Education and
globalization—United States. 3. Neoliberalism—United States. 4. Educational
change–Social aspects—Cross-cultural studies. I. Title.
LC191.4.S43 2006
306.43'2—dc22   2005027290

Printed in the United States of America

∞™ The paper used in this publication meets the minimum requirements of
American National Standard for Information Sciences—Permanence of Paper for
Printed Library Materials, ANSI/NISO Z39.48-1992.

To my wife,
Nedra

Contents

Preface

The last time Americans focused on school reform for social change was not in the United States, but in Japan. The time was 1946 and the purpose of educational reform was to change Japanese values. That empire had been, until the previous year, the mortal foe of the United States. Its society and its civil and military institutions were based on classism and militarism. Its emperor was worshiped as a god, public parliamentary debate was unheard of, popular disagreement through media was disallowed, and social discourse, even the least noxious, was not sanctioned. Yet, the most striking feature of Japanese society in 1946 was that few Japanese believed these restrictions to be socially or politically harmful. Nonetheless, it was important to the United States in those beginning days of the Cold War that Japan become the nation's trusted Asian ally.

The question most asked at the time, even by those instituting the reforms, was whether they would work. Could Japanese citizens embrace a society unlike any they had ever known? Could American-imposed civil and military institutions survive in a society historically committed to conservative values and structures? Would Japan become a democracy?

History tells us that the answers to these questions are yes. Within the life histories of the World War II generation, Japan regained its economic (now capitalistic) equilibrium and composed for itself an affordable standard of living while containing its military and enhancing its civil institutions. In short, by the turn of the millennium Japan had presented itself to the global community as a liberal democracy, an economic giant, and a trusted ally of the United States.

What has this to do with neoliberalism's reform of American schools? The imposed Japanese reforms taught neoliberal educational reformers something that few pay attention to today yet is profound: *Those who control schools govern societies.* That means schools have the ability to construct and conduct the social conversations about critical issues that affect our daily lives and the lives of those around us.

As globalization becomes the economic and social hallmark in this cross-millennial age, democracies are once again being threatened, but now from within. Unlike the traditional (and more recognizable) threats from totalitarian states such as that posed by mid-twentieth-century Imperial Japan, today's threats are couched in class and capitalism. It may sound strange to target an economic philosophy that is part of our social fabric, but I am not referring to that type of capitalism with which we have our daily experiences. Rather, I mean that raw, unbridled form of capitalism that was predominant during the Victorian period, which, without social controls, created the exorbitant wealth enjoyed by a handful of investors from the sweat of laborers. I am referring to that time of the robber barons when money and wealth replaced title and privilege as the measures of social rank.

Usually when educators talk about school reform, they are voicing their interest in improving classroom instruction and student learning. Reform for many teachers is an action word. But the reform movement in today's schools is not like those they have grown accustomed to. This reform movement is like that instituted by Americans in Japan half a century ago—with the difference that that effort was aimed at the democratization of a nation whereas this one is aimed at creating a class society based on unbridled capitalism. That is why we are witnessing the dismantling of the traditional school in favor of another that is privatized, therefore more competitive, less diverse, and more restrictive. Today's students are less likely than were their parents were to be welcomed into schools to learn about democracy and to experience a pluralist society. Instead, they are, depending on their life histories, often tolerated and shackled by the No Child Left Behind Act. In sum, what neoliberals learned from the Japanese postwar experience is if they want to reform American society, schools are the key to their success. Those who fear for their democracy and the education of their children have yet to learn who their adversaries are.

At the beginning of this research, my efforts focused solely on neoliberal educational reform. Even though we never wavered from that task, I was quickly reminded of what neoliberals had already learned—that schools do not exist in vacuums. They are part of society—influencing and being influenced by ideas, peoples, and events. That is why this discussion of neoliberal school reform is presented in such bright, broad strokes. Real schools must be painted in real colors, showing their development and challenges in this country and other lands. Schools are tangible, and to understand them it is important to talk about how they change students and the societies in which they live. Looking anew, we will also see how neoliberals are creating a different world in which they want us to live.

I would like to thank many students and colleagues for their interest in this project. Especially, I would like to thank Dr. Nedra Segall who took time from her professional responsibilities to read and comment on various parts of the text. Her insights were significant to the text's completion.

The copyright of the poem "America the Beautiful" quoted in chapter 2 was given to the American people by Katherine Lee Bates in 1923. Rudyard Kipling's poem "The White Man's Burden" in chapter 7 first appeared in the February 12, 1899, issue of *McClure's Magazine*. The poem "Eyes to Your Soul," also in chapter 7, is copyrighted by Kelly John Rose. It was written in 2001.

1

Reflections of a Different America: Surviving Ideology

Change is difficult. Sometimes welcomed, but often not, it represents transitions for peoples and societies alike. In its disruption, it disciplines, compelling us to see ourselves afresh—as if to look in a mirror for the first time. Our images can prompt us to recognize new opportunities. Or those reflections may give us feelings of foreboding about the future. Not fitful or intermittent, they are continuous and encompass societies, institutions, and the very people themselves. These are the images that spark reform.

Sometimes this reform is reactive and not creative. It may not challenge or demand responses to change. Engendered by nostalgia for a time past when life was simple and people were safe, it may be regressive. This is the nirvana that neoliberals hunger for but cannot achieve. They cannot return to that time past until American society is reformed and schools become agents of purity. The purpose of this book is to explore and learn why this is so.

The focus of this introductory chapter is to acquaint ourselves with these images, positioning them within the global turmoil change has created, and to learn who the neoliberals are.

GLOBAL SCHISMS: IMPRESSIONS OF THE MODERN WORLD

Traveling the world, His Holiness the Dalai Lama writes about his impressions of contemporary life. He fled Tibet in 1959 at the age of nineteen when the Chinese Communists invaded his homeland. He tells his readers that, although he is somewhat new to the modern-day world, it is this experience, uncluttered with Western life, that allows him to form impressions of people

1

and understand their innermost life stories. Certainly not naive, his insights show us the Dalai Lama is sympathetic and a sophisticated learner as he observes modernity and life in the new millennium.

> Everywhere, by all means imaginable, people are striving to improve their lives. Yet, strangely, my impression is that those living in the materially developed countries . . . are in some ways less satisfied, are less happy, and to some extent suffer more than those living in the least developed countries. Indeed, if we compare the rich with the poor, it often seems that those with nothing are, in fact, the least anxious, though they are plagued with physical pains and suffering. As for the rich, while a few know how to use their wealth intelligently—that is to say, not in luxurious living but by sharing it with the needy—many do not. They are so caught up with the idea of acquiring still more that they make no room for anything else in their lives. In their absorption, they actually lose the dream of happiness, which riches were to have provided.[1]

It is his impression, he says, that there is an intense global division among the world's peoples so profound that it overshadows those separations created by political and theological ideologies. The consequences of this division, now suffered throughout the world, he believes, are even greater than those precipitated by globalization with its obscene portioning of wealth. The division is elusive, he says, and not seen by most people because they are its participants, living their own personal tragedies. It is left for those who witness the unfolding of these human dramas to have the opportunity to understand the essence of this global separation.

While His Holiness will eventually draw his readers to conclusions, understanding why ethics is important in their search for personal happiness, it is the modernity he treats as a backdrop that is important for us in this investigation of neoliberal education reform. Even though I will spend considerable time tracing modernity's history in the next chapter and elsewhere in the text, we now can situate neoliberalism within the global division to which the Dalai Lama refers.

This is what neoliberals believe they have learned about global society. They understand the significance of the Dalai Lama's impressions. It is true, they say, that the global schism of which he speaks is also reflected in American society. But, they are unimpressed with his thoughts about ethics. Instead, they believe this schism is caused by immigrants entering the United States from Third World countries and is actively causing American society to become more diverse and less pure. Neoliberals allege this division is nothing more than a social barometer that measures immigrants' mediocrity. Their Third World personal histories and religions are threatening the traditional schools' Protestant values and curriculum and they are even threatening the schools' historic role of supplying laborers to the world of work.

They are weakening society's commitment to capitalism and assaulting the remnants of Victorian classism. Let us look at this neoliberal conundrum from another perspective.

Vulnerability's Sentiments: The Ideology of Social Deconstruction

Regardless of the sentiments they express, we must not discredit neoliberals' place within the global schism the Dalai Lama mentions. During recent decades, neoliberals have echoed the widespread concern in the United States about the quality of Americans' lives.[2] Like others in other societies of which the Dalai Lama writes, this American generation now pictures its future differently than its parents and grandparents did. Then, people were taught and brought up in families to envision their future as an absolute in which work, wealth, and community values were analogous with economic security and personal happiness. We can understand why these were this generation's convictions, neoliberals contend. They formed the social consensus that changed slowly, almost imperceptibly, within an international context.

However, these certainties are now being globally redefined, causing the present generation to witness unprecedented social upheavals. Growing more sensitive to continued technical, economic, and social disruptions, neoliberals insist people now should distrust social institutions that, within living memory, were considered sacrosanct and unchanging. Not surprisingly today, many parents, like the neoliberals around them, fear that their children will live in the same confusion they see about them, and that that once inviolable institution, the school, will fail to protect them.

Nevertheless, the upheavals experienced by this American generation are not isolated occurrences. In fact, in many developed countries, there is a deep-seated fear that social institutions, especially the traditional tax-supported school, will not protect the next generation. This is prompting educational reformers both within governments and outside of them to acknowledge the urgency of change by mimicking neoliberal educational reforms. Even the expressions of social vulnerability Americans believe unique to them are now voiced globally. Globalization has socially disenfranchised large numbers of young peoples in developing nations. Unable to work, they join the unsufferable poor, becoming more destitute, without food, schooling, and medicine. They watch their nations' wealthy elite become wealthier. Yet, the governments from whom they expect help are unable to assist because raw international capitalism has stripped them of their own financial resources. The impoverished governments, trapped by international loans to aid in their national development, are unable to provide for their own citizens.

This is the international plight, the terror, which neoliberals think they understand, even though they are not paying attention to the human costs of the global capitalism they parented. They imagine they are immune to its so-cial inequities. This is why neoliberals describe the international movements of peoples, not the *free-market economy*, as the cause of America's social pollution. Thinking they are the first ever to witness the massive changes in gender roles, disurbanization, family styles, morality, values, and work, they are appalled by the social upheavals these have engendered.

But, change is not new for Americans. During transition periods, they have traditionally expressed sentiments similar to those heard during the past several decades. Sometimes labeling these periods "social revolutions" or "awakenings," as we will learn in later chapters, Americans respond to them by looking inward to their institutions for answers. However, the sig-nificance of this specific social revolution is that neoliberals do not believe existing social institutions can help them. In fact, neoliberals, as I have men-tioned, believe the existing institutions are part of the problem. These, say neoliberals, are reflections of a corrupt or immoral society. In the name of re-form, to combat this corruption, neoliberals threaten to dismantle govern-ment social programs, arguing that public schools be reserved for the poor while the wealthy and middle class attend other schools controlled by peo-ple like them.

Reform: Fearing the Future

Let us look deeper and more specifically at neoliberals' dissatisfaction with the school. Rear Adm. Bill Rowley, who used a popular saying from Yogi Berra—The future is not what it used to be—as the title of a 1995 arti-cle,[3] draws the reader's attention to the extraordinary changes that have taken place during the past half-century. He notes that when he was grow-ing up in the 1950s he knew (along with everyone else during that time, he says) what the 1990s would be like: Robots would be mothers' helpers in the home, and fathers would travel to work in helicopters. The time parents saved, he said, would allow them more leisure time to spend with their chil-dren. Of course, he was wrong. None of his forecasts about that decade ma-terialized.

Yet, as those who have lived in both decades recall, Rowley was cor-rect from another vantage point. Change may not have resulted in robots in the home and highways in the sky, but technological advancements did occur as he expected. In fact, technology became the central feature of the 1990s even though it was different than what captivated the mid-century meanderings of a bright young mind. And, while Rowley in mid-twentieth-century America had not thought that technological change could affect society, he discovered that social values changed because of it. Admiral Rowley no longer could assume, as he had in his younger days, that fam-ily structures would remain the same. How else then, as a young man, could he picture a late twentieth-century America other than mothers remaining in the home and fathers working in an office or factory? His understandings of gender roles were completely modified in this case. At century's end, mothers were less prone to be stay-at-home moms, while fathers were more prone to home duties and child care. And, as both fathers and mothers learned new gender roles, they were also discovering the virtualness of the home computer and the Internet. This is significant, says Rowley. It is more than the inventions themselves we must understand; it is society's interpretation of them. These are the continued frustrations over which neoliberals anguish. They feel powerless, their personal futures less predictable.

Now we see what His Holiness the Dalai Lama is referring to when he writes of his impressions of the global schisms. He is talking about peoples' suffering, and that is why neoliberals are afraid (or unable) to strive for happiness, the very condition for life itself. This is the terror-filled life in which neoliberals find themselves. To their consternation, these are the good old days. They will remember them simply because these frustrations lack the complexity, measured against future global expectations.

OLD WINE IN NEW WINESKINS

Admiral Rowley's prediction of the present time becoming the good old days is exciting to consider. Change is not capricious, and that is why he marvels at its social consequence as much as the inventions that foster it. Focusing on the social dynamics of change—that is, the relationship between inventions and society—Rowley writes how life will become more orderly for some but more chaotic for others. From this, he theorizes that social change (caused by the information revolution) will allow individuals to become more involved in the governing process while allowing government to relinquish some tasks simply because of technology's increased sophistication. He refers to this as "direct democracy."[4]

Voicing their terror of the future, neoliberals insist that if Rowley's direct democracy becomes a reality, American society will degenerate. In fact, they argue, this is already happening. Those individuals who participate in a direct democracy are not all part of the nation's traditional European heritage. Many of them, new to the nation, represent different cultures that espouse non-Protestant beliefs and value different economic systems. They are not all proponents of capitalism and competition. Many of them, neoliberals believe, do not pay taxes, yet expect government to award them political and economic freedoms—even hand them a free education. These people want government to meddle with capitalism, to restrain businesses from creating profits, while expecting them to carry large tax burdens. This is socialism, say neoliberals, not the society they believe America once was or should be. Society is not intended to be progressive, say neoliberals. Government is based on capitalism, not on multitudes as Rowley and others like him think. The nation should distance itself from these demands. Individuals should be given the responsibility (freedom) to achieve their desires themselves. Individuals should compete for their personal futures, not expect others to give it to them.

This is the neoliberals' platform. Theirs is the twenty-first-century translation of Adam Smith's (1723–1790) and David Ricardo's (1772–1823) capitalist theories explaining the economic interplay among wealth, labor, and resources. Proposing those capitalist notions, these philosophers favored a class society rather than either an aristocracy or its opposite, democracy. They believed that societies should reflect capitalism in which individuals are free to compete.[5] If anything, they are classic liberals, favoring a society much like that described in the U.S. Constitution *without the Bill of Rights*. They want a government with minimum powers and schools committed to unregulated capitalism. Said otherwise by philosopher John Dewey, they favor a society in which individuals compete without protection from political degradation or economic exploitation.[6]

This is the seed bed of discontent from which we will explore neoliberal school reform. It is the conflict between two perceptions of school and society—one in which schools are the bastion against tyranny, the other one in which the free-market economy is the defense against social impurity. It is classic liberalism's capitalist philosophies woven into the neoliberal ideologies of its contemporary apostles Milton Friedman and Robert Fogel, not the multilateralism of Dewey and diplomat Joseph Nye Jr.

WHAT'S IN A WORD?

It is interesting during periods of social debate how words sometimes change their definitions or become social flags that arouse passions, sentiments, and assumptions which may be as diverse as those who spoke the word. This is especially true of the terms "neoliberal" and "liberal." Other terms such as *conservative* and *neoconservative* also share word histories that take on different hues depending on who speaks them or the audience that hears them. While this may appear confusing, we know that some terms share common histories in which one becomes the outgrowth of another. Interestingly, even though the definitions and connotations of the terms *neoliberal* and *liberal* change, their meanings constantly remain opposites.

This is not the history of the word *indigenous*. Its past is laden with cultural overtones, stereotyping good from evil, civilized from uncivilized, and intelligent from ignorant. It is a word that Protestantism and capitalism use to label others they do not understand. Unlike the terms mentioned earlier, this one remains constant. It is defined to mean diversity. Whereas the others may simply describe it, this term encompasses a third dimension that the other words do not. It is less the task of this word to act the role of the adjective as it is the commanding function of the noun.

Definitions: *Neoliberalism*

Neoliberalism is a relatively new term, becoming popular among scholars in the last decades of the twentieth century. It is now used by education researchers in many countries as they investigate the social and educational consequences of globalization. The term as they use it depicts dark attitudes about capitalist unilateralism practiced by corporations and international agencies and organizations. It is meant to infer cultural elitism, especially in the sense of social betterment and educational superiority. In some cases it also means colonialism but not in the traditional meaning such as we remember the British Empire. Instead, it is thought of as economic in the old Soviet fear of imperial domination.

Recently, the term *neoliberal* has been coupled with the word *unilateral* (usually associated with neoconservatives). In this case it implies cultural exploitation reminiscent of Christian knights attacking Jerusalem during the Crusades. The most vulgar definition of the term is expressed as an image of the World Trade Center.

Here in the United States, the term *neoliberal* is seldom heard or used. In fact, while the word is sometimes voiced by scholars, it has yet to enter education's vocabulary or the popular language of the street. To make the point clear, I suspect there are many neoliberals in this country who would be incensed if someone labeled them thusly. They do not want to be confused with those they hate the most, whom they call "liberal," even though that was what they once were.

Still, the term *neoliberal* has not matured into a single definition in this country. It lacks an agreed definitional thread to allow it to cross scholarly disciplines, even as it seems to satisfy the concerns of some about social and economic consequences of globalization, for example. With this understood, I define the term *neoliberal* to mean this century's reiteration of nineteenth-century classic liberalism with its focus on rampant capitalism and an untethered free-market economy. Neoliberals are, and as we will learn later, fundamentalists. They are found throughout society's institutions: economics, religion, governments, and schools. Their present purpose is to aggressively create a class society supported by raw capitalism and enhanced by a competitive school system.

American scholars sometimes compare *neoliberal* with other terms, especially *conservative* and *neoconservative*, suggesting they are related. Leaving the topic for discussion later in this chapter, I believe there is a joining of these terms. For example, as I will mention later, conservatives (and neoconservatives) generally agree with neoliberal educational policies, even though they approach these issues from different directions. The significant difference between them is that the conservatives are not terrified of the future (as are neoliberals). Even so, the point must be made that neoliberals, like these other classifications, are fundamentalists, wanting to purify society, and the institution they consider essential to their success is the American school.[7]

Definitions: *Liberalism*

While the term *neoliberal* has remained somewhat hidden from educational scholars in the United States, its opposite, *liberal*, has been the center of major controversy. *Liberal*, as used by neoliberals and others who share the trauma of educational reform, spells a strange mixture of feelings, attitudes, and definitions. Many in education's front line (teachers, administrators, and local school board members) misunderstand the term because of the heat generated by the neoliberal reform debate. Some, but mostly neoliberals as explained in chapters 7 and 8, have substituted the definition of *licentious* to mean *liberal*.[8] We will watch this term act as a neoliberal label for social impurity and educational mediocrity—the classic argument of those who advance a class society.

While neoliberals are committed to creating a class society in which there are clear economic demarcations among peoples, liberals want a society in which economic divisions among peoples are blurred. That is why neoliberal society is based on the social unilateralism of economists such as Milton Friedman, while liberal societies, speaking to the social inclusivity voiced by John Dewey, are multilateral. Pointedly, Friedman wants school reform so it will educate a quality workforce and increase corporate profits, while Dewey's thoughts are designed to educate students to manage their lives in conjunction with others. In other words, Dewey's school is democratic while Friedman's is investor centered.

To be clear about liberalism, it is that society which encourages individuals to become responsible decision makers, knowing their well-being rests in the community and their success impacts everyone's future. Liberal schools, with their curriculum centered on problem solving, foster a classless society. Students learn to be leaders and independent while practicing the process of democracy. Within this, students learn how to compete in a capitalist economy, barred from exploitation and the caveat emptorship (let the buyer beware) of unscrupulous capitalists.

Definitions: *Conservativism* and *Neoconservativism*

Let us now turn our attention to conservatives and neoconservatives within the neoliberal–liberal argument. I remind readers that conservatives and neoconservatives, and their sometimes partners neoliberals, share some overarching commonalities. This is partly because they either have shared similar histories, are the products of the other, or are redefined after meeting specific social needs in the past (as was the case of conservativism in the late Victorian period). It is possible, therefore (although confusing to the uninitiated), for neoliberals, conservatives, and neoconservatives to agree on school reform. That is why it is important to reiterate that, regardless of the particular fundamentalist ideology, school reformers voice neoliberal dogma. And, in this study, I do not distinguish between one label and the other simply because I am more interested in their neoliberal expressions.

To make the point, both conservatives and neoconservatives accept neoliberal educational reform doctrine not so much because of their capitalist heritage or visions of social impurity but because of their views on lessening federal government involvement in individuals' lives. On the other hand, neoliberals pointedly focus on reforming schools by using the power of the federal government. Said another way, while conservatives generally want parents to be the final arbiter of their children's education (using tax credits and vouchers), neoliberals, through high-stakes testing, want schools to meet the federal standards set in the No Child Left Behind Act.[9]

Now that we see the tangled connections between conservatives and neoliberals, we can understand the conservatives' views about capitalism and classism. Even though conservatives voice support for the free-market economy, it is less an article of faith for them than it is for neoliberals. Just as conservatives and neoliberals have intricate philosophic relations, so do they have with neoconservatives. While conservatives, like their neoliberal cousins, portray themselves as reformers, their philosophic emphases differ on such issues as globalization and a strong national defense. It is not so much that one thinks the other wrong; rather, it is that the former favors an American cultural global presence while the latter views America's global presence in a benign nationalistic mode.

Believing the United States is the globe's sole superpower, neoconservatives reckon the nation to be a model empire builder, especially in the Middle East. Neoconservatives, like neoliberals, are unilateralists. In this case, however, they are reforming nations while neoliberals are reforming schools. In some ways, although cynical, neoliberals and some conservatives agree with neoconservatives on school funding. They believe more public monies should be spent on a strong military and less on schools—assuming schools are privatized.

I will quickly state that we should not assume that conservatives are out of place or have nothing to contribute to school reform conversations. Conservative dogma, beyond that in which it agrees with that of neoliberals, should be discussed. Yet conservatives remain focused on themselves, unable to forget their historic defense of aristocracy two centuries ago. They lost their argument with classic liberals, neoliberals' inheritance, when the classic liberals became the Victorian economic and social champion.

It is perhaps this tangled history that causes some not to distinguish between the various conservative and neoliberal ideologies. They hear a calliope of criticisms about twentieth-century liberal pollution from neoliberals and those who flaunt different labels. Together, these economic fundamentalists, social elitists, school reformers, and political and theological minimalists are but the same representations of neoliberal ideology.

Definitions: *Indigenous*

> The next night, two hours after midnight, with a full moon, Juan Rodriguez Bermejo, also known as Rodrigo de Triana, a sailor from Seville on the Pinta, saw a white stretch of land [una cabeza blanca de tierra] and shouted, "Land! Land!" and he fired a lombard. The next day, October 12, Columbus made Landfall.[10]

This was not the first time Europeans had sailed to faraway shores, nor was it the first time they saw peoples unlike themselves. The difference between those earlier times and this in 1492 is that Europeans recorded their day-to-day sentiments and observations of others over a long period of time. What did Columbus and his fellow sailors say about these peoples he called "Indians"? He reported they were a simple people giving gifts of parrots, javelins, and cotton balls to him.

Of course, Columbus and his explorer colleagues viewed the world in simple terms, too. The world Columbus saw was divided into two parts: people like him and Others. He distinguished Europeans from each other (Columbus was from Genoa). Because Protestantism would not emerge until after his death, Catholicism, to Columbus, was just another word for Christianity. It was logical for him to consider Jews and Muslims as Others, and therefore evil.[11] That is why Columbus assumed the simple people he first met would be the template of others he would meet. They would all be the same.

This insular approach, learning about others, should be understood for what it was. Columbus considered himself and those he represented to be elite and masters of civilization. They were like the Greeks before him, he thought. Just as they labeled others who did not speak Greek "barbarians," he labeled those he met in the Caribbean "simple," never once thinking that the beads he gave might have been considered by them inferior products. Columbus was comfortable basing his elite culture's labels on others: primitives, savages, uncivilized and simple people. These words, along with the word *indigenous*, were the labels of invasion and colonization.

During the last century, the definition of *indigenous* has been modified. Striving to remove its colonial stigma, the term has gained an element of respect through formal definitions by international organizations such as the United Nations. In this case, the term refers to peoples who have cultural and social histories that are reflective of those that existed before colonialism. I understand the difficulty this definition holds for societies that define their histories differently: they conflict with others' views of their cultural universe.

Recognizing the traps these stereotypes present the unwary definitional traveler, I view the term to be less value-laden than that offered by the United Nations. It is presented here value-free to represent a world composed of diverse cultures and societies that speak about the meaning of their lives. In this investigation of neoliberal educational reform, *indigenous* is used as a foundational term upon which schools' purposes are best explained. It is that preservative term that when used in education means "curriculum."

To return to Columbus's simple people, he misunderstood them. When his simple people first met these strange-looking others who came from afar, they were afraid. But soon they assessed them within their own cultural and social context and then willingly went to war.[12]

SCHOOLS: NEOLIBERALISM'S GLOBAL CULTURE CLASH

Now that we know who the neoliberals are and the global society in which they live, we are more understanding, but less sympathetic, of their temperament. To them, the globe is full of change, technological revolutions, and social disequilibriums. As mentioned, it is a terror-filled world for these fundamentalists. In this book we will watch them become disgruntled with social crises they do not understand and listen to the reasons they think liberals threaten society. We will follow them as they search nostalgically for a time when diversity and mediocrity were not in the United States. Expressing Protestant values, these people search for an American nirvana, minimally governed and class structured. They seek that society in which parents know their children's future and each and all compete in a free-market economy. It is that society where schools will reflect values adults and children accept as truth, a society where schools educate lower-class boys and girls for the world of work while the children of the investor class learn about wealth and profit.

Did the nirvana the neoliberals long for ever exist? Or is it simply a pipe dream, a figment of their imagination, of some who cry for silence in a noisy world? Of course the answer, now that we have been introduced to neoliberalism, is more complex than a simple yes or no. It is clear in their minds that their nirvana did exist. They describe it as that period in the United States and Europe when classism defined society. It was when unfettered capitalism was the engine of the British Empire and the American "robber barons." It was that time before the age of social responsibility, the social concerns of David Riis, and the educational philosophy of John Dewey. It was when Victorian raw capitalism, dressed in elitism and classism, was the norm.

How, or where, did the nirvana for which neoliberals hunger begin? Although it was not at first called Victorianism, its seeds were planted at that social and economic moment when Europe and the rest of the world met. It was a struggle with violent clashes among societies, peoples, and values—much like that between Columbus and his simple people—that has yet to stop. It was a global campaign for Protestant, economic, and cultural domination of indigenous peoples in which schools, unexpectedly to some, became a recognized force sponsoring infant capitalism and its Protestant values.

Yet, liberal capitalists, the neoliberals' forebears, never thought accommodation was their responsibility when colonial domination proved uneconomic. The struggle for dominance continued into the twentieth century, culminating in globalization in its last decades.[13] The horns of the dilemma—to reconcile indigenous cultures with international capitalism—created a period in the twentieth century when newly independent countries tried to reform their schools. Yet, their reforms failed. None were able to develop a school curriculum that taught children their culture while learning how to compete in a free-market economy. In fact, some countries first attracted to capitalist utopias eventually rejected them in favor of other curricula. Some national school reforms simply collapsed, while others, their economies held hostage, succumbed to capitalism, parroting capitalist curricula. Even as indigenous educational reforms were being played out, capitalist formal schools were introduced to compete with theirs.

Much of the capitalists' reluctance to accept indigenous educational systems is still played out in the lives of peoples throughout the world. For millions, their personal lives are illustrations of the Dalai Lama's schism. They are caught in a quandary. Some, thinking the capitalist utopia was a dream come true, turned their backs on their cultural histories, only to discover the dream had become a nightmare. Forcing themselves, or being lured, young people learned in their formal schools the capitalist curriculum. Now, living their lives in capitalist cultures, disenfranchised by family and friends at home, they exist, ignored by those who educated them to hate their culture.

Neoliberal refusal to express some form of accommodation has proven offensive to most. Even in the United States, neoliberal judgments of minorities and immigrants have created economic underclasses separating poverty from wealth. At the same time, other nations' reactions are expressed in school reforms focusing not on capitalism but on curricula heralding Islam and other non-Christian theologies. And, neoliberal judgments have caused others to band together, forming their own economic and political platforms for school reform.

Why will neoliberals not accommodate others' schools, schools that do not base their beliefs on competition and oppose the free-educational-market economy? They are the schools that view teachers as professionals whose vision it is to create a classless community in which all, even the mediocre, participate. These are the evidences of socialism, say neoliberals, not capitalism. In these types of societies, investors are socially weak and a free-market economy will fail.

But in some ways these reasons are secondary to neoliberal unilateralism. Central to their view of education reform is that issues of great importance should be dealt with, using the hard reality of economics. To include other cultures in the decision-making process is a demonstration of weakness. Multilateralism diverts neoliberalism from its goal of reforming schools and creating a pure society for which it hankers.

A LAST WORD

While this book was written about neoliberals and school reform, I do not want you to think it is centered on economics, even though great attention has been paid to it. Certainly, some economists will take issue with some of my explanations of economic theories and philosophies, for that is as it should be in a book such as this. It is the same with the descriptions of the free-market economy. Just as educational philosophy is influenced by economic issues in this country, so it is in the broad avenue of international relations.

One problem in understanding neoliberal educational reform is that some researchers view it only within contemporary and local settings. But, the dramatic impact of neoliberal educational reform can be better understood by viewing it within its long-term global context. To make the point, the next five chapters of the text will explore the reforms' international influence before we investigate neoliberalism's American consequences. This is how neoliberalism should be understood: it is a rearticulation of classic capitalist assumptions set within educational theory. Neoliberalism is broad and is sparking international debate in fields other than education, including government and theology. It is reexplaining the elementary capitalist theories of supply and demand as if they were new, revolutionary ideas. Less obvious, however, are the neoliberal reexplanations, especially those of Smith and Ricardo (and many others, as well), who also advance notions of classism. It is not that classless societies existed before classic liberalism.

It is because their form of classism is based on raw, uninhibited capitalism. We last experienced that form of society earlier in our cultural lives. It was during the days of the robber barons. We refer to it as "Victorianism."

It may be obvious by now that classic liberalism and its neoliberal inheritors are not conspicuous supporters of democracy. In fact, during the Victorian period, classic liberals thought democracy (they called it "mobocracy") was a sign of social collapse. They feared their political and social powers and wealth would be drained from them by governments voted into office by the unwashed laboring classes. Is it difficult for us to sympathize with classic liberals who believed owning wealth was evidence of social superiority even when the majority of the people disagreed?

Finally, a variety of words have been used to make our point. For example, the word *capitalist* and its various adjectives (such as *raw capitalism* and *uninhibited capitalism*) are used to remind the reader of neoliberalism's classic liberalism. In the same regard, I emphasize the critical differentiation between *liberal* and *neoliberal* and use terms such as *free-market economy* and *free marketplace* to mean international capitalism and globalization. Similarly, the term *free-education-market economy* highlights the playing field upon which neoliberals want schools to compete and at the same time connects school reform with the free-market economy. I have used the term *European* in its cultural setting, acknowledging that the continuing Protestant Reformation is an international experience and is fundamental to the American economic and school experience. As such, the reader will be able to connect educational reform in this country as part of a globalized whole.

As mentioned earlier, the plethora of terms (including *conservative, neoconservative*, and *neoliberal*) used today in public discussions such as this do not have discrete agreed-upon definitions. It is not possible yet to draw definitional boundaries around these terms so that each means something so specific that it limits itself from all others. Partly, this is because these terms, and others that are emerging, are very much alive. Nevertheless, as they are used in the contexts in which they best perform, they will become more clear. All of this means it is possible that one person can express neoliberal ideas in educational reform and neoconservative views in diplomatic procedure all the while discussing a conservative social program.

The reality is that people do not draw margins around their ideas, segregating one from another. Rather, they develop a homeostasis, a logic, in which their ideas and viewpoints relate comfortably with each other regardless of the issue they are studying. It is from this position we use the term *neoliberal*. In fact, some educational reformers identified as neoliberals might, under the harshest cross-examination, prefer to call themselves by another name. Regardless, they are committed to neoliberal economic, educational, and social reform policies. For example, chapter 7 reports on the reform battles within the Southern Baptist Convention as an illustration of neoliberal education reform policies. Undoubtedly, the two leading revolutionaries, Paige Patterson and Paul Pressler, will insist they are conservatives, yet their actions to purify that evangelical sect are the same as those neoliberal educational reformers who are intent on reforming American schools. Therefore, they are discussed within that context.

In many ways, the present clash between neoliberalism and liberalism is but a reenactment of the battles between latter-day Victorian classic liberals and workers during much of the early part of the twentieth century. Those were the waning days of unbridled capitalism, trade unions, wars, and lockouts. Those were also the days in which unions, including the American Federation of Teachers, were formed to protect teachers from unscrupulous administrators and boards of education. Recognizable, neoliberal educational reform is merely classic liberalism's policies encouraging teachers to return to those days when their status was that of humble laborers and students were docile learners. Those were the days when investor wealth created worker poverty. It was John Dewey who saw the connections between classic liberalism's education (he called it "traditional education") and economic theories and wrote of their threat to American democracy.

Let us turn our attention in the next chapter to the neoliberals' capitalist past, as they created a new world through colonialism and indigenous domination.

NOTES

1. His Holiness the Dalai Lama, *Ethics for the New Millennium* (New York: Riverhead Books, 1999), 5. The Dalai Lama escaped the Communist invasion of his Tibetan homeland in 1959. A Nobel Peace Prize winner, he is the spiritual leader of his people and has demonstrated remarkable courage in his quest for world peace and the civil rights of people.

2. David G. Myers, *The American Paradox: Spiritual Hunger in an Age of Plenty* (New Haven, CT: Yale University Press, 2000).

3. This saying's connotation is that immediate events are more or less difficult to understand because of social and technological changes. For a discussion of these views, see Bill Rowley, "The Future Is Not What It Used to Be," U.S. Air Force Air University, Air War College, April 1995, www.au.af.mil/au/awc/awcgate/awc-ofut.htm. Admiral Rowley was deputy assistant chief of health care operations in Washington at the time of this article.

4. Rowley is voicing Rousseau's concept of the social contract as democracy's cornerstone. For an excellent discussion of the social contract, see Jean-Jacques Rousseau, *The Social Contract* (1763; reprint, trans. Maurice Cranston, Baltimore: Penguin Books, 1968).

5. Scholars who support this view, including Thomas Jefferson and Alexander Hamilton, refer to Adam Smith, who talked of the "invisible hand" of self-regulation.

6. John Dewey, *Liberalism and Social Action* (1935; reprint, New York: Prometheus Books, 1999).

7. Neoliberalism is the reemergence of the classic liberal economic philosophy proposed by Adam Smith, David Ricardo, and other European economists in the early and mid-Victorian period. Milton Friedman, of whom we will speak of in later chapters, is also a classic liberal. These school reformers—Smith, Ricardo, Friedman, and others—are *neoliberals* (we also refer to them as "raw capitalists" and other like terms). They, like their classic liberal models, equate democracy with unbridled capitalism like that during the times of the robber barons in the United States and in Europe of which Karl Marx (1818–1883) complained.

8. It is important to note that *liberalism*'s problem with neoliberalism is that the former focuses its attention on Rousseauian philosophy, while the latter focuses on unregulated capitalism in which individuals compete for their own welfare.

9. During the last decades of the twentieth century, as political philosophies began to shift from those expounded by the New Deal and Great Society, conservatives campaigned for government programs to be placed in the private sector. Neoliberals agreed with conservatives about privatization: Using the example of school choice, neoliberals want schools to be held accountable to the government (for example, the No Child Left Behind Act) while conservatives want parental choice. In the meantime, neoconservatives are interested in a strong military and national security. Ideally, neoconservatives prefer schools be privatized so public monies can be spent on national security.

10. Hugh Thomas, *Rivers of Gold: The Rise of the Spanish Empire, from Columbus to Magellan* (New York: Random House, 2003), 93.

11. Columbus's first trip was delayed a short period because the harbor was cluttered with ships carrying expelled Jews from Spain. Late in life, Columbus wrote of the need for Christian armies to free Jerusalem from the Moslems. See Thomas, *Rivers of Gold*.

12. Thomas, *Rivers of Gold*, 134–35.

13. I use the word *indigenous* to differentiate peoples, economics, values, and societies from capitalism and the Protestant value–laden European and American school curriculum. To make the point, I place Dewey's educational philosophy within that rubric.

2

How Eras Change: A History of Neoliberalism

In the introductory chapter we were concerned with identifying neoliberalism, neoconservativism, and other terms and showing how each related to school reform. Using the Dalai Lama's thoughts of global schisms and Bill Rowley's speculations of the relationships between technology and society, these definitions were constructed within the parameters of global social and technological change. At the same time, the chapter contributed to the discussion of how these terms, much alive and changing, relate to each other—that is, to understand their connections with educational policies, ideas, and schools. Of the terms, *neoliberalism* is the most important to our study. It was placed within the Victorian boundaries of classism and raw capitalism. Furthermore, it was highlighted as more potent than the others, signaling the neoliberals' thoughts of school reform as prerequisite to recreating their nirvana.

This chapter paints neoliberalism's capitalist heritage as a word picture beginning from its birth in the Protestant Reformation, watching its uneasy colonial relationship with indigenous societies develop and then wane, and finally noting its reemergence in the United States as the late twentieth-century expression of Victorian classism and capitalist fundamentalism. We will see that it continues today, marshaling the support of its neoconservative and conservative cousins, as schools' appraisers. Its intent is to re-norm global society.

Under different labels and flags, neoliberal history is long and has been interrupted only for a brief time in the twentieth century by John Dewey's ideas of democracy and pragmatism's utterances. Its colonial and Victorian economic reference points, now expressed in globalization, focus on investor and labor relations—that is, wealth harnessing indigenous labor and resources for profit creation. Let us look at the ideology that results in the social and economic relationships neoliberal schools champion against the reality of Dewey's schools for democracy.

THE EUROPEANIZATION OF THE WORLD

Columbus: Lessons in Indigenous Realities, Part One

> They [the indigenous peoples] are so ingenuous and free with all they
> have, that no one would believe it who has not seen it; of anything that
> they possess, if it be asked of them, they never say no; on the contrary,
> they invite you to share it and show as much love as if their hearts went
> with it, and they are content with whatever trifle be given them, whether it
> be a thing of value or of petty worth. I forbade that they be given things so
> worthless as bits of broken crockery and of green glass and lace-points, al-
> though when they could get them, they thought they had the best jewel in
> the world.[1]

In his first letter to Ferdinand and Isabella, Christopher Columbus recounted his westward experiences and his first meeting with indigenous peoples. His letter was immediately translated into Latin and published throughout Europe.[2] It was a rave success. The letter seemed to give readers an impression that the peoples Columbus described were just like those who were first put on Earth. It is fascinating, but, as mentioned in the previous chapter, Columbus was a product of his times and education; therefore it is important for us to know his meanings because he represented the understanding of the physical, social, and philosophical environment of his late fifteenth-century world.

At the end of the late Middle Ages, Columbus lived in a Europe just beginning to look beyond itself. Realizing that heaven's geography could not be explored, nor its rewards received until after death, many Europeans turned their attention to the world about them. The promise of wealth encouraged many nations to embark on colonization programs. Columbus's records show the profit he sought from the Spanish crown was political and economic control of the oceans surrounding the islands he explored. He is a good example for us to learn how Europeans were educated during that late Middle Ages period.

It was possible during Columbus's time to be educated without going to school, for in that day only princes of the realm or of the church needed instruction in the essentials: languages, mathematics, science, philosophy, and theology. Therefore, the universities he knew, such as Salamanca, intermixed ideology with theology in their curricula. Columbus probably learned how to read and write in the woolen craft guild he may have belonged to.

Later he was trained as a mariner. His school was life itself. At fourteen he sailed the Mediterranean and along Europe's western shores. In fact, evidence indicates he probably sailed into the North Atlantic toward Iceland. And it is recorded he participated in a sea battle off the African coast in about 1476. His educational opportunities (and adventures) to learn new things about others were, in many ways, daily challenges.

Columbus thought of his world much like others in that period. In this pre-science era, reason was not the testing of ideas against each other or collecting data to prove or disprove a hypothesis as Dewey and others postulated in the twentieth century. Rather, it was based on applying existing ideologies to world realities. For example, it was assumed at that time that if the weather was warm on some parts of the equator, then the weather would be warm regardless of where on the equator one found oneself. In other words, Columbus thought that if the realities of the world were different than the existing ideology, then the reality was wrong. You can imagine why he was not surprised when he discovered that those simple people he had written about to his sovereigns did not have the same type of hair or physical features as the Africans he had seen in his earlier travels. He thought he was in India.

Cortés: Lessons in Indigenous Realities, Part Two

Compared to Columbus's, the life of Hernán Cortés is better documented. He was born in 1485 filled with zeal for adventure. However, records also indicate Cortés was either lazy or, as it sometimes is said today, "he had not found himself." He attended the University of Salamanca, studying law, but did not graduate. Returning home, Cortés continued an indolent life, and after a series of minor adventures at the age of nineteen, sailed to the New World. Here Cortés's life became everything it had not been in Spain. It was almost as if he had spent his European years preparing for what he would do in Cuba and Mexico.

Looking back on Cortés's march to Tenochtitlán and subsequent military adventures, one can assume all was for gold and power. It is true he was not blind to wealth and honor, but for our understanding of neoliberalism's heritage, especially its views on social class, it is important we know his relationship with the Aztec. William H. Prescott presents the following word picture of Montezuma's retainers when they met Cortés in Vera Cruz in 1519.

> Teuhtlite then commanded his slaves to bring forward the present intended for the Spanish general. It consisted of ten loads of fine cottons, several mantles of that curious feather-work whose rich and delicate dyes might vie with the most beautiful painting, and a wicker basket filled with ornaments of wrought gold, all calculated to inspire the Spaniards with high ideas of wealth and mechanical ingenuity of the Mexicans.[3]

In this specific scene, Cortés highly prized the gold but not its ornamentation. In fact, to him the feathered crafts were works of the Devil. He destroyed them. Cortés could weigh the realities he experienced in Mexico only against the ideology he had learned in Europe.[4]

In Aztec society, religion was a central focus, with gods that understood people and were accountable for the functioning of this society. Cortés was shocked when he learned this. It simply affirmed his ideology, thereby hiding from him other realities. Even so, this sophisticated society was class conscious. By the time of Cortés's arrival, Aztec society was structured with a semigod ruler, priests, warriors, and administrators encompassing the aristocracy. The common class was composed of farmers, merchants, soldiers, and artisans. Unlike the European class system, this one was fluid, and people could move from one class to another. If a soldier was brave in battle, he could become a warrior. In fact, children could attend elementary schools that served each of Tenochtitlán's eighty districts to learn how to become members of the clergy so they could attain a higher class.

Schools: European Ideologies and Indigenous Realities, Part Three

It was not so much that Columbus and Cortés grappled with economic theories when they first interacted with indigenous peoples, although they were much concerned about Spain's treasury and their personal profits. While hunger for riches would certainly come, they did not see themselves as entrepreneurs as much as they saw themselves as royal representatives splendored in the firm ideology of the truth. Both wrote of their personal willingness to interpret that ideology to the indigenous realities they encountered. Neither waxed theologic about these indigenous societies. They interpreted what they saw, heard, felt, and smelled with European wisdom. As a consequence, Columbus expressed his worldview when he met "Indians" for the first time. Likewise, Cortés saw with his own eyes the reality of the gold given him, but could not grasp the value of the feathered artworks.

These were momentous times. They were revolutionary, marked by the violent birth of a Europe destined to become the globe's economic mother. But it was not intended this way. There was no European master plan that willed this international relationship take place. In fact, other than West African exploration, previous European contact with other cultures seemed to argue against the point. They had heard of Marco Polo, who was shocked by the advances made by China. His descriptions of cloth spun by worms, colored clothing, and luminaries speak of his firm conviction that it was Europe, not China, that was a thirteenth-century Third World.

In the sixteenth century, European society was revolutionizing itself. Technological advances, new understandings of Greek and Roman art, philosophies, and a militaristic history of Christian conflict allowed Europeans to view themselves as individuals. To explain these ideologies, theologians used schools. Therefore, it is surprising that both Europeans and Aztec placed their schools in similar social positions—the major difference between them was curriculum. Europeans formed their schools to reflect a Protestant ideology evidenced by wealth, church, state, and the individual. Aztec schools taught a curriculum based on an inward understanding of theology and skills. That is, emerging Protestant schools taught the concepts of individualism, nationalism, and capitalism, while the Aztec schools taught the somberness of theological existence.

It is difficult to pinpoint in Aztec history when schools began. Hugh Thomas speaks of Aztec cultural sophistication during the early 1500s.[5] Regardless, Aztec schools taught both written and oral languages. Elswhere, I have described the written Aztec language as picture-writing which families and government officials used to write to each other.[6] European schools continued their educational efforts, teaching Latin, Greek, and Hebrew. Unlike Europeans, the Aztec taught oral languages. On the other hand, like the Aztec, European students also had books or scrolls.

The sophistication of Aztec education could also be seen in higher education. Prescott wrote about a college of theology:

> In the colleges if the priests the youth were instructed in astronomy, history, mythology, etc.; and those who were to follow the profession of hieroglyphical painting were taught the application of the characters appropriated to each of these branches. In an historical work, one had charge of the chronology, and other of the events. Every part of the labor was thus mechanically distributed. The pupils, instructed in all that was before known in their several departments, were prepared to extend still further the boundaries of their imperfect science. The hieroglyphics served as sort of stenography, a collection of notes, suggesting to the initiated much more than could be conveyed by a literal interpretation. This combination of the written and oral comprehended what may be called the literature of the Aztecs.[7]

It is unclear whether the Aztec thought about who should attend schools. But they were open to the social classes, as mentioned earlier, although we might assume, as was the case in Europe, that few common-class children attended. There were perhaps only marginal class differences between the Aztec college of theology mentioned by Prescott and Cortés's University of Salamanca.

Understandably, Protestants saw their schools as a means to reinforce their theologies. Wanting all children to attend, these schools eventually were called "grammar schools" in England.[8] In Germany, they spurred the development of elementary and secondary schools. And in the United States, they became more functional, eventually identifying themselves with capitalism and the beginning middle class in the Victorian period. These are the unions of schools, capitalism, theology, and nationhood that neoliberals understand so well.

PRACTICING GLOBALIZATION

The Slave Trade: Indigenous Schools

Europe's first major problem in its colonies was developing a stable concentration of labor. While these difficulties were described in social contexts, they were in fact manifestations of new economic realities. Each colony experienced labor problems, and each tried to solve them within its own understanding of indigenousness. That meant England and France had great difficulty enticing Native Americans and First Nations to become laborers. The Spanish sidestepped that issue and simply made them slaves. It is to the classism of slavery, first important to early capitalists and later to their education, that we now turn.

Even though slavery still exists today, it is difficult for contemporary democracies to imagine this centuries-old enterprise. In most cases the history of slavery was written by Europeans. The oral literature of slaves, on the other hand, has been submerged or mostly forgotten. Within a short span of decades, European companies were transferring Africans to the Americas. They became laborers in colonial enterprises ranging from sugar plantations in the Caribbean to tobacco plantations on the mainland. Obviously, slavery was both an economic and cultural issue. That is why Europeans realized the importance of educating slaves.

The conversation about slave education is best discussed in the theologies of the sixteenth to nineteenth centuries. Voicing capitalism within an ideology, it was distressing to Christians that Africans had not heard of their Trinity. It was equally distressing that Africans could live all their lives in sin praying to false gods. It was a small leap, therefore, for them to conclude that slavery under a Christian master was far better than living in sin with friends and family. Connected to this ideology was the very important question of whether Africans were human. The topic was not multidimensional because Christians thought they were not, thus saddling capitalists, and later neoliberals, with indefeasible positions they publicly present for contemporary educational reform. While we will discuss these reform positions in later chapters, the sixteenth-century debate centered on how human Africans might be, or were, or could be.

As a consequence, teaching Africans how to be slaves became an urgent educational issue. Slave education began at the point of purchase.

Rounding them up, packaging them like merchandise in ships, oiling their bodies, displaying and selling them were, in actuality, school curricula of obedience, loyalty, and deculturalization. The graduate surviving these schools was well educated—becoming that *undesirable* now part of society's unseen working machinery.

But, slaves were also self-taught. They learned to be invisible to escape punishment. Developing subservient behaviors yet maintaining dignity, building family ties yet risking purchase, demonstrating worker loyalty yet staying immune to allegiance were all part of their curriculum.

However, the plantation was the slave's graduate school. Sold, and perhaps resold, slaves were placed in small plantation communities. Here they lived, slept, ate, and worked. Marching to the fields to plant, hoe, or harvest, they saw their manager riding horseback. They knew they were watched. They also knew that if the manager was not satisfied, he would draw a whip, use it, and repeat it again and again. Slaves ate in the fields. Children worked with their parents. Women and men were equal in their slave schools. They worked hard, fast, and long. The day ended after the sun had set.

At night after chores, slave education was expressed through entertainment. Songs and stories pleading their condition were sung and told and re-told. Perhaps a Sunday morning was reserved for church. But, beyond that, work was required. Slaves were constantly worried about their physical condition. They knew their economic worth was diminished if they couldn't work. Illnesses and accidents had to be treated by someone within the community, thereby learning a medical curriculum.

But the plantation-school gave no grades other than life or death. In fact, without using the words, slaves were being re-cultured into an economic and social underclass. They learned the mannerisms, social expectations, languages, theologies, and other subjects managers wanted them to know. Slaves understood this curriculum would not make their lives easier. In fact, they knew they were being educated to become expendable. This was the school in which labor was extolled as a virtue, loyalty was expected, and the slaves' culture was pronounced sinful. Perhaps, there was one part of the plantation-school upon which both managers and slaves agreed: Each knew the use of slave women to satisfy the sexual desires of managers was degrading to both the slave and the manager's wife.

In summary, slave education resulted in the devaluation of their personal histories. The plantation-school was really a concentration camp that taught the nonexistence of the future. Slaves were prisoners. What values were they to have other than those of their jailers? Managers, regardless of nation or colony, were united in making certain they would never know.

Corporations and Schools: India

Now that we understand the rudiments of neoliberals' social history, let us look at their economic heritage. It is at this time that European entrepreneurs recognized the extraordinary capital outlay required to transport labor from one part of the globe to another. The investment was immense and continued for centuries. To give one example, the business transaction by which slaves, or any other forms of merchandise for that matter, were sent to or from the Spanish territories began with a license from the monarch.

But much of this can be understood in a broader context when slave traders became part of an international economic system. With the advent of Caribbean sugar plantations in the 1640s, British, Dutch, and French interests created an increasing demand for African slave labor. Spending profits gained from selling sugar to Europe, ships were sent to the African coast to purchase slaves. They were shipped to the Caribbean sugar plantations, which in turn sold and shipped its produce to European homelands. The economic triangle continued its trade until the British dominated it in the eighteenth century.

Sugar and spice corporate interests were also represented by the Dutch, French, and English East India companies. Of these, the English East India Company was the most noted. This extraordinary company, begun by royal charter, remained in business until January 1874. During this period, the company governed India in its own name as well as that of the British crown. In many ways, the East India Company was one of England's first experiments in globalization. In total, however, the English East India Company, along with the others, signaled that the European economic community was sufficiently mature to advance its own economic interests and, at the same time, to assume the stature of a state within a state. The company spoke as equals to heads of states, appointed its own governors-general, maintained its company armies, selected its generals, and, in its own name, conducted business across nations. Modeling behaviors for international corporations in this century, its influence was all-encompassing.

The English East India Company and the Spanish viewed indigenous peoples in like manners. It is clear that they did not acknowledge Indians to be their cultural equals. Yet, Indians did not seem to be like the indigenous populations the English had previously met in the Americas and Africa. Probably this is because they were learning about India's centuries-old intellectual history in literature, languages, philosophies, and theology.

Like the Spanish in Mexico, English ideologies would not allow them to grasp the significance of this indigenous reality. Difficult as it seems today, the British were unable to understand Indian educational history. Many thought it impossible that in the fifth century, in Nalanda, an informal community of two thousand scholars could teach a curriculum including Buddhism, mathematics, logic, theology, medicine, and the Vedas. They could not comprehend that Indian students at that time were given aid so they could study (they were fed by villagers who lived close by). To listen with British ears that heard only Oxford and Cambridge scholars, it was unbelievable to them that as many as ten thousand students had learned in Nalanda. More so, their unbelieving minds dismissed the school, knowing it was destroyed by Turks in the twelfth century.

Much of what the Vedas students learned was oral, but through the centuries they were written for ease of learning.[9] In philosophy, students learned the Upanishads, which constituted some of the basic concepts of Hindu thinking. The historic epic poems of the Bharata dynasty were also studied. These poems, including those of Valmiki, were transformed into a literary form sometime in the third century. All of this is to say that the ideology of the English East India Company administrators judged Indian culture to be of no value. Sounding much like Columbus four hundred years earlier, Winston Churchill expressed his view in 1896 that Indians would follow any government that would not bully them and would guarantee economic security.[10]

Yet, the company seemed to sense that confrontation between European ideologies and indigenous realities could be explosive. For that reason, they discouraged missionaries from evangelizing. However, as the government became more involved, evangelicals quickly came. They almost immediately demonstrated the explosive results so feared. They outlawed *suttee*, which in some respects epitomized for English ideology the *backwardness* of Indian culture.[11]

Why they used *backward* rather than *savage*, as they did in Africa and America, is interesting. Perhaps, on a more sophisticated level, the backwardness the English thought they saw could be explained by the principles of Buddha. Regardless, they could not reconcile India's realities with their ideologies. The idea that life was full of sorrow and pain was absolutely foreign to the British mind. Nor could evangelists accept the idea that hell's escape could come without Christian learning.

The immediate consequence of the clash between English ideologies and Indian realities was first found in education. In 1835 all indigenous persons who had business with the colony's administration and courts were required to conduct their affairs in English. With the development of railroads, highways, bridges, and post offices, India's need for a European curriculum increased. Conversely, learning the ancient ways was minimized. In this colonial setting, Indian students were taught that ancient practices were backward and that knowledge of English history, literature, and language were the mark of an educated person.

Undoubtedly, the vehicle of colonial upward mobility other than the English language was the civil service system. Heralded as the world's most efficient, the civil service relied on high-stakes examinations.[12] The tests were based on the English classical curriculum taught in such schools as Eton and Rugby. Obviously, for the Indian, little could be done to become a member of this elite government administration. Even if the curriculum had been taught on the subcontinent, the graduate was still required to take the test in England. Consequently, few Indians joined the civil service.

In brief, these two cultures created a tension in which each, sophisticated and mature, warily viewed the other. What was it the British saw in India? Obviously, it was a place where their investments had found a home, exporting spices, silks, and luxury goods to Europe. The reason the British, who manufactured little the Indians wanted, managed this system so well was because of its concentration of wealth, in this case, silver. England had one other asset—a powerful standing army with a navy that could take it anywhere in the world. Also obviously, the second feature the British saw in India was cheap labor.

It is for these reasons England did not develop a labor education system in India as they had done with African slaves. Mandating that they learn the English language was the driving force for Indians to work for English capitalists. In short, investors learned, as they had in other colonies, that schools were intended to separate the managerial class from the laborers.

THE EUROPEANIZATION OF AMERICA

Teaching Labor

> O beautiful for spacious skies,
> For amber waves of grain
> For purple mountain majesties
> Above the fruited plain!
> America! America! God shed His grace on thee,
> And crown thy good with brotherhood
> From sea to shining sea.[13]

Katharine Lee Bates, a professor of English at Wellesley College, wrote "America the Beautiful" in 1893 to express her wonderment at the sight she saw atop Pikes Peak. She expressed the nineteenth-century Victorian attitude about the country she called America. Of course, the name "America" rightly belongs to all the nations in the two continents, yet this country expropriated it to designate only the United States. That explains much about how Americans viewed themselves and others at that time. They saw themselves living in a complicated, evil world controlled by conservative European monarchs and parliaments. European conservatives during this Victorian period focused their social and cultural philosophies on maintaining class structures in which a few, with the consent of many, governed.

While Americans disagreed vehemently with this philosophy, it is incorrect to assume that by the time Bates wrote her patriotic poem the nation was classless. But, as noted in chapter 1, Americans were busy redefining conservatism in ways by which, in later years, they could support a neoliberal school reform agenda. But now they expressed their restraint within the context of a constitutional republic. In short, conservatives wanted a United States committed to isolationism, Manifest Destiny, and unbounded capitalism.[14] This is why Americans believed they were a special people, recognized by God who, as Bates said, had "shed His grace" on them.

This land, which Bates poetically magnified, was based on wealth. In fact, the wealth she saw from Pikes Peak was in many ways the same seen then by her fellow citizens. Free, fertile land, space, minerals, and ores were all wealth that had been found or were there waiting to be mined. There was another wealth, however. It was called industrialization. In the middle decades of that century, communications and transportation inventions changed the way capitalists prospered and Americans lived. In an era in which horses were common means of transportation, travel distances were usually measured in days, weeks, and months. That meant that parents lost track of their children as they moved to the frontier, perhaps never to know where they settled or even if they were still alive. The consequences of learning about events suffered the same fate. For example, in 1865 westward travelers learned about the end of the Civil War by word of mouth.

The rapid change in technology had other major consequences. Factories demanded more laborers. As we will discuss in a later chapter, the factory was labor intensive. Men, regardless of age, were expected to work long hours, six days a week in primitive conditions. Many times, their jobs were dull and repetitive; other times, they were backbreaking. Men working in the steel industry found their work exhausting. Working close to blast furnaces, feeding them coal, workers were engaged with moment-to-moment expectations of physical hurt or death. It was a life in which the young aged quickly. Immigrant women, regardless of age, also worked in factories.[15] Believing women whose families had lived in America for generations were more delicate, wealthy factory owners stereotyped them as more "suited" to be secretaries and stenographers, thereby and unintentionally feminizing a male working position.[16] Of course, factory owners made certain they received the same quality work at lower wages.

Regardless, capitalists and labor agreed that factory workers needed an education if profits and wages were to increase. Public education had become the arena in which labor and wealth discussed how schools could be organized and who should be taxed.[17] While capitalists' interest in worker education was economic, labor's was in elementary schools. They thought these schools, teaching the basic skills, held the secrets to joining the skilled trades. And it was a place, they thought, where children could learn other subjects and make their lives better than their parents'. Interestingly, they did not foresee the time when their children would want to continue their education. Perhaps, labor and management informally agreed that the social line which separated their classes was entrance into high school. Mindful of that, Adolphe E. Meyer speculates that if labor had asked capitalists to increase their tax burden so their children could receive a high school diploma, they would have been severely rebuffed.[18] So, it was not until the last decades of the nineteenth century, at the end of the Victorian period, that labor unions, and especially the American Federation of Labor, demanded continued education for their children.

It was in the area of adult and industrial education that labor found a cause. Hopeful that these curricula would help their children, labor unions campaigned for federal financial support. Labor's success eventually materialized in the 1917 Smith-Hughes Act. This act and others that followed were confusing to the capitalist middle and upper classes. Expressing a European labor philosophy, vocational and technical curricula were instituted in schools. Meyer talks about how little public controversy followed worker education. He speculates that laborers, in their day-to-day life, did not see the specific need for any other type of schooling either. Of course, Meyer is discussing education in the early twentieth century, prior to the Depression.[19] Regardless, both labor and capitalists joined together to grapple another social problem created by industrialization—immigration.

Teaching Immigrants

> O beautiful for pilgrim feet,
> Whose stern, impassioned stress
> A thoroughfare for freedom beat
> Across the wilderness!
> America! America!
> God mend thine every flaw,
> Confirm thy soul in self control,
> Thy liberty in law![20]

Industrialization was also occurring in Europe. As will be discussed in chapter 9, by 1848 European conservatives, including the middle class, believed they had failed in their efforts for government and economic reform. In eastern Europe, nationalism caused empires to collapse. Germany, Italy, and France each experienced varying forms of civil unrest. Workers and peasants were dissatisfied with capitalism, which created greater levels of poverty, prompting Karl Marx to comment on laborers' lives.[21] The Industrial Revolution generated extraordinary social tensions as small agrarian communities were, one after the other, transformed. While the various rebellions eventually built a platform for European socialism, they stimulated, in the short run, major movements of people out of Europe. The country of choice for many was the United States.

Immigration, while continuing from colonial times, expanded greatly during the Industrial Revolution. In fact, during the period 1840–1920, thirty-seven million immigrants came to the United States.[22] After they left Ellis Island and other entry points, many settled near their port of entry, while others bought train tickets and flooded the country. Searching for employment but wanting to maintain their cultural ties, they usually settled in New York, Pittsburgh, Buffalo, Cleveland, Chicago, Minneapolis, and other urban areas where they had relatives, friends, or acquaintances. This is why immigrants were believed to be a social threat by capitalists and laborers alike. They focused on immigrant issues that centered around language, culture, and jobs. But, to grasp the complexity of the immigrant problem, it is important we understand both the impact of the West and urbanization on the American psychology. The result of the intermix of labor, wealth, and Protestantism culminated in the continued expansion of the common school. Its purpose was to assimilate immigrant children at taxpayer expense.

It is easy to understand the evangelicals' motives for social reform Bates referred to in "pilgrim feet, / Whose stern, impassioned stress / A thoroughfare for freedom beat / Across the wilderness!" Bates's pilgrims, impassioned for religious renewal, were in fact marching across the American West with the conviction of a new religious Great Awakening that focused on stopping a century of moral decline. Protestants voiced their fears that pioneers, associating with Native Americans, would lose sight of Christianity, and for the sake of their own souls, needed to be re-saved. Of course, there was the ever-present Columbus-like concern that Native Americans, like innocent children, were following the Devil in his handiwork. Evangelists recognized the same problems in urban areas. Now, yoked to crime and human misery, came the fear of immigrants.

Interestingly, labor unions were the first to present solutions to these social issues. Admittedly, unionism was in its infancy, yet labor voiced its support for such economic issues as higher wages. Unions wanted capitalists to devise a ten-hour workday. At the same time, unionism opposed monopolies and the appropriation of workers' tools because of indebtedness. Mostly, labor campaigned for common schools supported by public tax monies.

Not surprisingly, Protestant churches were divided over publicly funded schools. Presbyterians and Congregationalists crusaded for tax-supported common schools, while Lutherans and Quakers did not. Of course, none opposed the Protestant curriculum the schools offered workers' children. Rather, the two issues strongest in their minds were public taxation and the relationship between public and private schools. To make matters more complex, churches seldom agreed on a single social agenda. While they generally agreed on prison reform and better treatment of the insane, for example, not all were pleased about labor unions, and they traditionally opposed women's rights.

Yet, there were two causes for church alliances. Immigrants, many Protestants believed, simply refused to become assimilated or Americanized. That is, Protestants found immigrants' cultures a barrier to the nation Protestants pictured as theirs. In short, the Protestant problem with immigrants was that many of them were Catholic. The demographic growth of Catholics shocked and worried Protestants. They knew that in just one decade in the mid-nineteenth century, for example, the nation's Catholic population had doubled.[23] Immigrants also worked for lower wages, a sin in an urban setting revolving around labor and management.

As a consequence, especially in the burgeoning cities, the focus on school funding first centered on the growing middle class and Protestant clergy. Within the conflicting spirits of state constitutional responsibility and localism, the educational enterprise eventually would be administered by both state and local boards of education. Therefore, within the flukes and dissonance of labor–management, Protestant–Catholic, and state–localism issues, the curriculum was revolutionized. It moved rapidly from reading and writing to spelling, grammar, English, deportment, geography, and American history. In sum, the curriculum became both Protestant and secular. The English-language and deportment courses, and others such as American history and geography, gave students an awareness of their new home. In other words, these classroom subjects transported students from the world of their parents to their own new land. The common school was designed to develop a cultural breach between the old immigrant generation and their children. And it succeeded.

Perhaps the two books that helped this transition the most were Noah Webster's *American Spelling Book* and the *McGuffey Eclectic Readers*. In the spirit of nationalism, the *American Spelling Book*, published in 1783, was Webster's attempt to de-Europeanize the United States. In the same sense, the *McGuffey Eclectic Readers*, first published in 1836, were spectacularly profitable. While never outselling the King James Bible, the little textbooks continued to compete for that honor. These lighthearted books, filled with drawings, dealt with significant topics about how Victorian children were expected to live and act. Pictures of what families looked like, or how children played games such as hoops, or how they were to fly a kite explained the world these youth should belong to. Poems about George Washington and other heroes helped them develop pride in being an American. Stories about honesty and personal integrity underscored the Protestant morality they were expected to learn. Many immigrants agreed with Bates, the pilgrim's feet she romanticized in her poem were stern and impassioned as Protestantism marched across the nation.

Teaching Nontraditionals

The Protestantization of America would never be complete. Because of this, the nation was forced to recognize its diversity, causing today's neoliberals never-ending difficulty advancing their ideas of social impurity. Jews were one of the first European groups to migrate to the United States. Eventually, coming from many countries, Jews were diverse because of the societies they represented. With a strong belief in education, they were also different in other ways. The first Jewish immigrants were Sephardim, that is, Jews from Spain and Portugal. Increasingly, however Jewish immigrants were Ashkenazic, Jews from Germany and eastern Europe. During the decade prior to the Civil War, Jewish immigration totaled as many as fifty thousand people.

In some ways the impacts of these numbers were hidden from view because non-Jewish Germans were migrating to the United States at the same time. Another reason was that Jews remained in large cities such as New York. But, in the 1880s and beyond, Ashkenazic Jewish immigration was noticed, so others were aware of their social presence. Coming from Russia and eastern European countries, speaking Russian and Romanian, as well as Yiddish, these Jews were set apart.[24]

What Protestants were not always able to grasp was that not all Jews were alike.[25] They did not understand the cultural and social differences among Jews and, like Martin Luther, considered Jews to be the murderers of Christ.[26] Protestants also seemed to have difficulties understanding the European urban history Jews represented. Forgetting, or choosing not to remember, European economic policies outlawing Jewish land ownership, they assumed their family cohesion was based on theology rather than on social exclusion. Bluntly, the economics of the ever-increasing Jewish immigrants was based on retailing and not labor.

Retailing in the post–Civil War period was personalized by the peddler. During that period, stores were small and rare. Merchandise, mostly essential items like razors and scissors, with few accessories, were sold by peddlers. Not all peddlers were Jews; many were Protestants and Catholics. What set the Jewish peddler apart from his competition, however, was his familial economic structure. Being able to borrow from relatives and friends, Jewish peddlers were able to sell both staples and nonstaples, to the delight of their customers. Even more important, they were able to offer their customers something most other peddlers could not—credit. Family support gave the Jewish peddler an economic advantage.

If there was a common Jewish peddler, and there was not, it would be that man who started his retailing adventure in rural areas with saddlebags packed with merchandise, or if he lived in the city, a push cart. Slowly developing a profit history, he would graduate to a horse-drawn cart or corner stand and finally to a store. Peddlers continued to expand, developing retail stores such as the now famous Macy's, Gimbel's, Abraham & Strauss, Bloomingdale's, Altman, Saks, Bamberger's, Filene's, and Hecht. Perhaps Levi Strauss with his trousers is the most common picture of the Jewish retailer. Like Strauss, others such as Hart, Schaffner, & Marx and Florsheim fashioned merchandise that was sold in retail stores. Even in larger retail enterprises, Jews such as Sears, Roebuck, and Co.'s Julius Rosenwald, who supported schools for freed men, succeeded.

Unlike European Jews who came to the United States because of anti-Semitism and economic and cultural peace, Asians came because of Manifest Destiny. The demand for labor intensified as the economy expanded. For example, in Hawaii as early as the 1830s, entrepreneurs recognized that without a steady source of cheap labor, sugar plantations would eventually be threatened with bankruptcy. Their call for cheap labor was a reaction to the decline in Hawaii's indigenous population. In 1850, the Royal Hawaiian Agricultural Society contracted for Chinese laborers. Reminiscent of the time when African slaves were purchased in previous centuries, Ronald Takaki describes how Japanese and other Asian laborers were brought to Hawaii.[27] He says white planters or *haoles* ordered laborers from retailers in the same fashion as the Southern plantation owners when they ordered slaves—with other commodities.

Plantation work was difficult. Treated like slaves, the Chinese, Japanese, Filipinos, and other Asians struggled in sugar cane fields. The laborers' health was threatened. Many, after a life of work, were physically deformed, unable to stand in an upright position. And they had other difficulties as well. Unlike African slaves who were both male and female, Asian laborers were, by and large, only male. Obviously, the hiring *haoles'* rationale was simple—while African slaves were expected to stay in that station of life forever, Asians were to be life's sojourners. Even so, few men who came to Hawaii originally wanted to stay. Family, community, and marriage gave them reasons to go home. The culture of family was so important that many parents would not allow their sons to marry before they emigrated—giving them good reason to return. On the part of the men, they hoped to make sufficient profit from their labor so they would return home wealthy.

As Japanese laborers, for example, became more at home in Hawaii, and later California, their sentiments about their ancestral home changed. Now, their feeling of responsibility to their parents was replaced with wishes of bringing their wives, girlfriends, and relatives to the United States. Graduating from sojourners to settlers, laborers wanted to participate in the economic order and expand their educational opportunities. Not being allowed to own land, some developed small businesses; others became *coolies*.[28] Compared to Japan, labor pay in America was excellent, but their wages were far below that of whites. Here, for a daily wage of one American dollar, a Japanese laborer worked ten hours or longer. This was only one of the many reasons few Japanese were accepted in West Coast society.

But, it was the Nisei, the Japanese immigrants' children who understood what was happening. Inheritors of their parents' life choices, the second generation was bicultural. That is, they were no longer "those from Japan," whose homes were in Japan. Unlike their parents, they knew few people who lived in Japan. They had little or no awareness of their mothers' and fathers' families. For the Nisei, the United States was their home. While they knew the music, language, religions, and cultures of their parents, the Nisei were comfortably part of the American scene. It was as if they had leapt across the Pacific Ocean, embracing a culture foreign to their family history.

The Nisei went to two schools. They learned about America in public schools, and their parents taught them about their homeland at home. Yet, both generations agreed on the importance of an American education and the ability to speak English. For the Issei, the first-generation immigrants, America was the *gold mountain* where they lived but could not participate. Their children, the Nisei, believed that an American education, and the necessity to speak English, was the entrance into America society. Both generations were wrong. Protestant America evaluated the Issei and their children on who they were and not what they could become.

In this chapter, you may have noticed that Europeans and Americans are treated as if they were one people with a common history. In fact, their neoliberal heritage shows in many ways they were. The country was settled by the English at the start of the Protestantization of the globe when their ideas of schools, nationhood, and capitalism were new. American Protestants defined their ideology much like their European cousins. Beyond their partnering of theology and education, however, Protestants in the United States, like those in Europe, were also partners to capitalism. From the time of Columbus's voyages until the Victorian period's end, they participated with a powerful capitalist class that appreciated schools for their own reasons.

We now understand why this heritage will not allow neoliberals to equate their ideologies with indigenous realities. Just as the Victorian English were blind to the similarities between the Indian caste system and their class system, neoliberals and their robber baron forbears could not understand the realities Jews and Asians presented them. Just as capitalists could not accept Poles, Russians, Romanians, Hungarians, Italians, and French, neoliberals today cannot accept immigrants from Third World nations. They are *undesirables* to neoliberals in the same way Victorian capitalists judged those who were not English and German as *swarthy* or as Columbus characterized his *Indians* as childlike.

NEOLIBERALISM AND DEWEY

It is within this context of immigration in Chicago, at the beginning of the twentieth century, that John Dewey entered into a philosophic discussion about demographic changes in the United States. Without highlighting the conflicts between labor and management that were important to him, the question Dewey dealt with was on immigration and culture. He was involved with philosophers Alain Locke, Horace Kallen, and others such as W. E. B. Du Bois. In many ways the question was not exotic, but it was terribly personal for Dewey. It paralleled the ongoing public discussion taking place on the printed page and movies at that time. For example, in 1915 the first long-playing movie, D. W. Griffith's *Birth of a Nation*, recounted scenes that projected how blacks and eastern European immigrants were unwilling to assimilate into American society.[29] Increasing the social volume, in 1916 Madison Grant's book *The Passing of the Great Race* argued that eastern European immigration should stop.[30] He feared the diminished Anglo-American (Euroamerican) "race" would become powerless.

This is why Kallen immediately argued that American democracy should be willing to accept cultural differences. He said, using the term *cultural pluralism*, that is what democracy was about—it is supposed to be classless. He meant that people should be proud of their cultural heritages and willing to adhere to them. In fact, Kallen insisted that those who chose to forsake their cultural differences would be swallowed up by the newly emerging evil mass culture of cars and movies.

Believing that Kallen was proposing a form of self-withdrawal from the general culture, Du Bois argued in his classic book *The Souls of Black Folk* that cultural self-withdrawal is inconsistent with American history.[31] He described African Americans who, because of inflicted segregation, created for themselves a feeling he called *double-consciousness*. Double-consciousness, he said, was negative because it generated within blacks feelings of wanting to be loyal to both America and blackness. The result of double-consciousness was not internal conflict but, rather, black awareness they had no identity.

Within the European context, Locke supported Du Bois's position. Agreeing first with Kallen's term *cultural pluralism*, Locke's argument differed in its essence because modern, industrialized societies, he said, cannot tolerate cultural separation.[32] These societies are conducive to social assimilation because they foster creativity. This is why children who live in modern societies are different than those who live in agrarian societies. In these premodern societies, children learn what their parents know because that knowledge will help them live the same lives as their parents. In many ways, Locke says, life in these societies is enclosed. Parents know how their children's future will turn out. On the other hand, in a modern society, parents and children must be malleable because the children's future will be different than the present in which their parents reside.

Dewey developed the cultural pluralism argument further. Explaining *modernity* to mean the created future postulated in pragmatism, he positioned his argument of the created future to be the base upon which democracy exists. Dewey was not a socialist. Nor did he construct the philosophy called pragmatism by himself. In fact, he did not consider himself an educator. This Vermonter, one of the first Americans to receive a Ph.D. from an American university, became a pragmatist in generally the same manner as William James and Charles Peirce.[33] Dewey believed philosophy was a tool that helped persons understand the environment in which they lived. It was his thought that when ideologies clash with realities, merging resolutions will become part of the environment we call the future. Like humans, facts in a modern world have life spans. Dewey was talking about the tentativeness of modern society in which realities change from the old to the new.

How does one find out what is true? Dewey responded that truths are discovered through the scientific method. They are never permanent—their life span is controlled by new truths' discovery. This, he said, was why philosophy was the understanding and acceptance of experience, especially in the collective form. On the shoulders of Rousseau and in the company of reformers such as Jane Addams, Dewey defended his philosophy that schools were mirrors of society. To maintain an ideology in the adverse face of reality, said Dewey, was to deny democracy.

We now understand neoliberalism through the mind of Dewey. The neoliberal *self* is separate from others. The *self*, says neoliberal ideology, is moral and free while the *community* is not. Communities change helter-skelter without a firm ideological foundation. On the other hand, ideology is constant, regardless of the realities it encounters. This, says the neoliberal, is because it is the self, not the community, that is better able to describe the environment. Schools should give children an education based on ideologies so they can fit the environment to their worldview.

Although not knowing the word *neoliberalism*, Dewey understood its theory. It is part of the centuries-old conflict between ideology and reality. He termed what we once had, the teaching of ideology, "traditional education." It is a curriculum long since passed in the wake of science and democracy. To replace the new with the old, he says, is to return to a time when the common man was held hostage by the robber barons of his youth.

Placing Dewey's philosophy in a global context in which indigenous societies must come to terms with concentrations of wealth, the next chapter will discuss how four countries (the Soviet Union, Mexico, India, and Tanzania) experimented with different schools and curricula, hoping each would allow them to exist in a global society fast approaching globalization.

NOTES

1. Christopher Columbus, quoted in Samuel Eliot Morison, *Admiral of the Ocean Sea: A Life of Christopher Columbus* (Boston: Little, Brown, 1941), 231. Morison—an admiral in the U.S. Navy, a Harvard professor, and a Pulitzer Prize winner—traced Columbus's first voyages in 1939.

2. Morison, *Admiral of the Ocean Sea*, 231.

3. William H. Prescott, *The Conquest of Mexico* (1843; reprint, New York: Bantam Books, 1964), 173. See also David J. Weber, *The Spanish Frontier and North America* (New Haven, CT: Yale University Press, 1992).

4. It would not be until the scientific method became an investigative tool in the early twentieth century that ideologies such as these became less defensible. That method, a cornerstone of John Dewey's educational theories, became a hallmark of his New Education.

5. Hugh Thomas, *Rivers of Gold: The Rise of the Spanish Empire, from Columbus to Magellan* (New York: Random House, 2003).

6. William E. Segall and Anna V. Wilson, *Introduction to Education: Teaching in a Diverse Society*, 2nd ed. (Lanham, MD: Rowman & Littlefield, 2004), 118–19.

7. Prescott, *The Conquest of Mexico*, 69.

8. The first European school in the United States was founded by the Puritans in 1635 in Boston. It was known as the Boston Latin Grammar School. The school that would become Harvard University was founded the next year.

9. *Veda* means "knowledge." The general theme of the Vedas is the worship of both live and inanimate objects. It is Agni, the Veda god of fire, who was perhaps the closest god to humankind in his representation of eternity. To read a masterful translation of a Hindu scripture, see Sir Edwin Arnold's translation of the *Baghavadgita* (Mineola, NY: Dover Publications, 1993) and William K. Mahoney, *The Artful Universe: An Introduction to the Vedic Religious Imagination* (Albany: State University of New York Press, 1998).

10. Robert Blake and William Roger Louis, eds., *Churchill: A Major Assessment of His Life in Peace and War* (New York: W. W. Norton, 1993), 443–56. Churchill expressed this view throughout his life. He opposed India's independence.

11. *Suttee* is the Indian burial custom of the immolation of the wife on her dead husband's funeral pyre. English evangelists found this shocking and insisted that the funeral services were works of the Devil. If the evangelists had any concern for the wife because she was female, that interest was only marginal.

12. The British civil service was created to maintain Parliament's daily operations regardless of which party formed the government. Civil service positions during the Victorian period and later were highly prized both in England and the colonies because it was a public statement of personal prestige and power.

13. Katharine Lee Bates, "America the Beautiful," verse 1. Bates originally wrote the poem in 1893 and updated it in 1904 and 1913 to protect it from some who wanted to change the words. She gave her copyright as a gift to the American people.

14. These terms, in the broad sense, belong to the English social philosopher Herbert Spencer. He believed human society would improve if those who were fit continued to outpace the unfit. Wealth and poverty, for example, were clear indicators of

who were fit and unfit. His philosophy supported the 1896 Supreme Court case *Plessy v. Ferguson,* 163 U.S. 537 (1896). Herbert Spencer, *Social Statics: The conditions essential to human happiness specified, and the first of them developed* (1851; reprint, New York: Robert Schalkenbach Foundation, 1995).

15. Jacob Riis, a reporter for the *New York Tribune*, wrote a newspaper essay about a fire in a cigarette factory that killed young women who, trapped, jumped to their death. His subsequent book, *How the Other Half Lives: Studies among the Tenements of New York* (New York: Charles Scribner's Sons, 1890), revolutionized New York city administration. Riis is credited with the development of parks and other social assets for children who live in congested areas.

16. Alice Hanson Cook, Val R. Lorwin, and Arlene Kaplan Daniels, *The Most Difficult Revolution: Women and Trade Unions* (New York: Cornell University Press, 1992).

17. Ibid.

18. Adolphe E. Meyer, *An Educational History of the American People*, 2nd ed. (New York: McGraw-Hill, 1967), 356–57.

19. Ibid.

20. Bates, "America the Beautiful," verse 2.

21. Karl Marx was keenly aware of the social consequences of these economic problems. He and Friedrich Engels wrote *The Communist Manifesto* (1848) to explain their views about labor and capital.

22. Variously, many Germans, Italians, English, Welsh, Austrians, Hungarians, Scandinavians, and Russians came to the United States as their homelands experienced social dislocations and economic depressions while changing from agrarian to industrial economies. Probably the most dramatic example of the European exodus to the United States occurred during the middle decades of the nineteenth century when 4.5 million of Ireland's population emigrated to America.

23. The Catholic population increased from 650,000 in 1840 to approximately 1,300,000 in 1850.

24. Yiddish is a Judeo-Germanic folk language.

25. Of course, the Jewish immigrant experience was different than others, yet there is a feeling that immigrants, regardless of personal histories, were forced to cope with the realities of learning about others while trying to keep their own culture alive. See Joan Morrison and Charlotte Fox Zabusky, comps., *American Mosaic: The Immigrant Experience in the Words of Those Who Lived It* (Pittsburgh: University of Pittsburgh Press, 1993).

26. Martin Luther was anti-Semitic. He wrote a polemic, expressing in the most vehement terms Jews' responsibility for Christ's death.

27. Ronald Takaki, *Strangers from a Different Shore: A History of Asian Americans* (Boston: Little, Brown, 1989).

28. *Coolie* was a derogatory term used by Europeans to label unskilled contract Asian laborers. A coolie was a sojourner.

29. It is interesting to note the first long-playing movie in the United States considered a social topic of such depth. The controversy reverberated throughout academic, political, social, and religious circles. For an excellent discussion of this controversy, see Louis Menand, *The Metaphysical Club: A Story of Ideas in America* (New York: Farrar, Straus and Giroux, 2001).

30. Grant's book was shocking to that generation. He expressed the same concern that Winston Churchill voiced during this period and later, except, in this case, Grant was speaking about the United States and not India. See Madison Grant, *The Passing of the Great Race; or, The Racial Basis of European History* (New York: C. Scribner, 1916).

31. Du Bois, W. E. B., *The Souls of Black Folk* (1903; reprint, New York: Penguin Books USA, 1996).

32. This is a critical argument about agricultural and urban societies. Locke's point is that in modern societies, social groups must come together in some fashion so no group may be dominant. Dewey agreed, insisting that in this democracy immigrants should not all be required to assume the values of English and German Protestants. See Menand's *Metaphysical Club* for an extensive discussion on this point.

33. Menand discusses how both James and Peirce were instrumental in the development and naming of the philosophy. See Menand, *The Metaphysical Club*, 227–28.

3

Postcolonial Educational Reformers: A Global Perspective

With education as a backdrop in chapter 2, we focused on neoliberalism's capitalist colonial history. It was argued that the early 1500s was a crucial period in global history because it was the first moment when European ideologies interacted with indigenous realities. The chapter contended the Protestant Reformation defined the European neoliberals' worldview within the parameters of education, nationhood, economics, and theology. It also noted that the parameters were not discrete. Rather, all were related because each supported and explained the others. These are the underpinnings of globalization experienced through colonialism. In this regard, chapter 2 described the yoke worn jointly by neoliberal ideologies and indigenous realities. Through this lens, wealth and labor, portrayed by entrepreneurs and indigenous colonials, structured the neoliberals' contemporary conversation about the specialized educational needs of both groups. While dominant entrepreneurs required an elite, literate education to manage complex global economic enterprises, indigenous peoples also needed an education—in this case a nonliterate curriculum that focused on deculturalization and increased work output.

In this chapter, we will see that the mid-twentieth century challenged much of that. With the decline of colonialism, the fledgling nations were immediately confronted with the formidable task of constructing schools. Some new nations revised existing colonial schools, while others experimented with quite different institutional models. In either case, postcolonial reformers quickly discovered that it was imperative their schools focus on the twin priorities of reflecting the indigenous cultures while creating economic enterprises that competed in the international marketplace.[1] These reformers

expected schools to educate citizens to appreciate their cultures and the
virtue of labor in agriculture or industry.

Of course, the question asked by most postcolonial reformers was what
type of school could accomplish these tasks. There were existing national
school models that postcolonial reformers looked to for guidance. The
school model that immediately attracted international attention was the Soviet Union's. Even though the Soviet Union had no formal history of European colonialism as had Africans, Asians, and others, its revolution was considered by postcolonials to have been a contest between labor and a
European-influenced aristocracy. Consequently, Soviet educational reform
was attractive to postcolonial reformers because it focused on nation building, which, in this case, aimed at creating a new socialist workers' utopia. Socialism was also attractive to some postcolonials because its economic theory appeared to be a viable alternative to capitalism.

A second model, although a less prominent one, was that of Mexico.
While seemingly less economically promising than the Soviet Union, Mexico's school system appeared more mature because it had successfully
passed through a history of social and governmental upheavals. Rejecting
Marxist-Leninist socialism and championing central government control,
Mexico had been exposed to centuries of European and American capitalism. As a result, its economic problems were familiar to the newly formed
countries. In all probability, Mexico's major attraction was its educational experience in a society composed of both indigenous and European cultures.
All of this is to say that the Soviet and Mexican school models were equally
important to postcolonial reformers because they were viable alternatives to
those in developed capitalistic societies. Let us turn our attention to each of
these models so we can understand their attraction to postcolonial school reformers.

REVOLUTION: HOW SOVIET EDUCATION WAS BORN

> Long, long ago, when the Big War had just ended and the Red Army was
> driving out the White troops of the cursed burzhuins there lived a boy
> called Malchish Kibalchish. He lived in a little house amidst thick orchards
> and raspberry bushes with his father and elder brother. And he had no
> mother. His father worked, mowing hay, and his brother worked carting
> hay. And Boy Malchish helped, first his father, and then his brother, and
> when he wasn't helping with the work he played with the other boys and
> got into mischief. No bullets were whining, no shells were bursting, no
> need to fear the burzhuins—it was a good life.[2]

Arkady Gaidar's hero in this children's story is Malchish Kibalchish. Gaidar
describes him as about twelve years old. His hair is blond, and he sports

freckles on his nose. Malchish is a good-looking youngster who wears pants, shirt, and hat that suggest a soldier's uniform. While fictional, Malchish is important to Russia's revolution because he personalizes the resolve to fight the enemy, offer his life as a sacrifice to the nation, and die a hero's death. But, Malchish demonstrated he was an ordinary person his readers could relate to—Gaidar would not allow him to wear shoes in this story, for example—because he understood the utopian society Marxism-Leninism constructed. Gaidar wanted his young readers to relate to Malchish as the personification of the "Soviet Man."

Gaidar wrote this story, *Tale of the Military Secret*, for domestic literary consumption. As youth literature, it stood the test of time, becoming one of the favorite young Soviet stories of the twentieth century. Dressed in the clothes of Communism, Malchish spoke on several levels to emerging Soviet society. Beyond the obvious messages of Communism, Malchish represented the difficulties indigenous agrarian societies experienced living with the continued threat of European capitalism. Gaidar recognized this when he clothed his overweight, cigar-smoking *burzhuins* with top hats, monocles, and tuxedos.

Malchish represented the result of the Soviet educational reform movement during the 1920s as the government developed a national school system. An example of how quickly Moscow recognized the importance of educational reform can be seen in Anatoli Lunacharsky's welcoming speech to representatives at the First All-Russia Congress on Education on August 26, 1918.[3] As the Soviet Union's first people's commissar for education, he explained what the government expected of schools. Basically, Lunacharsky wanted students to be products of polytechnic schools, schools that produced persons who were socially well-rounded yet understood the value of manual labor. Lunacharsky thought of the school as a commune in which collective self-determination was critical, especially as it related to mental and manual labor.

Underlying these thoughts, Lunacharsky's Marxist-Leninist educational philosophy emerged. How is one to meet the goals of Soviet society, he asked, other than through the study of human culture?

> The history of human culture is inextricably linked with nature. It is the science we have studied best of all, and there is no science which is not a branch sprung from it. Such an approach is dictated to us by Marxism, but some eminent teachers who had nothing in common with Marxism have come close to the same approach in which natural science . . . grows.[4]

Even though Lunacharsky wanted schools to mirror Marxist-Leninist social and economic philosophy, he gave no direction to the delegates about how Marxism-Leninism could accomplish the government's reform goals.

Regardless, Marxism-Leninism was committed to the overthrow of prerevolutionary schools. These, he reported, were the play toys of the aristocrats and the clergy because they kept workers ignorant of who were the beneficiaries of their labor. Said he:

> First of all, we did away with the remains of the old apparatus, discontinuing the posts of district guardians, directors and inspectors of schools . . . and we issued the decree forbidding the teaching of Scripture, and removing Latin from the curriculum; we did away with matriculation as such, replacing it with certificates attesting that courses in sciences had been followed; we abolished the award of marks, and introduced co-education of the sexes. Any teacher will admit all these reforms to be an essential condition for anything approaching a normal school.
>
> And we had only removed the rubbish weighing down the school, only freed it from some only too evident deformations. After that we must set about the real, creative reform of the school.[5]

Soviet Experiments in Educational Reform

The 1920s was a decade of educational experimentation, the goals of which were to construct schools that produced Soviet citizens and socialist economics. It is apparent now that the reformers were creating a new language to achieve these goals by introducing such terms as *scientific socialism*, *pedagogical science*, and *socialist realism*. It was equally important for Soviet educational theoreticians to discount European and American ideas, although James Bowen points out that as late as 1929 major educational theorists such as Albert Pinkevitch glorified American educational philosophy.[6]

> The mere enumeration of the names of Hall, Dewey, Russell, Monroe, Judd, Thorndike, Kilpatrick and many others, known to every educator in our country, is a sufficient reminder of the tremendous influence which American education has exerted upon us. . . . We study carefully and transplant upon our soil whatever of value we may find elsewhere.[7]

Pinkevitch argued that while there were noticeable philosophical differences between the Americans and socialism, Soviets should recognize American reform successes for what they were. It is for that reason he wanted Soviet pedagogical science to study the project method, standardized tests, statistics, the Dalton Plan, and other ideas created by American educational reformers.

Within that spirit, others such as Pavel Blonsky, a Rousseauian, proposed that Soviet children be left to their own devices so they would naturally become aware of their own creativity. That was why, said Blonsky, the traditional prerevolutionary teaching methods based on memorization failed. Other reformers such as S. T. Shatsky thought schools could be Soviet and Deweyan at the same time. Shatsky, the director of a school for *besprizorniki* (street urchins) named the Colony of the Cheerful Life, considered schools to be culture's midwives. Schools had the resources to build culture although none had.

> No nation has done so yet. True culture must be founded on the good of all. School, educational philosophy and political life must be united. . . . To lay the educational bricks in building socialism is the high duty of current pedagogy.[8]

Actually, Shatsky's articulations about schools acting as culture builders of a disciplined, *collective* society rather than a free society that glorifies individuality illustrates the confusion of Soviet reformers during the 1920s.

Makarenko: Marxist-Leninist Educational Reformer

But not all reformers were confused. Anton Makarenko, a Ukrainian, insisted the world beyond the Soviet Union had little or nothing to teach him. Also an experimenter, Makarenko voiced his abhorrence that some of his colleagues believed Deweyan methods could be used to reform Soviet schools. He wanted a unique educational system equipped to create a new workers' utopia based on Marxist-Leninist philosophy. Communism, he stated, would be poorly served if reformers insisted they use methods that could not guarantee known or agreed-upon ends. Unlike his colleagues, Makarenko thought the ideas of John Dewey were dangerous. Even though both were social reconstructionalists, Dewey thought the education of individuals was the purpose of schools. Makarenko, on the other hand, thought the purpose of schools was to serve Soviet society. In blunt terms, Makarenko explained the Marxist-Leninist curriculum:

1. Labor is the basic school curriculum.
2. Students should learn (and work) in school using techniques learned in collectives.
3. Learners will contribute in the collective as part of a whole and not as an individual in a collection of individuals.
4. Schools will declare the morality of the collective to be above that of the family.
5. Educational reformers will conduct educational experiments within the boundaries of known and agreed-upon Communist outcomes.[9]

Like Dewey, Makarenko developed an experimental school to test his ideas. Although he framed his experimentation within the purposes of Marxism-Leninism, it is clear from his writings the philosophical frontier he was exploring. Makarenko's *Road to Life* is engrossing and engaging.[10] Written almost like a mystery novel, it invites readers into his life and experiences as well as those of his fellow teachers and students. He took a small group of besprizorniki with him to an abandoned estate outside Moscow and started a school. Named after his hero Maksim Gorky, Makarenko's Gorky Colony began its existence with Makarenko and his students living in hovels. He describes the hovels as filthy structures with dirt floors, broken windows, and entrances without doors. In fact, they offered little protection against the cruel Russian winter. Makarenko writes how the students hated their existence and wanted to leave the colony. Even though Moscow offered nothing better, their feelings of despair were obvious. Insolent, the students refused to help the teachers repair the buildings. With all the government money spent, food could not be purchased, and Makarenko's punishing demands that nothing be stolen from surrounding villages created chaos.

It was during this desperate revolutionary moment in which the students were beginning their rebellion that Makarenko abandoned his "philosophical tightrope," as he called it later, and faced the student revolt in dramatic fashion. The result of this teacher–student standoff became a central part of Makarenko's educational philosophy. First, he discovered that, as soon as the students saw him for what he was, a bonding among the students and teachers developed. Thus, the students and teachers, including Makarenko, found they could work together. He had birthed his *collective*. Not once thereafter, he wrote, were the students thinking of themselves as individuals. Now they were working for something more important than themselves. They were working for the benefit of the collective. In fact, the collective had become more than each of the students and, in many ways, had become more than all of them together.

Continuing, the Gorky Colony would move to other locations in its history. Each time, Makarenko mentions, his educational philosophy became more mature. He had, said he, succeeded in demonstrating Marxist-Leninist educational philosophy. In his writings he made clear he was not in search of a new, or unused, or capitalist educational philosophy. Makarenko did not want others to think he was simply another reformer like Blonsky or Shatsky. His experiment did not create something new but, rather, supported Marxist-Leninist theory, which had been his original intent.

What were Makarenko's contributions to Soviet society? Within Marxist-Leninist theory, Makarenko wanted the school to develop citizens so they reflected Soviet society. But he saw schools as only one part of Soviet education. All social units should think of themselves as schools, he said. Factories, farms, even families—which he hoped would become extinct—should teach students to fit into the collective. Makarenko was committed to polytechnic education. He believed that an educated student was a person who understood the relationship between manual and intellectual labor. The result of this type of education was that students appreciated industrialization and exhibited a *collectivist* behavior pattern that allowed them to live in Soviet society. In other words, he created Arkady Gaidar's Malchish Kibalchish.

How did Makarenko put his educational reform philosophy into practice? In his Gorky Colony, he divided each school day into half. In the morning, students learned about human culture formulated through Marxism-Leninism. In the afternoon, students worked in shops, repaired buildings, tended crops, and carried on other productive affairs needed by the colony. Student understanding of the relationship between the morning and afternoon activities, thought Makarenko, gave them opportunities to live as successful members of a true communist society.

REVOLUTION: HOW MEXICAN EDUCATION WAS BORN

"Poor Mexico! So far from God, and so close to the United States!"[11] This comment, attributed to President José de la Cruz Porfirio Díaz (1830–1915), is the lens through which Mexico describes its relationship with the United States. It reflects Mexico's frustration with American entrepreneurs interfering in its cultural and economic affairs. It also reflects the nation's frustration with the Catholic Church's insistence that education was the clergy's responsibility. To illustrate, during Mexico's postcolonial period (1821–1917), schools remained in the grasp of the aristocracy and the clergy. Children of the aristocracy attended primary schools (*primeras letras*), secondary schools (*colegios*), and the prestigious Universidad Real y Pontifica de México while suffering through formal, rigid, elite curricula designed for Spaniards living in Madrid. Taught by the clergy, students knew their future was in the legal and theological professions, for this was the avenue they traveled to join the ranks of bureaucrats, legislators, governors, or influential members of the government.

Indigenous children were taught in rural schools. If the students came to the schools at all, they found their teachers to be clergy who taught them their culture was evil and governed by the Devil. The rudiments of Spanish culture were taught through language and religion. Students were also taught that God's purpose for their existence was to labor on the land. Food and shelter was their reward for tending crops on lands upon which they may have been born but did not own. On the other hand, rural schools were not usually accessible, so few indigenous children were exposed to this.

Part One: Benito Juárez and *La Reforma*

Even with the rise of the anticlerical liberal reformer Benito Juárez (1808–1872), a hero of indigenous Mexicans, little could be done to remove the permanent, powerful grasp of the clergy over schools. Juárez, born in Oaxaca de Juárez, attained the position of president of Mexico through the then typical method of military revolution. His efforts to provide universal education and stop clergy interference helped only a short time, yet Juárez's importance to Mexican education was long term. His reform philosophy focused on developing an educated citizenry participating in a democratic government much like that of the United States. In fact, his reform philosophy—*obligatoria, gratuita, y laica*—meant that urban and rural children should have equal access to schools. Schools, Juárez stated, should be secular, controlled, and financed by the central government. That is, the clergy should not use schools to evangelize students and purposely discount their culture. The liberalization of education came to an abrupt end, however, during the *afrancesado*, or Empire period (1862–1867). With Juárez's death in 1872, Mexican schools returned to the normal pattern of serving an elite. However, another type of elite forced its demands on schools.

Part Two: Porfirio Díaz and the Great Mexican Giveaway

Porfirio Díaz's presidential regime viewed education through a lens different from either Juárez or the clergy. Using the argument of decentralizing schools in the American sense, only schools in Mexico City were to be financed by the federal government. As a consequence, the clergy quickly filled the void and dominated urban and rural schools until the end of the dictatorship in 1911. But Mexican education was revolutionized within the Díaz regime by intellectuals who, to varying degrees, believed Mexico's economic success could only be realized if schools taught scientific thinking and French positivism. In fact, what the intellectuals intended was to Europeanize Mexico's indigenous culture so it appeared as a more attractive labor force to foreign entrepreneurs. The intellectuals thought indigenous workers had the potential to be economic assets.

A proponent of this rural education reform plan was Justo Sierra. He believed Mexico's last opportunity to develop as a society was during the Díaz regime. Sierra proposed that rural schools teach European values and lifestyles to indigenous peoples who, as good laborers, would willingly work for low wages. He spoke passionately at the First Convention of Primary Instruction held in Mexico City in 1890:

> We will have made ourselves worthy . . . then we will merit the words of the great French orator Eugene Pelletan, who in speaking of Latin America . . . said, "New generations are arising in Latin America who will transform those societies, because their generations bear the light of hope before them and the thirst for progress in their hearts."[12]

Another intellectual, Felix Palavicini, looked toward the United States as a font of culture and industrialization. Although Palavicini represented a growing Mexican middle class sympathetic to capitalism, he understood capitalism's impact on indigenous cultures and was adamant that schools lead Mexico's modernization movement. Like Sierra, Palavicini wanted schools to change Mexico's culture, although in this case, to a Mexico which, like the United States, would symbolize economic wealth, political power, and a modern culture. But all of this was merely a prelude to the Mexican Revolution.

Part Three: José Vasconcelos and the 1917 Constitution

The Mexican Revolution was long, remarkable, bloody, and confusing. Unlike other twentieth-century revolutions, especially the Russian Revolution that was being conducted at the same time, the Mexican was considered unique by its participants. And, indeed it was. The cast of characters included ex-president Porfirio Díaz, the intellectual Francisco Madero, and the bandits Pancho Villa and Emiliano Zapata, along with others. Each had his own set of revolutionary goals, and some were accomplished, although at different times and under different circumstances. School expansion at the end of the Díaz regime had improved negligibly. Madero was interested in political reform and paid little attention to schools while he was president. Zapata and Villa, both illiterate, were interested in reform. Although they concentrated on land reform, each inherently understood the value schools represented to the rural indigenous peoples.

But, the real revolution for education reform was the Constitution of 1917 and the reformer José Vasconcelos. The Constitution of 1917 gave purpose to educational reform that resonated throughout Mexico. It was the schools' sole voice heard by the people throughout the twentieth century. Recalling Benito Juárez's *La Reforma* and Díaz's Americanized decentralization failure, the constitution awarded the federal government control of the schools. Thus, the government was responsible for the free, secular education of all children between the ages of six and fourteen. Recognizing the clergy's pervasive influence in education and Juárez's failed attempt to oust them, the Catholic Church was constitutionally allowed a voice in education—but, this time, under central governmental supervision. Entrepreneurs were also held accountable for financial aid to schools. Usually, this was accomplished by companies establishing schools for their workers' children or paying the state. Even so, it remained the federal government's constitutional responsibility to establish the levels of financial support from federal, state, and municipal governments.

The potency of the 1917 Constitution was experienced immediately in the Álvaro Obregón administration. Chosen to fill the position of minister of public education was Vasconcelos, the eminent intellectual and writer. With a zeal, Vasconcelos undertook the responsibility of popularizing educational opportunities for indigenous children in rural areas. Officially described as the *Escuela de Acción* (the active promotion of education in rural areas), Vasconcelos lobbied the federal government for this program to be given priority and receive a greater share of the federal government budget.

Yet, the idea of compulsory, free secular education meant more than children simply attending school. Vasconcelos wanted cultural and economic purposes to mirror each other in the national curriculum. Schools developed programs to jointly introduce urban and rural children to Mexico's cultural heritage. He created a centralized ministry, which expanded the cultural awareness of urban and rural children by introducing them to the art, history, music, and folklore of indigenous Mexico. Respect for indigenous cultures became a central tenet in the ministry's curriculum. Vasconcelos also introduced the *misiones culturales* (social action programs). These literacy programs were intended to help indigenous children become more skilled as workers and give them the intellectual tools to live in urban areas. Vasconcelos wanted indigenous peoples to free themselves from the land and have equal opportunities in Mexico's social and economic life. His efforts were a successful beginning, for schools were finally divorced from the established elitist educational system mirroring Sierra's and Palavicini's capitalist models. He developed a nationalistic model in which students, proud of their various cultural heritages, were learning to live in an industrialized, tricultural society. What was less successful, however, was Vasconcelos's attempt to develop a curriculum based on social criticisms. Instead, what emerged was the use of schools to speed the nation toward industrialization and economic progress.

Part Four: Post-Vasconcelos Reform

Organizationally, the Mexican school structure continued to evolve in the twentieth century. Divided into three distinct sections, students now begin their education in primary schools (*primarias*) at the age of six and remain there for six years. Studying a national curriculum, students learn Spanish, mathematics, history, geography, natural sciences, social sciences, the arts, health, and physical education. Secondary schools are divided into two components. Students in the junior component (*secundaria*), much like the U.S. junior high school, continue to study the elementary curriculum, but in more depth. The senior component (*preparatoria*) is composed of the last three years in which students prepare for university. It is during the higher-education experience that students concentrate on their specific majors in professional schools called *carreras*. Although students may major in many disciplines, the most popular careers, other than medicine and dentistry, are business administration and engineering.

Plagued by problems familiar to most postcolonial countries, Mexican schools have severe troubles that continue to beg for reform. Confounded by changing demographic patterns, schools serve urban areas to a much greater degree than the rural areas. While 74 percent of the population resides in urban areas (1998 estimate), fewer schools per capita have been available to those who live on the land or in small villages. It has been pointed out elsewhere that, because of lack of facilities, as many as 9 percent of Mexican children do not have access to primary school. In fact, of those who live in rural areas, school access may be such that children attend primary school for only two or four years or some other short period.[13] As well, Mexico's population explosion places extraordinary pressures on its schools to educate increasingly larger numbers of students.

Schools are discovering other pressures as well. With the persistent threat of poor community health and public medical services in urban *barrios* and rural areas, children continue to drop out of school. At the same time, uncounted numbers of rural youths leave villages for the opportunities of urban life in settings such as Mexico City and Juárez. They are attracted by television and the voices of friends and family who emigrated earlier. Yet, urban life has continued the downward economic spiral for young rural immigrants. Fighting poverty and poor health, few are able to attend schools. In fact, many are not attracted to an education they view as insufficient for their needs. Urban social and economic pressures have exposed their vulnerability to a future they cannot control. Willingly admitting their desperation, Mexico's youths forsake their homes and homeland for the dream of poverty in the United States.

SOVIET AND MEXICAN EDUCATION: SCHOOL REFORM MODELS?

At first blush, commonalities between Soviet and Mexican education systems seemed to be either lacking or so minor as not to warrant investigation by postcolonial reformers. Yet, as more colonies became independent and educational issues better defined, both models appeared more attractive because of the varying manners in which they approached similar problems. It was not that postcolonial reformers wanted to replicate these school systems. They were interested in how the Mexican and Soviet school systems reacted to the differing consequences of European and American capitalism. The Soviet Union, for example, while never an "official" European colony in the same sense as Mexico, experienced the same massive effort of creating a new, emerging postcolonial state. While the Soviet experience was based on

Marxism-Leninism, Mexico's experience was based on a strong central government. What was unique in Mexico's case was that its nation-building struggle took place under the watchful eye of the United States.

But, in other and more important ways, both countries were comparable to newly emerging nations. Each had extensive educational histories in which schools served the interests of social and economic elites. Postcolonial reformers understood Commissar of Education Lunacharsky's criticism of traditional Russian education as aristocratic because they had the same histories. For the same reasons, postcolonial reformers applauded Vasconcelos's programs to increase educational opportunities for indigenous Mexicans because they had similar problems of diluting their elites' influence on schools. Rejecting capitalists' schools was a significant accomplishment for both the Soviet Union and Mexico in the minds of postcolonial reformers because capitalist schools never gave indigenous laborers the opportunity to join the dominant culture. Even in capitalist nations, postcolonial education reformers recognized that schools were used to separate managers from laborers.

Yet, none of this meant that capitalistic educational systems did not contribute to their nations' economic welfare. In fact, the opposite was true. Lunacharsky, Vasconcelos, Mohandas Gandhi, and Julius Nyerere, of whom we will speak next, recognized the capitalist influence on workers. This was because capitalist schools created class differences by educating workers to become docile. It is for this reason that Soviet and Mexican educational reformers investigated John Dewey's educational philosophy. Let us first look at Dewey's ideas about education for workers and then trace the Soviet and Mexican responses.

Continuing our discussion of Dewey from the previous chapter, we understand that he knew schools were influenced by society and economics. Like Jane Addams in Chicago and Jacob Riis in New York, Dewey thought the social consequences of uncontrolled economic growth would be devastating to workers. After all, he had witnessed the Chicago Pullman strikes. Yet, Dewey was not capitalism's opponent as much as he opposed industrial disregard of laborers' quality of life. He wanted planned growth in which laborers and managers cooperated to develop the world they both envisioned. However, Dewey did not define planned growth in socialistic terms, nor did he believe labor was docile. Rather, he thought managers and laborers, participating in the democratic process, could come to an agreement about the social consequences of their combined actions. The notion Dewey advanced, as we will witness in a later chapter, was that both managers and laborers had, within their cooperative power, the ability to create their own social future. That creation came about through a process of negotiation in which both labor and management cooperatively solved mutual problems. Of course, the process of negotiation Dewey had in mind was the scientific method. The social future he wanted labor and management to create centered on society's quality of life. Quality of life could never be a reality to Dewey as long as the process was dictated by capitalism. Instead, capitalism's responsibility was to serve society and perhaps advance its quality of life. Otherwise, said Dewey, the democracy was threatened.

Within this framework, Dewey constructed his reform philosophy. Schools, he argued, should teach children how to cooperate and think scientifically. Learning how to use the scientific method and solving mutual problems gave students experiences in working together. This, to Dewey, was the essence of what he termed "community." This active education—or as he called it, "new education"—demonstrated the importance of scientific thinking as the active ingredient that sustained American democracy.

In the most elementary manner, both Soviet and Mexican educational reformers disagreed with Dewey. Notwithstanding his philosophy, Soviet and Mexican reformers, for different reasons, classified American society as predatory. Both the Soviets, who wanted to create a workers' utopia, and the Mexicans, who were creating a tri-cultural society, believed the purpose of schools was to be an arm of government to build a nation. We can now understand why Vasconcelos's reform movement divorced Mexican schools from European and American curricula and why he developed a nationalist curriculum that included all parts of Mexican society.

In some ways, the Soviets' immediate educational response to Dewey was less clear, although it was immediately understandable to postcolonial reformers. The Soviets were interested in using schools to help develop their workers' utopia. It was left to Makarenko to explain why they could not accept Dewey. In his experiments with his besprizorniki, Makarenko witnessed their interactions when he and his students formed a collective. This Communist organization was composed not of blood relations like a family but a utopian camaraderie in which all in the collective worked together for the good of the collective. As a consequence, Makarenko had no regard for Dewey's concept of community, because it was not based on order, discipline, and uniformity. Makarenko viewed the individual to be that person whose goal it was to reflect the Soviet utopia as experienced in the collective. Dewey disagreed; he understood the individual to be an active member of a community in which the person participated in the decision-making process.[14]

It is this conversation about capitalism and labor that postcolonial reformers' experiments would expand upon. It is obvious Makarenko's criticism of Dewey's community was significant. Marxism-Leninism focused on a workers' utopia outside the culture of most postcolonial societies. In the same fashion, Mexico's criticism of Dewey was understandable. It was obvious Vasconcelos understood Dewey's educational reforms reflected a predatory society and, as a defense, took immediate action to reform Mexico's schools systems to be more inclusive. Yet, the conflict between wealth and labor and resources remained. With this, let us first turn our attention to Tanzania's attempt to create a socialist state while preserving a rural oral culture.

SCHOOL REFORM IN RURAL ORAL CULTURES

The human accomplishment of lengthy verbatim recall [fifty words or more] arises as an adaptation to written text and does not arise in cultural settings where text is unknown. The assumption that nonliterate cultures encourage lengthy verbatim recall is the mistaken projection by literates of text-dependent frames of reference.[15]

Ian Hunter's statement about learning or verbal recall was a condemnation of elitist provincialism. Hunter reported how literate capitalist societies evaluate the knowledge base of nonliterate indigenous societies. He described contemporary literate, capitalist societies' inability to acknowledge that nonliterate societies may not suffer educational handicaps because of cultural differences—in this case, lengthy verbatim recall. That is, the perceived educational handicaps literate societies recognize were those they would place upon themselves, if they all of a sudden were to become nonliterate.

At the same time, Hunter's description is an excellent illustration of the perceived cultural relationship postcolonials believe they maintain with European capitalists. Even though the Soviet and Mexican societies were literate, Hunter's comments about elitist provincialism are worthwhile because they are descriptions of the problems both Soviet and Mexican educational reformers understood and wanted to avoid. Yet, a purpose of postcolonial schools was to prepare indigenous peoples to live in a literate, elite, capitalistic world. Perhaps Negussie Ayele explains the conflict best with a specific illustration:

A story is told about a child who had just started going to school, a modern school where he was learning mathematics and he came home to his illiterate, unschooled grandfather and said, "You know, grandfather, you do not know what you have been missing by not being young now and going to school." His grandfather nonchalantly says, "Oh! Is that so. What do you think I am missing?" The youngster says, "Well, I'll tell you. If you had twelve cows and you had four children and you were to divide these twelve cows among these four children, how many would each one get?" And the grandfather looks at the boy and says, "Well, son, that depends on how I want to divide them."[16]

This encapsulated the fundamental problem facing government education reformers in oral cultures.

If indigenous peoples were to receive an education to live in a world dominated by the capitalist elite, what type of world were they leaving? In many oral cultures, the world indigenous peoples lived in centered around their immediate environment and the person's place in it. The purpose of education was to create *valued beings*. "Valued beings" were those who, in adulthood, were respected because they exhibited approved social values and performed the majesty of work. Fafunwa described *valued beings* as those who were honest, respected elders, participated in family and community affairs, worked hard, and respected and contributed to the community's cultural heritage.

The education of valued beings was the responsibility of parents, relatives, friends, priests, and community members. Each had a responsibility to praise a child whenever a worthy deed had been performed and to rebuke the child when he or she did not meet the expected mark of behavior. Traditional education also required children to publicly participate in village ceremonies. Usually ceremonies marked passages from one part of life to another, for example, recognition of leaving childhood and becoming an adult. Ceremonies, however, were not intended to be graduation ceremonies, although it was expected the community would celebrate with the young initiates. Rather, ceremonies focused on learning experiences, such as instructing a young man how to behave as a husband or a young woman learning about restrictions on food. In some cases, the education of the young was conducted through mimicry. As children grew, they learned from their parents what was expected of them. Even though it was common for both boys and girls to work together in the fields or other activities, they also learned about division of labor according to gender.

Perhaps the most successful teaching method used by the child's many teachers was the telling of proverbs, myths, legends, and verse. Each conveyed, as we learned about slave education in the previous chapter, complicated information that was intended to advance the child's education. For example, proverbs were used to help children learn how to reason, and myths helped explain in a simple way how great events, such as the creation of the Earth, took place. Legends helped children understand the great work of heroes or others that helped the community. Verse, of course, was used in both serious and entertaining settings to tell stories of major importance. The unifying theme of all these teaching methods was that they were used in every living setting, for education was a lifelong experience.

Nyerere's Rural Socialism

Now, we understand the conflicting ideas about schools and national development in postcolonial nations. They were created by the push-pull of capitalistic and indigenous social value structures. In Tanzania, for example,

Julius Nyerere's educational philosophy was pro-African. Nyerere, born during the height of early twentieth-century colonialism, experienced the cultural duality and conflict between European capitalism and African resources and indigenous labor. He understood the personal investment Africans had in their cultures and the raw terror they felt when Europeans minimized, depreciated, and marginalized them. Because of these experiences, Nyerere as president was single minded in advancing his educational and political reform philosophy. Tanzania would not survive in the global community unless it represented its indigenous cultures. Nyerere did not think of this as a negative statement about European culture. Rather, just as European nations represented Christian cultures internationally, African nations should be allowed to represent indigenous cultures. In fact, he believed no African nation could survive in the international community unless it advocated its own culture and people. As a consequence, Nyerere focused on the prospect that Tanzania would become a potent political, cultural, and educational leader in Africa and, at the same time, a respected member within the community of nations.

Nyerere understood the growing economic difficulty Tanzania had with European nations. Basically, Tanzania was viewed by capitalists in the same manner as in previous centuries, even though the nation was now independent. Using cheap labor to mine or grow needed resources for European markets was, in most cases, Tanzania's only source of revenue. On the other hand, the growing appetite for European manufactured goods, merchandise, and professional resources, such as medicine and transportation, cost more than the nation's income. In other words, Tanzania, if left to its own consequences, would eventually become an international nonentity, again open to the whims of predator nations. This was why Nyerere thought of schools as an arm of government. Schools had the ability to develop educated persons who could assist Tanzania to become less dependent on European capitalists. Nyerere wanted schools to make Tanzania self-reliant.[17]

To do this, Nyerere developed his educational philosophy called *Ujamaa* (Swahili for "familyhood").[18] Ujamaa was specifically chosen for its focus on Tanzanian life in which valued beings in communities cooperated for the good of all. Nyerere did not differentiate among various parts of the government. Therefore, education, social, economic, and political policies were interrelated and reflected the Tanzanian oral culture. This was Nyerere's *rural socialism*. To explain this, especially as it related to schools as nation builders, Nyerere spoke about children becoming national assets when they were taught how to be self-reliant.

Blending the oral culture of valued beings and cooperation centered in villages, Nyerere believed European technologies could be transplanted into African life without causing cultural disruption. To reinforce these goals, schools taught Swahili so students could become qualified for government service and communicate with Tanzanians who spoke another language, including English.[19] Swahili was taught as an emblem of national pride. Self-reliance also meant students were expected to become valued beings by learning how to work and solve problems together. For example, in secondary schools, teachers encouraged students to think of common objects that could be used in their lives, their school, or their community that would take the place of imported technical objects. Not only was this beneficial for student learning, it also contributed to nation building.

Yet, education for nation building created structural problems for Tanzanian schools. The colonial model inherited from the British divided the school structure into three components: primary (grades 1–7), secondary (grades 8–11 or 12), and university (University of Dar es Salaam). This structure created major handicaps for indigenous students. For example, during the 1971 academic year, it was thought that no more than 50 percent of school-age children attended primary school. While not all students finished primary school, many dropping out before grade 7, large numbers also failed the final exams (primary leaving examinations), Nyerere complained.

> The most simple thing about the education which we are at present providing is that it is physically an idealist's education designed to meet the interests and the needs of a very small proportion of those who enter the school system. It is designed for the few who are intellectually stronger than their fellows. It induces, among those who succeed, a feeling of superiority and leaves the majority of the others hankering for something they will never obtain. It thus cannot produce either the egalitarian society we should build or the attitudes of mind which are conducive to an egalitarian society; on the contrary, it induces the growth of a class structure in our country.[20]

At the same time, secondary schools suffered an extensive dropout rate. This was compounded with failure rates on the final exams (secondary leaving examinations) as well.[21]

Tanzanian secondary schools also suffered other problems. At independence, most of the secondary schools were small, the few students studying only a British university-entrance curriculum. Secondary school expansion, therefore, became a national priority. Increasing student attendance in small schools, increasing the number of curriculum options (streams) for students who were not planning on attending university, and building more secondary schools throughout the country were the immediate aims. Yet, because of financial costs, these attempts failed. Therefore, efforts to increase student enrollment, while decreasing costs, meant changing the school structure. New regulations included reducing by one the number of years students were required to attend secondary school, while decreasing the number of days students in each academic term were required to attend school. Other less radical cost-cutting measures were also taken. Each of these was largely unsuccessful.

These measures were devastating because the secondary school system was central to the economic and social health of the nation. In many ways, Nyerere's valued beings were represented by the graduates of these schools. The numbers of those wishing to continue their studies at the University of Dar es Salaam or universities in Kenya and Uganda diminished. That meant there were fewer veterinary science and agriculture graduates, which consequently had disastrous impacts on rural economics. Perhaps Nyerere's greatest disappointment was in the area of primary teachers. Fewer primary teachers were available because fewer secondary school graduates entered teaching. Recognizing that many primary schools (and some lower secondary grades) would suffer teacher shortages, qualifications were decreased so that primary school graduates or even students in their last years of primary school were eligible to teach. The same process was used to encourage less-qualified students to staff secondary schools.

Had Nyerere's rural socialism and self-reliance reform philosophies failed? Some argue they had. For example, Nyerere's primary schools did not close the serious economic gap between urban and rural Tanzanians, nor had schools noticeably improved the living standards in rural areas. In fact, much of the curriculum was seen by students as irrelevant to their everyday lives. Because of this, as well as structural and curricular problems, few rural students passed the primary school leaving examinations. Of those that did, most stayed home, refusing to leave their villages to attend secondary schools in other communities. And, as detractors stated, even if the students had passed the primary and secondary leaving examinations, most would have chosen to remain in urban areas, causing continued rural decline.

Others judged Nyerere's school reform program unsuccessful because it had not closed the economic gap between Tanzania and the capitalist nations. Had Nyerere's education reform programs changed the economy sufficiently that Tanzania was becoming less a concentration of resources and labor? Or did the schools have no impact on creating national wealth by developing domestic industry? In some ways, these questions were unfair, yet it was obvious that secondary schools were the linchpin for nation building. Except in specific areas such as veterinary medicine and agriculture, university graduates were not absolutely required. Education for rural existence, as Nyerere pictured it, was difficult because schools did not teach skills relating to agricultural life and technology. As a consequence, Tanzania's primary schools did not motivate students to stay in school.

If Nyerere thought these questions were unfair or his reforms were judged too soon, he must have realized they were the proper questions to ask. After all, these are the benchmarks oral cultures must pass if they want to live in a literate, capitalist-dominated world. These are also the questions

Gandhi had tried to answer when he articulated his educational reform philosophy at the end of World War II.

Gandhi's Satyagraha

Of the postcolonial educational reformers, Mahatma Gandhi was unique. It is impossible to speak about his educational reform philosophy without understanding his life. Gandhi saw all things in the universe as interrelated. Like most educational reformers of this period, Gandhi had participated in his country's independence movement and had a European education. Unlike some reformers, Gandhi brought an early freshness to postcolonialism because of his lived experiences in England, India, and South Africa. Like Nyerere later in Tanzania, Gandhi experienced British colonialism and understood the grating relations between elite, capitalist societies and traditional oral cultures. And, though he experienced those issues in British colonial India, he also witnessed as a foreigner those same grating relations caused by British South Africa's apartheid policies. It is this that allows us to see Gandhi's reform philosophy in three-dimensional detail. Gandhi was able to identify with others beyond the boundaries of colonialism. It is this that set him apart.

It is not surprising that India's independence carried with it a sense of disappointment for Gandhi, for the nation was in the process of reshaping itself theologically. India, he learned, could be either Hindu or Muslim, but it could not be both. With this, Gandhi, like Nyerere, recognized that the fate of the nation could culminate with capitalism's dominance. Except, in this case, no conclusion could be negotiated because India had already won its independence. How wrong he was!

It was not that Gandhi was opposed to capitalism or favored Marxism-Leninism. Rather, it was his reform philosophy, known as *Satyagraha*, that he favored. In it, he maintained the interrelatedness of elite literate and non-literate cultures. Gandhi did not rank one better than the other, although he recognized the provincialism of European elites and talked about how damaging they were to workers regardless of where they lived. In fact, education, he pointed out, was not about literacy and nonliteracy, as many reformers believed. The purpose of education was to become more spiritual, and spirituality was not dependent on literacy. For Gandhi, the well-educated person lived an active nonviolent (*Satyagrahis*) life. He stated:

> The term *Satyagraha* was coined by me in a demonstration of its permanence and invincibility. It can be used alike by men, women and children. . . . It is impossible for those who consider themselves to be weak to apply this force. Only those who realize that there is something in a man which is superior to the brute nature in him, and that the latter always

yields to it, can effectively be Satyagrahis. This force is to violence . . .
what light is to darkness.[22]

Satyagraha was a powerful force for those who understood it. It was not
education that gave strength to the weak, he said; rather, it was the eternal
law of unconditional love. He didn't want schools to embrace the narrow-
mindedness of literacy so children learned only about the past with its dead
white heroes. Education was about eternity. Educated people were those
who saw their lives as a consequence of major forces unfettered by artificial
boundaries. Gandhi wanted teachers to teach children that they were not
discrete individuals separated from others. Children, he said, should see
themselves as a part of a great whole that began before they were born and
would not end at their death. Like Thoreau, Gandhi believed that whatever
children should know, society or others could teach. Schools should only
teach spiritual attitudes—those things that were essential for a person's life.
Yet, Gandhi recognized evil, for he had experienced it in England, South
Africa, and India. Nevertheless, he did not think of it as an opposite to that
which was good. Goodness was spiritual, and evil was the creation of humans. To remove the world's evil, Gandhi said, schools should teach compassion, a subject area which did not have literacy as a prerequisite.

Indeed, Gandhi was not in favor of India's parroting capitalist cultures
by industrializing. When he lived in England, Gandhi saw British laborers
working in factories and felt their lives were minimized. Although he sympathized with them because of the difficulty and tedium of their work,
Gandhi saw that workers were happy with their material rewards. How
could peace of mind, harmony, and satisfaction come about if laborers were
happy with rewards that were only temporary possessions? He cautioned India's laborers that they, too, would become like English workers if they accepted the tedium of working in factory assembly lines. They would never
reach those high levels of mysticism because the capitalistic entrepreneurs
would drag them down to the intoxicating depths of materialism.

However, Gandhi recognized that manufacturing was essential for India.
Because he wanted India to be self-sufficient, he believed that economic suf-
ficiency should occur village by village and not because of government mandate. Gandhi thought of self-sufficiency as an all-encompassing economic,
social, and educational activity that could come about through village production or cottage industries. Keeping with him a spinning wheel, Gandhi
continued to demonstrate the worthiness of villagers working together to
produce only what they needed. He saw the village as the basic social unit.
It was here children first became aware of the ethics of living and learning
by doing.[23] Cottage industries taught children self-control. As children labored with adults, creating goods the village needed, they learned the discipline that resulted in wisdom. This rural economy would be the mainstay of

Indian life, the only place where children could learn the relationship between theory and action.

Gandhi focused India's debate about its postcolonial economics and schools by comparing its history of British capitalism with his philosophy of cottage industry. He reminded the new nation that during *swaraj* (Sanskrit for "self-ruling"), that period immediately before independence, Indian consumers had boycotted British industries because capitalists demanded laborers work for starvation wages. He also reminded them that before British colonization, cottage industries created village wealth. In those days, adults and children produced what was necessary for all the villagers. The only economy that left India destitute, he pointed out, was British capitalism.

As for schools, Gandhi's argument was the same. Regardless of how schools were organized, in buildings as the European preferred or in the open village as he favored, the question of what curriculum children should learn was paramount. European capitalism, he said, taught a curriculum of elitism, expressed through literacy. While he did not discount literacy, Gandhi thought teaching Indian children how to become good factory workers was unacceptable. Pointedly, he compared capitalism with peasant production. While one rewarded Indians with material goods which would wear out, the other rewarded Indians with mysticism and wisdom, both of which were eternal.

Gandhi's educational philosophy would not be accepted by the Indian government. Led by his protégé Jawaharlal Nehru, India adopted a subdued economic plan that included government ownership of major industries.[24] It was not that Nehru disagreed with his mentor, but he feared that, without industrializing, India would never be freed from European capitalistic servitude.[25] Nehru fostered central government planning and, while inviting foreign entrepreneurs to invest in the economy, encouraged the growth of domestic industry. In a succession of five-year plans, the government expanded domestic industrial development in rural areas so that villagers would not move to urban areas. In the same manner, Nehru encouraged community development programs to bring electricity, water, and other essentials to rural areas. Included in this economic design were his government's programs to increase agricultural production.

In retrospect, some postcolonialists faulted Gandhi, arguing his concepts of cottage industry and educational reforms would not have helped the people. As support, they point to Nehru's industrialization policies. Nehru, they mentioned, believed India would never succeed within the community of nations unless the nation industrialized. Fixedly, Nehru wanted the Indian economy to compete in the international marketplace. Yet, Gandhi's cottage industry philosophy should not be rejected because of Nehru's decisions. To Gandhi, cottage industry was more than economic competition. It was a method of maintaining the lives of people within the social and economic environments they knew best—the village. Further, cottage industries were many things, including schools. Here, children learned a curriculum of working with village adults acting as teachers. They learned they needed to produce only what was needed. Education was lifelong, and the rewards were eternal.

REFLECTIONS OF EDUCATIONAL REFORM

Of the four school systems (Soviet Union, Mexico, Tanzania, and India) discussed in this chapter, none accomplished its stated economic and social goals, although Mexico might argue its educational reforms are still on track. In fact, one of the governments (Soviet Union) that experimented with schools as nation builders no longer exists. Two nations (India and Tanzania) failed as they discovered theological or economic differences were more important than nationalism. But for some school reforms, setbacks were only partial. For example, while Juárez's *Reforma* melted away after his death in 1872, his educational reform philosophy was revived in Mexico's Constitution of 1917. On the other hand, one plan offered by Gandhi was immediately dismissed by the country's first prime minister. Before we dismiss the reformers and their reforms, let us look at the commonalties we inherit.

Of course, none of the school reforms was viewed by the others as a model worthy of replication, although, through the Cold War eyes of capitalism, it seemed that Marxism-Leninism was showcased in Tanzania. In reflection, that was not the case because Nyerere was not building a utopia. Self-reliance and rural socialism were not to be founded on Marxism-Leninism. Each reformer, except Gandhi, using different words or presenting different philosophies, imagined schools as an arm of government. In fact—unlike the Soviet Union, which used schools to develop the true Soviet citizen—Gandhi's and Nyerere's educational reforms intended schools to enhance village or rural life and improve domestic industry. Perhaps the reason their reform philosophies viewed schools within this milieu was because both understood oral cultures and wanted schools to reflect this. As a consequence, Nyerere's rural socialism and Gandhi's cottage industry are similar for the same reason: each wanted schooling to be a community affair

Mexico, on the other hand, presented a different picture. Because of its long postcolonial period, interrupted by revolutions and foreign invasions, its understanding of rural indigenous peoples was not clear. Until 1917 education was reserved for Mexican elites, who pictured themselves as Europeans. Rarely were schools open to indigenous peoples in rural areas, except when the elites thought they had the potential to be economic assets influencing foreign investment. After 1917, the educational reform administered by Vasconcelos focused on domestic economic development, but mostly on indigenous inclusion and the development of a tri-cultural nation.

A commonality among the four educational reformers was their interest in using schools as laboratories to experiment on social issues. The most obvious of the four, the Soviet Union, was open in its declaration of developing schools that would create the Soviet person. For example, Makarenko's Gorky Colony experiments helped develop his concept of the collective. For Makarenko, the collective was the embodiment of socialism in which people acted within the group and responded within group purposes. The collective was the equivalent of the state-sanctioned family. On the other hand, Gandhi's and Nyerere's educational reforms were not socialistic within these definitions. The traditional cultural heights to which a well-educated person could climb was not to be a member of a collective as much as it was to be a valued being who spoke Swahili, accepted rewards of mysticism, and lived in peace and harmony. Although Nyerere used the expression *rural socialism*, it was much closer to Gandhi's term *cottage industry*. Each was interested in rural (village) production.

Of the four, Mexico was unique. Unlike the others, it lived next door to a wealthy capitalist nation. Although not suffering military invasions or incursions, the American threat was primarily cultural. Exporting its mass culture worldwide, Mexico was a prime target. As a consequence, Mexican educational reform faced much more complicated problems than the others. Domestically, schools were focusing on developing tri-culturalism while attempting to minimize American mass culture. In some ways, the constitutional reform Vasconcelos was implementing in the early twentieth century was similar to Nyerere's concern about developing national unity among Tanzanians a half-century later. Each chose schools to change national attitudes and abilities. While Nyerere used Swahili to attack his problem, Vasconcelos chose a curriculum enhancing indigenous cultures and social respect.

Perhaps the most significant commonality among the reformers was that they thought schools could protect them from unregulated international capitalism. And, that may have been the reason they were attracted to John Dewey's philosophy. As we discussed earlier in this chapter, while the Soviet Union and Mexico at first expressed deep curiosity about Dewey's philosophy, both nations, led by reformers Makarenko and Vasconcelos, rejected him. Even though those rejections were understandable, Dewey's attraction to Nyerere and Gandhi was based on the concept of community and lifelong learning.

It is interesting how Dewey, Gandhi, and Nyerere thought of themselves as education reformers. Each agreed that European colonialism had

created an international indigenous worker class whose purpose was to labor for capitalist profit. Using different words, each defined the worker class
similarly. Dewey defined workers as those who were slaves or were
thought by capitalists as undesirables. Nyerere thought of them as representatives of a nonelite oral culture, and Gandhi viewed them similarly but
feared they would be willing to accept capitalists' materialism as their pay.
Each believed capitalists had been successful in maintaining the existing
cultural divisions because they controlled schools. Therefore, each assumed
his education reforms would contribute to the independence of the international working class.

Each used labels to designate capitalist education. For example, Dewey
labeled elite schools as "traditional education." This was the schooling he received in Vermont as a child. He described it as passive, in which students
quietly accepted what was taught by teachers. Nyerere and Gandhi, as well
as Vasconcelos and Makarenko, had the same type of passive education in
their home countries. They referred to it as *colonial* or *aristocratic*. The reformers agreed that student success was based more on class, race, gender,
and economic advantage than on ability.

Each reformer proposed different philosophies of education in which
children learned a curriculum that was meaningful to their environment and
allowed them to be actively engaged in the learning process. Except for
Makarenko, each assumed the rewards for education was a form of personal
growth rather than class solidification. For example, Gandhi proposed
schooling in his cottage industry model. Nyerere's rural socialism reflected
Gandhi's cottage industry in many ways. However, he expected schools to
be arms of government. Both Makarenko and Vasconcelos agreed with this,
except their goals were much different. Lastly, Dewey defined his "new education" to mean children would learn to think scientifically and cooperate,
thereby becoming useful members of society.

What were the consequences of these reforms? Actually, Gandhi, like
Dewey, did not see his educational reforms put into operation. Gandhi's reforms were rejected in favor of an elite school system that was designed to
compete with capitalists on an international level. Nyerere saw his schools
become part of his nation-building efforts but was frustrated because of his
inability to finance the reforms. Lastly, Makarenko's collective, at first a glow-
ing success, passed into the same historical dustbin all utopias eventually enjoy. If there is cause to think these reforms failed, it was because the European dominant capitalist cultures refused to accept them.

Perhaps, that is what the reformers should have expected. Each of the
four national reform models we investigated in this chapter stood as discrete
entities alone on the international stage. The reformers wanted to include laborers, indigenous peoples, and nonliterate cultures in their schools. But
they were measured against the elite standards of European capitalism. If

these educational reformers had stood less discretely and had been part of international organizations, would their reforms been judged less harshly? In fact, this is what they wanted when they joined a family of nations. The Soviet Union developed an empire through which its education was exported. Tanzania, along with Kenya and Uganda, joined an African federation to combine their resources. India chose to remain aloof as a Third World leader to be courted by both socialism and capitalism. Mexico joined its wealthy neighbors to the north in an economic agreement. In the next chapter, we will investigate these international organizations and their influences on schools and watch them prepare themselves to live in a global village.

NOTES

1. The postcolonial period is that time frame when new national governments established major institutions such as schools. During the early postcolonial period, many nations turned to Marxism-Leninism to solve educational and economic problems but found it unpromising. Eventually, most countries turned to some form of modified capitalism in which governments played a central role.

2. Arkady Gaidar, *Tale of the Military Secret, Boy Malchish Kibalchish and His Firm Word* (1935; trans. George Kittell, Moscow: Novosti Press Agency Publishing House, 1974), 1–2. As a youngster in the early years of the Russian Revolution, Gaidar was active, supporting the Bolshevik-Leninists. He organized street gangs. At sixteen he commanded a Red Army regiment. Gaidar's children's books center around love of country and faith in those around you. Children learned they were to be straightforward in their relations with others, loyal to the Soviet Union, and steadfast with their friends. For adults, Gaidar's theme is that the simplicity of absolute truth can even be understood by children. Gaidar died in 1941 as a soldier in World War II.

3. Anatoli Lunacharsky, "Speech at the First All-Russia Congress on Education," in *On Education: Selected Articles and Speeches*, comp. E. Dneprov, trans. Ruth English (Moscow: Progress Publishers, 1981), 10–30. Lunacharsky was first nominated for the new position of people's commissar for education by V. I. Lenin in 1917. Both were instrumental in creating preschools and vocational education. One can hear in his opening address to the All-Russia Congress delegates Lunacharsky's frustration with teachers (especially university professors) who were not committed to forging a new Marxist-Leninist educational system. Lunacharsky was appointed chairman of the Academic Committee of the Central Executive Committee of the Soviet Union. In 1933 he was promoted to envoy plenipotentiary of the Soviet Union to Spain. Lunacharsky reportedly died in France on his way to take up his appointment in Madrid. Educated in Switzerland in philosophy and the natural sciences, he also wrote a number of plays, including *Barber to the King* (1906), *Faust and the City* (1918), and *Don Quixote Liberated* (1922).

4. Lunacharsky, "Speech at the First All-Russia Congress," 22–23. Lunacharsky is referring to John Dewey in his comment about "some eminent teachers who had nothing in common with Marxism."

5. Lunacharsky, "Speech at the First All-Russia Congress," 18–19.

6. James Bowen, *Soviet Education: Anton Makarenko and the Years of Experiment* (Madison: University of Wisconsin Press, 1962), 16–17.

7. A. P. Pinkevitch, *The New Education in the Soviet Republic*, ed. George Counts, trans. Nucia Perlmutter (n.p., 1929), vi, quoted in Bowen, *Soviet Education*, 16–17. Pinkevitch was the president of the Second State University of Moscow.

8. Shatsky had no difficulty blending the ideas of Dewey with that of culture building. See Thomas Woody, *New Minds, New Men?* (New York: Macmillan, 1932), 49, quoted in Bowen, *Soviet Education*, 138.

9. Bowen, *Soviet Education*, 43.

10. Anton S. Makarenko, *The Road to Life* (Moscow: State Foreign Languages Publishing House, 1955). Makarenko wrote a trilogy (the other books are entitled *Learning to Live* and *A Book for Parents*). In many ways, it is a deeply personal story of how he and homeless adolescents (*besprizorniki*) learned to live together though difficult conditions. See also Anton Semenovich Makarenko, *The Collective Family: A Handbook for Russian Parents* (Magnolia, MA: Peter Smith Publishers, 1990).

11. This comment has been used to explain how Mexicans feel about living so close to a global superpower. In Mexico the comment also hints at the disgust Mexicans may feel when they read the history of Mexican-American relations.

12. Justo Sierra, *La Educación Nacional, Obras Completas*, vol. 8 (Mexico City: Universidad Nacional Autónoma de México, 1948), quoted in Edward Ignas and Raymond J. Corsini, eds., *Comparative Educational Systems* (Itasca, IL: F. E. Peacock, 1981), 291.

13. William E. Segall and Anna V. Wilson, *Introduction to Education: Teaching in a Diverse Society*, 2nd ed. (Lanham, MD: Rowman & Littlefield, 2004), 123.

14. Dneprov, Anatoli Lunacharsky's compiler, believes Lunacharsky understood the difference between the terms *collective* and *community*. In a lecture delivered in May 1928 in Leningrad (St. Petersburg) entitled "Education of the New Man," Lunacharsky mentioned Dewey as a follower of Soviet educational philosophy. Yet, within the specifics of the speech, he referred to Dewey as a pragmatist who developed a curriculum that had little content or logic. "Only those things were taught which could be practically applied." Lunacharsky, *On Education*.

15. Ian M. L. Hunter, "Lengthy Verbatim Recall: The Role of Text," ed. Andrew W. Ellis, in *Progress in the Psychology of Language: What Happened in the Years Immediately after the Execution of Jesus* (Hillsdale, NJ: Erlbaum, 1985), 1:207–35. Quoted in John D. Crossan, *The Birth of Christianity* (New York: HarperCollins, 1999), 69.

16. Ayele Negussie, "The Political Culture of Ethiopia," in Institute of International Studies, Office of Education, Department of Health, Education, and Welfare, *Education and Culture in Eastern Africa* (Washington, DC: GPO, 1973), 1:16.

17. Tanzania's economic relationship with European and American capitalists and international banking systems was not unique. Postcolonial nations had great difficulty controlling their budgets. The ever-increasing costs of imported capital goods could not be met with revenues gained from exported natural resources. National deficits were covered by international bank loans, many of which had high rates of interest. See Roger Yeager, *Tanzania: An African Experiment*, 2nd rev. ed. (Boulder, CO: Westview Press, 1989).

18. *Ujamaa* also means "cooperative economics," and it has become one of the seven principles (*Nguno*) of Kwanzaa. The other principles are *Umoja* (unity), *Kujichagulia* (self-determination), *Ujima* (collective work and responsibility), *Nia* (purpose), *Kuumba* (creativity), and *Imani* (faith). See Julius Nyerere, *Ujamaa: Essays on Socialism* (London: Oxford University Press, 1973).

19. Nyerere wanted both Swahili and English as official languages. While Swahili's purpose was to unite the various cultural and social groups of the nation, English was reserved for international economics and politics.

20. W. S. Kajubi, address to seminar on Tanzanian education, in Institute of International Studies, *Education and Culture in Eastern Africa*, 3:21–22. Kajubi was the director of the National Institute of Education at Makerere University College in Kampala, Uganda, at this time, when the Uganda, Kenya, and Tanzania universities were part of the East Africa Community. He is explaining Nyerere's views on education while commenting on the Ugandan minister of education's position in relation to the Tanzanians.

21. Few Tanzanian students were able to pass the stringent European examinations and therefore were left to live with failure.

22. Mohandas Gandhi, quoted in Frederick Mayer, *A History of Educational Thought* (Columbus, OH: Charles E. Merrill Books, 1962), 339.

23. Like Dewey, Gandhi had experienced a European education in which students remained passive, inactive, and learned a curriculum others had defined for them. Therefore, it was not difficult for Gandhi, discussing cottage industries, to understand Dewey's New Education in which he extolled active learning. He also agreed with Dewey that practical experience was more important than shallow memorization, as typified by Dewey's description of traditional education.

24. Jawaharlal Nehru (1889–1964) was India's first prime minister. Born a Brahman, Nehru was trained as a lawyer in England and returned to India in 1912. Nehru and Gandhi had a long, positive relationship prior to Indian independence, in which Gandhi acquainted Nehru with the political, social, and educational problems of rural villages. With Gandhi's public blessing, Nehru became prime minister of India's transitional government and then prime minister of India. Nehru's daughter Indira and grandson Ravi became prime ministers during the twentieth century. See Beatrice Pitney Lamb, *The Nehrus of India: Three Generations of Leadership* (New York: Macmillan, 1967), and M. J. Akbar, *Nehru: The Making of India* (New York: Viking, 1988).

25. Nehru's concern was well justified. As early as 1974, Inkeles and Smith noted that schools cause people to participate in modernity. Yet, Fagerlind and Saha have also credited television and social incidentals in fostering change. See Alex Inkeles and David Smith, *Becoming Modern* (London: Heinemann Education Books, 1974), and Ingemar Fagerlind and Lawrence J. Saha, *Education and National Development: A Comparative Perspective*, 2nd ed. (Oxford, England: Pergamon Press, 1989).

4

Schools in a Global Society: From a Family of Nations to a Global Village

In the previous chapter, we investigated postcolonial educational reform. Exhausted as laborers and resource suppliers, postcolonial governments wanted schools to meet their economic and social aims rather than those of the departing European colonizers. Therefore, many reformers looked for educational models that would help them develop economically and, at the same time, acknowledge their culture. Of the viable models that existed in the mid-twentieth century, two met most of the reformers' benchmarks. These schools were based on indigenous philosophies. While neither exhibited every part of the criteria, together they illustrated it was possible for national school systems to be unique to specific cultures. The first model was from the Soviet Union. Forged by Ukrainian reformer Anton Makarenko, this system modeled the Marxism-Leninism philosophy that schools, as arms of government, were critical instruments in the creation of a Soviet workers' utopia. The second model was Mexico. While not studied for its economic failures and successes, educational reformers examined its postcolonial experiences of creating a tri-cultural society in social defense of capitalist mass culture.

The previous chapter also investigated attempts by postcolonial educational reformers Mahatma Gandhi (India) and Julius Nyerere (Tanzania) to develop national school systems that incorporated nonelitist oral cultures. Neither Gandhi's cottage industry or Nyerere's rural socialism was accepted by elite, literate capitalists as equivalent, however. Bluntly, Europeans dismissed noncapitalist educational models as irrelevant and insignificant.

In this chapter, we will look at the postcolonial reformers' response to the reactions of the dominant elite nations by noting the reformers' participation in international organizations. Postcolonial educational reformers thought their views would be better understood, and more resources would be made available, if their educational needs were expressed in the aggregate rather than on a country-to-country basis. As members of a "family of nations," they assumed they would continue to experiment with their educational models. They also believed their importance would be enhanced to dominant nations as discrete political, economic, and cultural entities within the context of the Cold War. Recognizing this, and the significance of educational reform for social survival, this chapter will focus on indigenous educational reform as these nations have been irreversibly drawn to a new form of global economic structure called globalization. In short, postcolonial educational reformers discovered they were becoming members of a "global village" in which they competed with their neighbors for the promised largess of a free-market economy.

POSTCOLONIAL SCHOOLS AND THE FAMILY OF NATIONS

In some ways, Gandhi and Nyerere were typical postcolonial educational reformers. They, like others then and now, recognized the relatedness of schools and society. They articulated how the schools they envisioned would be different from those of their colonial masters. They understood that capitalist economics meant mass production of goods. And, to increase profits, they asserted, indigenous laborers were paid minimum wages, while their natural resources were exploited. It was because of this, partly, that reformers wanted schools to voice the peoples' cultures.

Through this lens, it was easy for postcolonial reformers to understand why Europeans regarded their educational experiments as irrelevant and insignificant. These postcolonial systems did not prepare children to become good industrial laborers. Students were not taught the elements most laborers were expected to know—to work hard and be loyal to European managers. Of course, as Gandhi, Nyerere, and other reformers realized, international economic competition also caused indigenous laborers to become capitalists' customers, buying goods they produced from resources they mined or grew. The result of this economic reality was that postcolonial nations never reaped the rewards of capitalism and were fearful they would forever remain poor. For these reasons, they joined international organizations. Let us first look at the United Nations.

United Nations

Aptly, the United Nations' motto—"Let us beat swords into plowshares"—signified for dominant and indigenous nations alike a dream come true.[1] At the conclusion of World War II, dominant nations dreamed of a time when military costs would not be a line item in their national budgets. And postcolonial nations dreamed of the time when those who labored with plowshares could live lives touched by the affluence of health, education, and welfare. Peace and human dignity, it seemed, finally were to be reached in postwar years. Immediately, and in many ways, these two national groupings (capitalists and postcolonial reformers), realized some of their dreams.

The UN General Assembly legitimated postcolonial nations. Here, those who experienced empire, colonizers and colonized alike, met for the first time on an equal basis. Each, dominant and postcolonial, was politically and socially discrete, without political bonds in which one was tied to the other in managed servitude. With equal votes (one country, one vote), postcolonial nations had the opportunity to express their views about issues that touched them the most. Besides participating in every international committee and action of the United Nations, the aggregate power of legislating membership dues of all nations, including their former colonizers, was, in their eyes, the most important.

But these emerging nations quickly discovered the power of the United Nations rested elsewhere. Other than developing budgets, the General Assembly had minimal influence, only recommending actions to the Security Council. With veto power and guaranteed membership in the Security Council, the dominant nations remained in control. Because of this, many postcolonial nations expressed deep interest in the various UN committees, for collectively they assumed they could enter into meaningful dialogues with dominant nations. The committee that most appropriately allowed postcolonial reformers entrance into these discussions was the United Nations Educational, Scientific, and Cultural Organization (UNESCO). In short, it was this international committee that acted as a platform upon which the world's indigenous confronted the dominant nations.

UNESCO

UNESCO became a reality in 1946, when twenty countries made application for membership.[2] Its purpose was exactly that which postcolonial countries believed was their avenue for economic assistance and international regard. Defined by its constitution, UNESCO was committed to helping nations discover ways in which they could solve mutual problems in education, communications, science, and culture. At the same time, the organization helped member nations through research, technical assistance, and professional expertise, all contributed by dominant nations. Within this milieu of expectations, both postcolonial and dominant nations learned about each other. In this case, unfortunately, it was through conflict and disorder.

Much of the conflict and disorder focused on the organization's budget. The dominant nations, concerned that the majority of monies was awarded to favored postcolonial nations and unable to develop sunset clauses, thought themselves excluded. As well, they argued that too much of the organization's budget was spent on pointless conferences and seminars. All of this caused mini-dramas that focused on specific individuals.

Yet, these issues, taken separately, were not significant. Rather, they were symptoms of distrust between the two cultural perspectives. Believing issues such as these were illustrations of an anti-Western bias, the United States in 1984 and the United Kingdom in 1985 withdrew their membership for a time. In short, postcolonial educational reformers discovered little international assistance could be expected from an organization that was founded on an unshared dream. Or they learned that, if they wished to discuss mutual issues with dominant nations, different parliamentary avenues would have to be discovered.

Regional Associations

Postcolonial reformers continued to direct their economic and cultural conversations with dominant nations through membership in other international organizations. While participation in global organizations such as the United Nations and its various committees allowed some postcolonial countries to meet some of their objectives, most felt their numerical majority was dwarfed by their lack of economic independence. Specifically, postcolonial educational reformers understood their relations with dominant nations were framed within the context of the Cold War. That meant their importance was measured by the quality of their labor and resources.

To minimize these feelings, many newly independent nations joined regional associations in which they believed their social interests and educational concerns would be discussed. Still, most of the regional partnerships, as many were called, including the Organization of American States (OAS) and the Commonwealth of Nations were controlled by dominant nations. For example, the OAS's major thrust during the Cold War was supporting American Cold War foreign policy, even though countries such as Mexico were more interested in economic and cultural issues. In the same fashion, the Commonwealth, meaning the previous British colonies, centered its agenda on postcolonial loyalty to the British monarchy and Cold War policy. Neither of these organizations realized its goals, although the OAS has in the post–Cold War era become interested in economic and social problems facing the member states. In the same manner, the Commonwealth has voiced an interest in encouraging democratic and parliamentary procedures in some postcolonial dictatorships.

International Partnerships

During this period, there were other forms of international partnerships. Mostly to advance Cold War foreign policies, some dominant nations such as the United States, the United Kingdom, and the Soviet Union supported some corrupt postcolonial leaders through military, industrial, and cultural aid. While intending to curry favor, these efforts were designed to establish diplomatic and economic zones of influence within the Cold War confrontation. Other, more minor industrial nations and social groups, in the spirit of reaching out, were willing to support selected cultural institutions such as hospitals and schools. Yet, these efforts, especially from the European nations, were actually in support of the various Cold War antagonists. At the same time, many postcolonial nations were willing to become involved in the international power politics of the Cold War. Their interests were not so much a reflection of their political philosophies as it was an expression of their desperate need to solve their economic and educational problems.

The diplomatic-cultural dance between postcolonial nations and Cold War antagonists included school development. Dressed in humanitarian terms such as cultural assistance, or using the graphs of economic development, both reformers and dominant partners understood the conflicting purposes of educational development. Simply put, postcolonial nations wanted schools to contribute to the nation's affluence, while dominant nations wanted schools to win over the hearts, minds, and talents of the indigenous population for their Cold War political advantage. Two of the many examples of such mutual cultural assistance are the Soviet sponsorship of the Patrice Lumumba Peoples' Friendship University in Moscow and the American support of Haile Selassie I University in Addis Ababa, Ethiopia.

Patrice Lumumba Peoples' Friendship University

Renamed in 1961 for Patrice Lumumba, an assassinated African nationalist,[3] postcolonial educational reformers viewed the Peoples' Friendship University as an opportunity to send their bright students to a university less expensive than the high-priced European and American colleges and universities. Using precious hard currency, higher education was draining national budgets. The secondary costs of students traveling from continent to continent were inordinate. Living costs, even if graduate students' wives and families remained home, were still excessive.

Further, educational reformers were not always happy with how students reacted to capitalist cultures. While pleased with the extraordinarily high educational quality students received, reformers were displeased that some students returned home espousing Western values. Many, having driver's licenses and actuating different social values, showed little tolerance for their indigenous cultures. Their resultant impatience with indigenous social values was illustrated by their frustration and elitist attitudes.

Yet, the difficulty returning students represented was based on significant issues. Some students, now using different learning styles (especially those of John Dewey), continued their interest in learning through questioning. While that approach was acceptable in academic institutions, it was threatening in political and social circles. In short, many graduates returned to their homelands only to become reformers themselves, challenging the political and social processes created by the older reformer generation.

Regarding Soviet interest in the university, its use as a Cold War propaganda tool quickly became apparent. Espousing an educational philosophy in which postcolonial students would have the opportunity to learn with many others like them, young secondary school graduates traveled to Moscow to study engineering, economics, medicine, and other disciplines important to their nation's economic development. In this ostensibly non-corrupting social atmosphere sponsored by a university committed to international respect and friendship, students were expected to succeed in their studies. Although flaunted by Soviet educators as a world-class higher education institution, many postcolonial reformers, who were themselves graduates of English, French, German, and American universities, remained quietly skeptical. Regardless, many educational reformers believed that in this social-academic atmosphere students had the opportunity to receive an education beneficial to society and also have opportunities to meet, study, and live with students from other postcolonial nations. To meet the next generations' leaders, becoming personally acquainted with those they might work with on the international stage was an advantage not expected from all European universities.

But troubles soon emerged. Although students who enrolled at Patrice Lumumba Peoples' Friendship University knew the language of instruction was Russian, their colonial legacy had prepared them only in European languages. Even though many postcolonial reformers knew this, they continued to support the teaching of European languages, thereby placing students at an academic disadvantage. While learning Russian caused some delay, students also found themselves unable to become acquainted with Soviet society. Almost in social quarantine, some students became less interested in their studies and more concerned with transferring to schools outside the Soviet Union. Of course, transfer was difficult because of the political and academic obstacles. Beyond this, as students returned home, postcolonial educational reformers also discovered graduates were interested in social reform, especially when they believed their government showed symptoms of becoming a dictatorship.

Haile Selassie I University[4]

Unlike Patrice Lumumba University, Haile Selassie I University in Addis Ababa reflected a different Cold War philosophy. For example, in what would eventually become the university's College of Agriculture, rather than offering higher education programs in the elite mechanical arts and sciences, as had the Soviet Union, the American approach was to export low technology in the form of practical land-grant agricultural training. This was because the Ethiopian college students the Americans wanted to train represented an oral culture. The college therefore developed a preparatory school in which students learned to read and write while enrolled in agricultural courses.

The second mission garnered immediate results. The College of Agriculture invested much of its professorial talents hosting field days in which local farmers learned new low-technology agricultural methods. As the students increased their academic credentials and the school increased its social credibility, college classes began. In fact, the structure of the educational aid mirrored traditional U.S. land-grant educational history in which small state colleges first developed preparatory schools that taught students the rudiments of reading and writing while learning agricultural fundamentals. Graduation from the preparatory school allowed students to enroll in college courses.

The first agricultural education experiment using this model in Ethiopia was at Alemaya (Imperial Ethiopian College of Agricultural and Mechanical Arts) and Jimma (Jimma Agricultural Technical School). Unlike the Soviet approach, the Americans allowed their professors to contend with culture shock while the Ethiopian students learned in their specific culture.

Like the Moscow experiment, the Ethiopian enterprise was a reflection of a national effort to befriend an indigenous people who would willingly enter a specific Cold War zone of influence. And, like the Moscow experiment, it too ran into difficulties. As students graduated from the Imperial Ethiopian College of Agricultural and Mechanical Arts, many chose to continue their education in the United States. Entering prestigious graduate programs at elite land-grant universities, Ethiopian students became familiar with American culture. While many felt the sting of racial disharmony, other experiences seemed to offset their assessment of the people. For example, the ease of learning how to drive a car (and owning one), the mechanical servants (dishwashers, vacuum cleaners, and clothes washers), free public education, medical assistance, and air-conditioning appeared to compensate. As a consequence, many new Ph.D.'s chose to remain in the United States. Searching for positions in industry and higher education, graduating scholars discovered their dreams of affluence could be realities in their new land of opportunity.

For those graduates who returned to Ethiopia, life seemed less fulfilling. Not wanting to return to rural areas, most settled in Addis Ababa. Creating an intellectual surplus in which the government could not digest their creative talent, many took jobs that had been reserved for the less educated. It was not uncommon to see Ph.D.'s in agriculture education working as television commentators reading the news or discussing the weather. Some drove taxi cabs. Unlike most Ethiopians, these graduates had seen firsthand the measure of affluence dominant cultures possessed and it was difficult to return to less. Like their Moscow colleagues, they too were interested in political and social reform.

Pan-Africanism

While regional associations such as the OAS and the Commonwealth of Nations represented postcolonial reformers' best efforts to cooperate in development projects, few were successful. Nor were the partnership programs such as Patrice Lumumba Peoples' Friendship University and Haile Selassie I University. Perhaps this was because higher education was part of the dominant nations' Cold War policies rather than their honest desires to give educational assistance. Certainly this was the case with both Moscow's and Ethiopia's educational experiments. Each was aimed at developing zones of influence, and neither had the dramatic impact on the people originally thought possible. It could also have been the capitalists' and socialists' inability to understand the cultural bridges they were required to cross in order to understand postcolonial educational needs. Perhaps, it was that neither the socialists or capitalists wanted to.

Such was not the case with Pan-Africanism.[5] Insisting that its philosophy and movement's purpose rested solely on black unity in Africa and the brotherhood of blacks worldwide, it was looked upon with suspicion by most capitalist nations. In particular, U.S. concern with Pan-Africanism was multilayered. On one level, Pan-Africanism was thought by the Federal Bureau of Investigation to be a front for Communist activities. On another level, Pan-Africanism was presented in the United States as a civil rights movement centered in part on school desegregation. Pan-Africanism, however, became clearer as an international issue when the Cold War receded and regional economic associations or trade blocs developed in Asia, the Americas, and Europe. Encouraging African regional associations such as the Economic Community of West African States (ECOWAS) and the Southern African Development Community (SADC) to integrate their economies, Pan-Africanism believed these would become the stepping stones to continental unity.

Perhaps the best illustration of Pan-Africanism is the East African Community (EAC). Discussed here and later in this chapter, the EAC—comprising Tanzania, Kenya, and Uganda—conceivably had the best opportunity to demonstrate the economic and cultural goals of Pan-Africanism. Certainly this was true in education. Each partner-state had a strong educational history. For example, both Kenya and Uganda agreed they would keep their British colonial educational structure and curricula. And, while Tanzania experimented with various forms of pre-university educational models, the University of Dar es Salaam and the University of Nairobi mirrored Makerere University in Uganda. In fact, the three partner-states agreed schools were essential for national development and that development allowed all partner-states to become viable members of the family of nations.

In the same regard, the partner-states recognized economic development as the product of an educated citizenry. Therefore, the economic priority of each partner rested not in the elitist fields of engineering, for example, but in teacher education.[6] Of course, each faced similar cultural problems. For example, the partner-states were generally multicultural, hosting different languages, social orientations, and theologies. Offsetting this, however, was that they generally maintained good relations with their neighboring states, allowing each to concentrate on domestic issues such as schools.

Education and Schooling in the Family of Nations

As stated at the beginning of this chapter, a major reason that postcolonial reformers were attracted to global and regional associations was that they believed they were marginalized by the elite, literate capitalist nations. Even as independent developing countries, reformers believed dominant nations were continuing to view them as colonies whose importance rested on their concentrations of labor and resources. Therefore, postcolonial reformers argued that if they presented themselves in an aggregate within international and global associations, their educational, social, and economic interests could be more clearly articulated. Dominant nations would have the opportunity to view the newly independent nations through a lens of collective interests rather than simply economics.

Generally, as has been discussed, postcolonial experiences in the international organizations were unsatisfactory. In global organizations such as the United Nations, postcolonial reformers discovered that the democratic principle of one-country-one-vote was not always the determining factor. In fact, they were experiencing old-fashioned colonialism newly framed within the economics of wealth and resources rather than through political discussion and compromise. Even within the UN subgroups, postcolonial nations experienced the economic power of dominant nations who felt their values threatened. Therefore, the type of international assistance expected in school development by the postcolonial nations was generally not forthcoming. Obviously, the cause for this was because each nation group focused on different agendas. While postcolonial reformers were interested in schools to help them develop their societies, the dominant nations were in the midst of an international tug-of-war called the Cold War. Accordingly, while postcolonial nations saw themselves as part of the international family of nations in which each nation was equal in stature, dominant nations saw them as pawns in a political chess game in which there were no rules.

For the same reasons, educational reformers found regional associations unsatisfactory. Many of the associations included at least one dominant country. As a consequence, postcolonial reformers discovered their interests were usually subverted or marginalized in favor of some dominant nation's political and economic interests. Because the Cold War was an overriding concern of capitalist nations during this period, many postcolonial reformers experienced anew their inability to interact in these differing formats. In short, postcolonial reformers learned that the differences between colonialism and postcolonialism in the minds of capitalists were simply a matter of semantics. Their ability to interact with capitalist nations was framed by interests not of their choosing. For these reasons, many postcolonial nations, such as India and Mexico, recognized from the beginning how few choices they had to become an equal member within the family of nations.

However, there were some opportunities for developing nations to discuss their educational, social, and economic issues on the international stage. Looking beyond the political and economic horizon peopled by elitist capitalist nations, some postcolonial reformers discovered they were their own best audiences. They understood the international assistance many postcolonial reformers wanted from global and regional associations had to come from nations like themselves. It was this type of regional association to which postcolonial reformers were attracted. Yet, the difficulties represented by culture, language, religion, and social differences were, in many cases, insurmountable. In those specific circumstances when these were less apparent, the success of regional associations was greatly enhanced. Such was the case of the first East African Community.

Supported by Pan-Africanism, the EAC came into existence in 1967 and remained a potent force for a decade. The partner-states included Tanzania, Kenya, and Uganda; however, neighboring countries such as Ethiopia were closely aligned. While the community's interests were wide ranging (such as developing a custom union and health programs), its concerns for education were specific. Each of the partner-states recognized that schools were the crux from which economic and social issues would be defined and solved. Specifically, the economics of the Community rested on two mutually exclusive problems. First, recalling Nyerere's discussion of postcolonial economics in the previous chapter, the partner-states understood their exports to dominant European nations would never create sufficient revenue to pay for the imports each nation expected and at the same time finance specific social needs such as schools. But, thought the Community, if the partner-states were willing to join together in an economic common market, domestic industry could produce imitations of imported European goods. As a consequence, with increased revenues, foreign debt would be reduced, domestic labor would work for domestic enterprises, and needed institutions such as schools would be built.[7]

In many ways, the collapse of the East African Community could have been expected, not because of cultural and social issues, but because of economic and political turmoil. Reflecting the wider international stage, both Kenya and Tanzania found their central economic foci becoming more divergent. Kenya, a vibrant ex-colony of Britain, understood the significance of international economics and was interested in industrialization and urbanization. Tanzania, on the other hand, followed Nyerere's ideals of rural socialism and was concerned with central planning and maintaining a national indigenous culture. Meanwhile, Uganda succumbed to the holocaust of Idi Amin. Yet, the EAC remained as an example of what positive results could occur when postcolonial reformers came together to solve mutual problems, experiment with regional associations such as Pan-Africanism, and economically defend themselves in a capitalist world order.

But, the collapse of the EAC illustrated something else as well. The partner-states viewed each other as discrete political entities within the Community, cooperating for their collective good. Economic and educational decisions were developed within the partner-state system, as a result of which reformers assumed the Community could become industrialized. Certainly not believing their industrialization would threaten European capitalists, reformers thought the mere ability to manufacture imitations of some European imports was the signal postcolonial nations needed to create profits using their own resources and labor. This is a dramatic break in the historic economic circle in which colonies supplied indigenous labor and resources to capitalists for their profit. Manufacturing imitations, more than international associations and educational importations, was the expected graduation exercise postcolonial reformers wanted so they could join the family of nations as equal siblings. In this effort, they failed totally. Yet, globalization had not called the Community an educational malfunction.

POSTCOLONIAL SCHOOLS AND THE GLOBAL VILLAGE

AND WHEREAS the said countries, with a view to realising a fast and balanced regional development are resolved to creating an enabling environment in all the Partner States in order to attract investments and allow the private sector and civil society to play a leading role in the socio-economic development activities through the development of sound macro-economic

and sectoral policies and their efficient management while taking cogni-
sance of the developments in the world economy as contained in the Mar-
rakesh Agreement Establishing the World Trade Organisation, 1995 referred
to "as the WTO Agreement" and as may be decided by the Partner States,
the development of technological capacity for improved productivity.[8]

The preamble to the Treaty for the Establishment of the East African Community (1996) represents the culmination of a series of treaties in which the
three partner-states of the EAC discussed their failure to join the global family of nations. It was not their inability to manufacture imitations of European
goods that caused their downfall. In fact, as the Community recognized during the two-decade period between its collapse and reemergence, the ability to manufacture, even at a most elementary level, would not have given
them what they wanted. Like other postcolonial reformers, the Community
reformers recognized that joining an international family of nations was now
an impossibility. The family of nations they understood was based on the
politics of international associations and regional organizations. While this
was still true, it was also true that international corporations had, in most
cases, become supranational entities. These corporations, though generally
housed in dominant nations, had for all practical purposes, become nations
themselves. Without borders, they related economically and politically to
postcolonial nations as if they were dominant entities. In short, beginning in
the late twentieth century, these corporations began controlling their global
economic environment in much the same manner as did the East India Company during the first period of British colonial rule—except in this case, there
were *many* corporations rather than just one, and no single government had
the power to control them.

Joining these supranational corporations were international economic
associations such as the World Trade Organization (WTO). Unlike the previous political organizations, including the United Nations, these organizations were global economic policy makers. It was they who developed the
rules global commerce obeyed. And, as postcolonial reformers quickly
learned, unlike the political organizations of post–World War II years, they
were eligible to join only if they agreed with the organization's economic
policies—that is, if they were invited. To help postcolonial reformers who
had difficulty financing social institutions such as schools, other international organizations were developed to lend them money. Postcolonial reformers discovered the globe they shared with dominant European nations
had changed. The twentieth-century political experiment with international alliances, in which nations were considered discrete entities, had
matured into an early twenty-first-century reality in which alliances were
now defined in economic terms. The family of nations in which countries
related to each other politically had become a "global village" in which

they competed with each other economically. This borderless world was called globalization.

Because of this, postcolonial reformers recognized that schools had become even more central to their future, except, in this case, schools' curricula were designed to educate indigenous peoples to dominant capitalist cultures and values.[9] This must have been offensive to many educational reformers. They were becoming agents of change in which the culture of colonialism was reemerging. Now indigenous laborers were considered economic assets not only for their ability to work cheaply but also for their intellectual ability to work like elite, literate Europeans.

East African Community Revisited

In many ways globalization placed the EAC in peculiar situations that were not always understandable to the partner-states. As members of a family of nations, the various partner-states saw their focus as an illustration of Pan-Africanism. Here, the Community expected its economic and social policies to transcend cultural differences and be of mutual help to all. For example, in the field of higher education the partner-states combined Makerere University College (Uganda) with emerging universities in Nairobi and Dar es Salaam to form the new University of East Africa.[10] Reformers also hoped that standardization of entrance requirements and establishing centers of excellence would influence the quality of secondary and primary schools in the partner-states.

In fact, it is for this reason that the Community stressed they revisit the Inter-University Council for East Africa begun in 1967.[11] In many ways, the reformers understood the important role the national universities served in the waning years of the twentieth century. Unlike the Nyerere period in which secondary schools were expected to produce primary teachers, this now became the responsibility of the universities. The focus of higher education had changed to include new and unique missions that reflected the reality of international competition in which the Community was required to present its economic uniqueness to the world. It is for this reason higher education's newfound interest in the research fields of science and technology becomes important.[12]

The global village also expanded the purposes of preuniversity schools so that students in Kenya, Tanzania, and Uganda learned a common curriculum. What is so interesting about this decision is that that common curriculum was the exemplar of elitist capitalist educational philosophies. It confirmed that the postcolonial reformers had learned an axiom the dominant nations taught them—globalization is a world reality and all nations are influenced by it whether they participate or not. The bluntness of this learning experience for East African reformers was the lesson that the oral cultures were out of step in the new world order.

Mexico and the Return of Porfirio Díaz

Mexico learned about its entrance into the global village in much the same fashion as the East African Community. Like other postcolonial nations, Mexico understood the political concept of the family of nations and had projected itself internationally as a discrete, independent nation. Although not a postcolonial nation in the strictest sense of the term, for Mexico had gained its independence from Spain a century before, it still experienced international relations in global and regional associations similar to newly independent nations. Like the EAC, Mexico had considered various economic policies of breaking the economic cycle that destined it to endless poverty. Certainly the postcolonial cycle would never allow Mexicans to be anything other than laborers. Nor would Mexico ever be able to create revenues, except through the traditional exportation of natural resources. None of this allowed Mexico to create the economic profits necessary to improve the lives of its indigenous peoples through schools, social programs, and land distribution. As a result, Mexico chose during the immediate post–World War II years, as the EAC considered several decades later, to implement an economic policy increasing tariffs on imported goods while encouraging local industries to manufacture cheap imitations. The name of this policy is protectionism.

In this case, the lessons learned by the EAC reformers were learned by Mexican reformers. However, their lessons were mastered a little at a time as their protectionist policies collapsed in the 1970s. Living next door to the United States gave Mexican reformers another understanding of its capitalist philosophy and perhaps better awareness of the use of indigenous labor. They knew the reasons (all economic) why their northern neighbor was willing to accept illegal immigrant laborers in the United States.

Yet, reformers were not opposed to these American policies, for there were economic and social advantages for Mexico as well. The resulting flow of American monies into the Mexican rural economy supported villages that otherwise would have been the responsibility of the central government. And, as Mexican economists recognized, the continual inoculation of hard currency helped rural Mexico develop and prosper, although at a marginal level. Perhaps, even more urgently, Mexican emigration of young laborers to the United States staved off social unrest that otherwise would have developed because of poverty and unemployment. Mexican reformers were aware that the United States had also developed an educational philosophy called multiculturalism or diversity. It incorporated Mexican laborers' children into its school milieu by giving them a free education. American schools seemed as if they could, through the curriculum of race and class, successfully deal with the conflicting elements of multiculturalism and capitalism. Reformers understood the importance of this as they continued their rural educational programs.

But, as reformers became more familiar with American educational philosophy, particularly higher education, they recognized a significant difference between the two countries. Historically, Mexican educational philosophy had mirrored European higher education. In this case, university life and studies centered around the well-schooled person. Emphases on traditional curricula, therefore, placed a greater importance on undergraduate education, while the Americans seemed to favor graduate schools. Of course, wealthy Mexican families still enrolled their children in U.S. colleges close to the border so they could live in their culture. For those few who were interested in graduate study, however, elite universities were chosen.

These, the reformers recognized, were the limitations of their universities. While American higher education supported large numbers of professors who were committed to research, many of Mexico's brightest scholars were drawn to government and industry. Involved in other types of research, few scholars were given the time, or funding, to investigate festering social problems that adversely impacted Mexico's economic structure. As a consequence, environmental, urbanization, and health problems continued to plague Mexican society. As early as the mid-1970s, it became clear that, while universities were hotbeds in which social problems were described, little was being done to solve the problems.

Regardless, it was the education of the new Mexican politician that changed Mexico in the last decades of the twentieth century and placed it securely within the grasp of globalization. Educated at elite graduate schools such as Harvard or Yale, focusing on economic philosophies, the new politicians returned to Mexico advancing the theories of a free-market economy. These "technocrats," as they were called, encouraged foreign investment. Wanting government to become smaller and the marketplace more vibrant, they campaigned for the privatization of government-owned corporations. And, for the same reasons, they reneged on the government obligation to protect rural peasant farmers. Social programs were canceled. In short, the free-market economy returned Mexico to the prerevolutionary period of Porfirio Díaz's presidency.

It is important to give two examples of how the technocrats envisioned the Mexican free-market economy so its impact on schools can be better understood. The first example concerns peasants. The technocrats revoked Article 27 of the 1917 Constitution, which protected peasants who owned *ejidos*, small parcels of land, from unwarranted intrusion by private and public lending agencies.[13] The ejidos were now vulnerable to the marketplace. The revocation of Article 27 was politically and socially revolutionary. The second example concerns laborers. *Maquiladoras*, or assembly factories, were developed in free-trade zones, many of which hugged the northern Mexican border. U.S. manufacturers trucked unfinished goods to assembly factories to finish the manufacturing process at low cost. In many cases, laborers completed the process within one or two days, returning the finished goods to its U.S. manufacturer.

The result of the free-market economy in these two examples is not complicated, as it illustrates how economics supports and enhances social classes. The result of the technocrats' revocation of Article 27 was that rural unemployment increased to extraordinary levels. Indigenous peoples were forced to make major changes in their lives, either by remaining in their villages, emigrating to large urban areas such as Mexico City, working in *maquiladoras* for low pay, or escaping to the United States to work at menial jobs. Not surprisingly, almost every option deprived indigenous and rural farmers of educational opportunities. Yet, agricultural production soared. Large foreign agricultural corporations grew produce for export. It was difficult for laborers to understand how Mexico could increase its national assets at the same time it was increasing unemployment. In urban settings, low labor salaries and long work hours were some of the incentives the technocrats used to entice international corporations to the maquiladoras. Beyond the physical requirements of the assembly line, laborers must have found bittersweet humor in finishing goods they would never be able to afford.

These two brief illustrations of the impact of the free-market economy on Mexican society showcase fundamental changes in Mexican educational and economic philosophy. Economically, the technocrats resurrected the prerevolutionary policies of Díaz. Díaz's commitment, as discussed in the previous chapter, was that Mexico would participate in international economics by inviting foreign investment into the country. An advantage Díaz wanted to advertise to investors was that educated Mexican laborers worked for low wages. At the same time, foreign investors were encouraged to export the nation's natural resources to dominant countries. It is here the twin elite educational philosophies of Justo Sierra and Felix Palavicini became apparent. Sierra's original philosophy spoke of educating indigenous peoples to be good laborers who, maintaining a strong loyalty to the foreign managers, were willing to work for cheap wages. Of course, large, mechanized agricultural corporations were in less need of laborers than Sierra originally envisioned, but that was of little consequence because the technocrats had forsaken them. They were insignificant players in the free-market economy. Sierra's philosophies were appropriate for maquiladoras, though. In these assembly plants, laborers were encouraged to work together, whether they were sewing, constructing, or piecing together parts. Regardless of whether the assembly work was to assemble car parts or trouser parts, laborers still worked long hours for low wages. The education of the laborer was minimal. If a worker knew how to read and write (perhaps to understand written directions) and knew a little arithmetic (perhaps enough to make out the amount stated on a paycheck), Sierra would have considered him or her a laborer worthy of Mexican economics.

In some ways Palavicini's educational philosophy was also revived. While his ideas of Mexico mirroring American culture are unacceptable in contemporary Mexico, his views of Mexico's future as modeled by the American present are heady to those who strive for wealth and political power. To join the First World like the United States is a goal the technocrats want to see realized quickly. Nonetheless, educational reformers continued to compare the effectiveness of the 1917 Constitution to late twentieth-century social and economic philosophy.[14]

Reformers, recognizing the need to standardize school curricula, passed an amendment to the Constitution in 1992 and a General Education Law (1993) in which the federal government took responsibility for determining curriculum issues at the elementary and lower secondary schools and in teacher education. All of this was part of a structured effort to detail the specific responsibilities the various states and the federal government had toward schools. Here, the various states were held responsible for early and basic education, education of indigenous children, special education, and teacher education. States were also responsible (with some federal assistance) as a promoter of upper secondary schools, higher education, and adult education. In addition, states were required to develop work-training programs to satisfy the labor needs of local industry. Belatedly, the same amendment established, as a legal obligation, parents' responsibility to send their children to school.

All of this in the last years of the twentieth century culminated in the North American Free Trade Agreement (NAFTA). Joining the United States and Canada, Mexico willingly entered a global economy for which its educational system was being positioned. It would educate a workforce that could compete with workers from other nations.

India in the Third World

But Mexico was not the only postcolonial nation marching toward globalization. India too had, by the waning decades of the twentieth century, given up its dream of a socialized state. Gone were the days of central planning, high taxes on the wealthy, and protectionist policies. Also gone were the days in which the poor were helped.

Following the pattern of other postcolonial nations, India flirted with international organizations. Like the East African partner-states, Mexico, and other postcolonial nations, India joined the United Nations and regional organizations. And, like other postcolonial nations, India's interests were both economic and social. The government wanted to participate in international discussions about social issues such as how to expand educational opportunity to a vast, growing population. In some ways, in the first years of its independence, perhaps because of the continued international regard of Mahatma Gandhi and his personally chosen prime minister, Jawaharlal Nehru, India's international political stature seemed to be above that of most postcolonial nations. Indian reformers were quick to take advantage of their developing role as political leaders within the newly developing Third World. Somewhat as moralizers, Indian reformers positioned themselves as judges of dominant countries' Cold War foreign policies. Indian reformers were not willing to follow traditional postcolonial foreign policies of playing off the various dominant countries against each other. They were more interested in the dominant countries competing for India's recognition.

In many ways, India's immediate political success seemed to be mirrored in its economic policies. Beginning slowly, Indian economic policy was based on self-sufficiency. Although that policy was directed to manufacturing, self-sufficiency was first met in the agricultural sector in the 1970s. This tremendous feat, however, did not give Indian reformers what they wished. Recognizing by the last decade of the previous century that the nation would not be able to afford specific social programs, the government began to slowly privatize government businesses while deregulating such economic institutions as banking. Developing new economic policies, reformers had, by the end of the twentieth century, encouraged foreign investment rather than merely encouraging a fledgling domestic industry. India's economic policies mirrored those of Mexico, the East African Community, and other postcolonial nations. And like them, India's social costs of joining a globalized economy were great. For example, child labor, although illegal, increased in agriculture and in the small, continuing cottage industries Gandhi highlighted as the village school.

In the twilight of the twentieth century, as India opened its economy to foreign investment, its efforts in mass education became more measured. Having a history of education in which the elite were superbly schooled, educational reformers understood the need to improve higher education. As a consequence, under the guidance of the central government, new universities were created and others quickly improved. Adhering to the conventional British system in which the traditional three-year baccalaureate and one year honors degrees were the norm, universities expanded their curricula in the disciplines of law, medicine, science, engineering, and business administration. Cynically, the most noted illustration of the success of this higher educational system has been India's ability to produce atomic weaponry to forward its political-religious foreign policy regarding Kashmir against its equally armed historic Muslim enemy, Pakistan.

But preuniversity education did not enjoy the same sentiment of many Indian reformers. It was not that the reformers were opposed to elementary and secondary schools; it was that they as elite male students were able to attend schools in which they were prepared for advanced study. They thought this was normal and therefore assumed lack of schools for the lower classes and women was not a problem. This position of academic segregation, also experienced in European countries, was defended by elite Indian reformers who contended that not all children and adults were handicapped by illiteracy. Forced to respond to a grassroots social movement in the 1990s, reformers were criticized for withholding primary education from girls and others they defined as the lower classes. As a consequence, the various states were charged with developing primary schools, although the central government had jurisdiction over the various curricula and textbooks. The central government also maintained an interest in education by sharing the costs of schools with the various states.

Indian reformers, by last century's end, were willing to develop a ten-year educational structure in which elementary and secondary education became a shared national experience. Yet, maintaining the traditional Indian elitist educational philosophy, the schooling experience also included an upper-secondary curriculum. In total, this twelve-year preuniversity program was considered essential for those capable of university entrance. Indian education is still an example of elitist reformers attempting to come to terms with globalization. Recognizing the importance of education in an economically competitive world, India remains at only two of every three men and two of every five women literate. Perhaps this is explained by the vast numbers of rural elementary students still taught in one-room or open-air schools.

Russia: Yesterday's Good News

When Anton Makarenko was chastised by Varvara Victorovna Bregal, a local education authority, for his philosophic superficiality, Makarenko replied:

> You seem to regard the young, or shall we say, the child, as a kind of box. There's the outside of it, the packing material, I suppose, and the inside— the entrails. You seem to think we should pay attention to nothing but the entrails, and yet, if it's not properly packed all those precious entrails will be lost.[15]

In specific language, Bregal told Makarenko that what he had accomplished with his young charges was based on the force of his personality, not on a sophisticated system of ideas. As intimated by James Bowen, Makarenko said more to Bregal than perhaps he intended, for he defined for her the essence of his educational philosophy. Equally as important, Makarenko deftly stated the essence of the Soviet workers' utopia.

Makarenko wrote that the Soviet utopia was based on the Marxist-Leninist idea of the collective, which positioned the person within its embrace. Makarenko's educational philosophy highlighted that relationship—the box's "packing material." Soviet citizens were expected to accept their relationship with the collective because they were part of it. It was not just Makarenko that advanced this theory of the collective. There were others such as youth author Arkady Gaidar, who illustrated the philosophy when he portrayed young heroes such as Malchish Kibalchish as contributors to the collective. And it was this philosophy that became the Achilles' heel of the Soviet school system. In short, Makarenko's good news about the collective in the 1930s became the 1990s educational anvil upon which the Soviet implosion was forged.

Although the Soviet Union was considered a dominant nation during its seventy-year existence, in many ways it experienced much of the same history as did most postcolonial countries. Prior to its implosion, it, like many postcolonial nations, was interested in joining international organizations such as the United Nations. It also entered into regional associations, but like many postcolonial reformers, found those conversations minimized because of its own Cold War policies. In short, while the Soviet Union was not treated like a postcolonial country by capitalist nations during its existence, the effect of the Cold War upon it was much the same. They were excluded from elite Western culture, and while the Soviet utopia readily accepted capitalist exclusion to remain philosophically pure, the price it paid came at the cost of an economy based on labor and natural resources.

Within this economic rubric, educational reform in the post-Soviet period focused on changing a failed utopian experiment into a *marketplace economy*. Interestingly, but not surprisingly, the debate among educational reformers centered around the Makarenko-Dewey disputes during the 1930s. Although Makarenko would not enter the debate, simply disregarding Dewey's intellectual supporters, it was clear that pre-Stalinist reformers were interested in Dewey's educational philosophy. These are the thoughts twenty-first-century Russian reformers are examining. For many current reformers, the ideas of such early educational leaders as Lunacharsky are now contemporary.[16] For example, Lunacharsky is admired for quickly recognizing that schools, once controlled by the aristocrats and clergy, need to be revamped from an elitist, male-oriented curriculum to that which focuses on all children. Equally, reformers appear to be impressed with Lunacharsky's understanding of the negative impacts of memorization on student learning and of a passive curriculum that encourages class division. In the same fashion, Pavel Blonsky's proposals that Rousseau's social definition of childhood be accepted by teachers is now being reconsidered. Rousseau's argument that young human beings not be thought of as miniature adults supports Russian reformers' concern about new teaching methods and student learning.

Scolding Makarenko, who glorified the theory that all knowledge was housed in Marxism-Leninism, reformers are being reintroduced to Albert Pinkevitch's ideas about U.S. education. Reformers are willing to look elsewhere for differing or new educational ideas. To illustrate the significance of post-Soviet educational reformers, the contemporized ideas of Lunacharsky, Blonsky, Pinkevitch, S. T. Shatsky, and others are found in such Russian educational legislation as the Law on Education (1992) and its 1996 amendment.[17] While this legislation speaks about the importance of human values such as life and health, continuing social problems including drug abuse, prostitution, robbery, and other crimes caused by the marketplace economy are forcing teachers, parents, and others to question whether Russian society might return to the Soviet calm, once thought normal. It was this same conflict Makarenko was thinking about when he responded to Bregal's criticism of his philosophy. Comparing children to boxes, it is the calmness of the packaging that is important he said, not the complexity of the entrails.

POSTCOLONIAL SCHOOLS AND THE NEW WORLD ORDER

From our perspective in a post-Soviet world, Makarenko and Bregal's brief discussion about boxes and entrails has more to offer us than each of them perhaps recognized. Obviously, Makarenko's response to Bregal was to defend his philosophy from what must have appeared to him to be almost random criticism. But with the advantage of time, if we look closely at Bregal's comment, we notice that it also deals with larger issues that question the broad purposes of school–society relations. Is it possible schools can contribute to society's welfare if their relationship is as superficial as Makarenko suggests? Or, to put the point within Makarenko's context, can schools exist for society's purpose if they interact boxlike, unopened for examination by the other? From this point of view, Bregal suggests that schools and societies are partners in survival. There must be mutual understandings between them if they are to know of each other's vulnerability.

It is these entrails, the supplying of cheap labor and resources to concentrations of wealth, that postcolonial reformers realized was the central issue with capitalists. Postcolonial cravings for political interaction with dominant nations through international and regional associations were not significant to the capitalists because they were viewed as superficial. But, this would not just be the case for the newly independent nations such as Tanzania and India. It was also the circumstance of others, including Mexico and Ethiopia, both of whom had proven their political independence. And, it was the economic box in which Russia, the inheritor of the Soviet Union, discovered for itself.

For postcolonial schools, therefore, the curriculum of political and cultural independence was shallow. It did not ring true in a world controlled by capitalists. Educational issues addressed by Nyerere, Gandhi, and others were unacceptable to the capitalists for the same reasons Bregal criticized Makarenko. Capitalists visualized postcolonial education as superficial because it dealt with indigenous and oral traditions rather than an elite, literate curriculum. While postcolonial educational reformers wanted to picture their educational philosophies as the marriage between indigenous cultures and economics, the capitalists did not. Capitalists viewed the world in terms they valued and controlled. Unfortunately, none of this surprised postcolonial reformers because their centuries-old colonial relationship with them was based on servitude and dependence.

In retrospect, the postcolonial reformers, excluding Russia, shared the common experience of being pawns in a Cold War chess game. Moved from one part of the global chess board to another, postcolonial reformers discovered their voiced educational and economic needs were not heeded. Regardless of the external boxlike trappings of international organizations and actions, postcolonial reformers were not able to successfully articulate their agenda. Simply, while the reformers spoke of realities they considered important, capitalists listened for economic ideologies they understood. It is this critical relationship that postcolonial educational reformers reluctantly came to accept. After all, they were expected to live in the global village.

Postcolonial reformers came to terms with living in the global village in various ways. It is surprising that so many thought they could escape that new world ideology by using old capitalistic protectionist policies. Having experienced capitalism as colonies in which they were judged by their economic assets of labor and resources, postcolonial reformers were willing to add schools as their third asset. Each of them searched their educational history sufficiently to rebuild their educational past. For example, elite Indian educational policies reflected the old British colonial educational system that, at another time, kept even elite Indian children within the English colonial enclave. Similarly, Mexico discovered that if it wanted to live in the free-market economy it also had to reconstruct its educational past. Recalling Sierra and Palavicini, the elitist philosophers of the Díaz dictatorship from whom they escaped in 1917, Mexican technocrats reconstructed Mexico within the parameters of an economic agreement with the United States and Canada. As in the Díaz era, salaries became the property of Mexican labor and profits the possession of foreign investors.

Like India, Mexico also realized its international economic position rested on schools. Mirroring India, technocrats moved to reform the Mexican higher education system to include research and development. And, also like India, Mexico excluded its poor so the free-market economy could work effectively. Similarly, the East African Community discovered that, regardless of its Pan-African history, its entrance into the free-market economy rested on constructing a higher educational system that trained teachers and developed areas of excellence. Like India and Mexico, the three EAC partner-states paid for their first steps into the free-market economy at the expense of the poor, who suffered nutritional, health, and environmental problems.

What most postcolonial reformers discovered as they entered the global economy was what Mexican and Indian reformers had already learned. They were forced to center their schools within an economic process that produced graduates who would work and could compete in the free-market economy. It meant for most reformers that they had to become change agents and articulate the capitalist economic structure in which wealth controlled indigenous labor and resources. Again, reformers expected the school to bridge the economic gap in which profits and wages remained unequal and segregated.

In educational development, it is interesting that after the Soviet Union's implosion, Russia first remained aloof from, but quickly became part of, the free-market economy. While grasping globalization at the expense of Makarenko, Russian educational reformers have had a more difficult time reconstructing their educational history so their schools can succeed within the reaches of capitalism. Unable to return to prerevolutionary periods like the Mexicans and Indians, Russian educational reformers have centered their hopes for the future on pre-Stalinist golden age reformers such as Blonsky and Lunacharsky who viewed Dewey's (and others') progressivism as the schools' purpose. It is difficult for us to understand the Russian dilemma within this lens, for it reminds us of the discussions Dewey and others had during the beginning years of the twentieth century when they talked about scientific thinking, multicultural democracies, and learning through problem solving.

It is almost as if in post–Cold War years, capitalism and Russian reformers have momentarily traded philosophical positions, in which the reformers consider education to be the platform upon which their form of political democracy rests while capitalists herald schools as the free-market economy's workhorse. Regardless, in the twilight of the twentieth century, the free-market economy reaffirmed the Protestant reformers' sixteenth-century tenets that education, economics, nationhood, and theology were the cornerstones of the free-market economy.

Just as postcolonial nations were compelled to compete in the free-market economy, developing schools that produced workers, capitalist nations were reforming their schools to produce managers. Yet, capitalists had experiences, or tools, to judge the purposes of their children's schooling while postcolonial reformers did not. To understand the complications postcolonial reformers contended with, the following chapter will paint a face on issues that confront them and how their schools are responding.

NOTES

1. The motto of the United Nations is taken from Isaiah 2:4 in which the last days are described: "He shall judge between the nations / And rebuke many people. / They shall beat their swords into plowshares / And their spears in pruning hooks. / Nation shall not lift up sword against nation, / Neither shall they learn war anymore."

2. As more nations joined the United Nations, UNESCO grew. Presently, the organization includes more than 180 countries.

3. Patrice Lumumba was a nationalist in the Belgian Congo independence movement. He was assassinated and a mystique quickly developed around his life and violent death. Books, movies, plays, and resurrected letters have kept his views of Pan-Africanism alive. However, Lumumba's life was that of a bureaucrat (a Belgian colonial government clerk). He was sent to jail (found guilty of embezzling money from the post office). Lumumba was educated in a colonial missionary school and was deeply attracted to the ideas of Karl Marx and Jean-Paul Sartre. In the Cold War world of political intrigue, Americans thought Lumumba was a friend of the Soviet Union. See Ludo de Witte, *The Assassination of Lumumba*, trans. Ann Wright and Renée Fenby (London: Verso, 2001).

4. The university's name was changed after the revolution to Addis Ababa University.

5. Pan-Africanism is both a philosophy and a social-political movement. It expresses the brotherhood of all Africans and those of African descent. As a consequence, many view such social revolutions as the American Civil Rights movement as representations of Pan-Africanism. These ideas are discussed in Julian Kunnie's *Is Apartheid Really Dead? Pan Africanist Working Class Cultural Critical Perspectives* (Boulder, CO: Westview Press, 2000).

6. The partner-states thought of education in almost vocational terms. While they understood why dominant nations' educational philosophy conflicted with theirs, each partner-state (other than Nyerere's Tanzania) was willing to accept the required cultural trade-off.

7. Dr. Assefa Mehretu, a professor in the Department of Geography at Haile Selassie I University, insisted in 1970 that the community would enjoy a budget surplus by 1980 if it expanded its membership to include Ethiopia, Somalia, and Sudan. Education obviously became more urgent because the economics of manufacturing required literate workers. See Assefa Mehretu, "Regional Integration for Economic Development of Greater East Africa," in Institute of International Studies, Office of Education, Department of Health, Education, and Welfare, *Education and Culture in Eastern Africa* (Washington, DC: GPO, 1970), 1:1–7.

8. Treaty for the Establishment of the East African Community (Organization of African Unity Treaty Registration No. 001/2000, United Nations Treaty Registration No. 37437), Arusha, Tanzania, November 30, 1999, preamble.

9. Postcolonial reformers were learning that educational experimentation was not important in a world of economic competition.

10. Bernard Onyango, "Introduction to Makerere University College," in Institute of International Studies, *Education and Culture in Eastern Africa*, 3:5–6.

11. The Treaty for the Establishment of the East African Community was signed on November 30, 1999, by the heads of state for Kenya, Uganda, and Tanzania.

12. The revolutionary change of higher education philosophy can be illustrated by the Visitation Committee Report, better known as the Sheldon Report, in which Makerere College was admonished to become a national university rather than a colonial imitation of European institutions. See "Report of the Visitation Committee to Makerere University College," June 1970, ix, quoted in Onyango, "Introduction to Makerere University College," 3:17.

13. *Ejidos* are small plots of land in rural areas that are usually owned by the rural poor. The original purpose of giving land to indigenous farmers was to help them become economically and socially independent.

14. In 1992 an act entitled the National Agreement for the Modernization of Basic Education gave the states the responsibility of financing preschool, elementary, and lower secondary schools. The act and its rationale are somewhat similar to the Díaz government's educational policies in the last part of the nineteenth century.

15. Quoted in James Bowen, *Soviet Education: Anton Makarenko and the Years of Experiment* (Madison: University of Wisconsin Press, 1962), 123. According to Bowen (*Soviet Education*, 123), Bregal had said to Makarenko, "All your banners and drums and salutes—they only organize the young superficially."

16. Nikolai Nikandrov states that Lunacharsky, Blonsky, Shatsky, and Pinkevitch were focused on developing new educational philosophies. Each returned to Dewey, Rousseau, the Dalton Plan, and the importance of statistics. See Nikolai Nikandrov, "Education in Modern Russia: Is It Modern?" in Kas Mazurek, Margret A. Winzer, and Czeslaw Majorek, *Education in a Global Society: A Comparative Perspective* (Boston: Allyn & Bacon, 2000), 209–24.

17. Nikandrov describes the Law on Education and the 1996 amendment as a contemporary Russian acknowledgment of early twentieth-century Soviet reform ideas about Soviet schools. For a wider discussion see Nikandrov, "Education in Modern Russia," 209–24, and Ben Ehlof and Edward Dneprov, eds., *Democracy in the Russian School: The Reform Movement in Education since 1984* (Boulder, CO: Westview Press, 1993).

5

Globalization, Schools, and Children in Developing Nations

In chapter 4 we charted the course that postcolonial nations traveled as they moved from political autonomy to global economic interdependence. Moving from colonialism to political sovereignty was an understandable goal of educational reformers, but in the waning decades of the last century they reluctantly became aware that the free-market economy had developed the parameters within which their schools could operate. These nations were reintroduced to capitalism, in which corporate entrepreneurs, international organizations, and others played the role once reserved for colonizers. Educational reformers, striving to relate politically to capitalist nations in the global village, were stymied by the differing agendas underscored by economics and the Cold War. It was not until the aftermath of the Cold War that postcolonial educational reformers recognized they were being drawn into a global village in which their relationships with capitalist nations and international organizations were defined less politically than economically. In this capitalist-controlled globe, educational reformers reluctantly understood their survival was still positioned on the economics of labor and resources. Yet, reformers, now understanding the purpose of the school was to support the free-market economy, positioned it as an asset adjacent to their concentrations of labor and resources.

This combined third asset, once supportive of indigenous cultures and teaching children the curriculum of national development, now concentrated on teaching economic development and the free-market economy. Joining the global village, educational reformers discovered they were becoming change agents, supporting capitalist values and economic institutions. By following the lives of five individuals, we will put a face on indigenous populations as they became "little Europeans."[1]

LIVING IN TWO CULTURES: EDUCATION AND SOCIAL CONFLICT

In 1960, writing about the sixteenth-century Spanish conquest of Native Americans, George Foster observed, "At no time in history has there been such a significant degree of culture contact between peoples of completely distinct traditions."[2] He noted that the European–indigenous cultural conflict was so specific and violent that legends and myths were created to explain their histories. Foster's remarks are interesting because they were published in the Cold War era, as the indigenous peoples he was writing about began to demonstrate their political independence. In fact, the different worlds Foster wrote about, and lived in, were the same. Both periods, even though separated by centuries, hosted global clashes between Protestant Reformation Europe and indigenous peoples. In both periods, each culture, as we discussed in chapter 2, attempted to explain its political, theological, economic, and educational values to the other. While the Europeans were able to voice their values through colonialism, indigenous peoples were, in the main, unsuccessful.[3] Partly, this was because indigenous peoples had no vocabulary through which they were able to articulate their cultures, except during that brief mid-twentieth-century moment when schools became cultural conduits.

We now realize, as educational reformers had earlier, that twenty-first-century capitalism demands indigenous societies return to those dependent periods when indigenous schools were their economic partners. This is what Turkey's Ambassador Volkan Vural was referring to when he spoke of Turkey's plan for joining the European Union: "It is not like joining an international organization; it's like joining a new way of life. You don't lose your identity, but you put a new identity on top of it."[4] Vural's comment is insightful. He recognizes domination to mean that Turkey will adjust its social, political, and educational institutions to reflect those of the capitalist nations. Georgie Anne Geyer describes Turkey's efforts to Europeanize itself as a staggering task. She acknowledges that Turkey's elites, educated in Europe and Turkey, loosely think of themselves as windows of modernity through which Turks can safely glimpse the capitalist, Protestant future in which (they think) Muslims will live. It is this enticing, pervasive, economic relationship, which is stronger than any political partnership, that has created conflicting indigenous perceptions that they will equally share in the free-market economy's wealth.

Tanzania: Language, School Fees, and the Recolonization of Schools

For Ambassador Vural, Turkey's planned efforts to join Europe's prosperity is government policy; as he described it, "We set priorities, and we translated what this meant to helping our relevant agencies reform."[5] Yet, in other postcolonial countries, the Turkish road to wealth is less straight and more narrow. In some nations such as Tanzania, European prosperity is characterized as a slippery slope to recolonization in which economics, not politics, is the binding issue. It is the result of this conflict between developed and indigenous societies that Tanzanian schools, disadvantaged by government school funding and renewed British economic and cultural interests, acknowledge as their reason for their inability to maintain an indigenous society in the global village. Crushing poverty, brought about by government debts owed to international organizations, trade imbalances aggravated by industrial and agricultural government policies, and uncontrolled urban migration, prompts major Tanzanian economic and social dislocations.

The revolutionary social and economic consequences of twenty-first-century postcolonial poverty have fallen unevenly on women and children. For example, Tanzanian women and children, whether in a rural or urban setting, like their sisters and siblings in other postcolonial countries, are purposely employed by male managers because they work harder than their brothers or husbands and are willing to accept lower wages. As Tanzanian women continue to be a major part of the national workforce, their social responsibilities increase because of family issues, especially health care. Even though diseases such as diarrhea, malaria, pneumonia, cholera, and typhoid are treatable in capitalist countries, they continue to ravage postcolonial families and plague national governments' health budgets. As a consequence, women's work accentuates their traditional role of caregivers, causing them to become even less effective as income producers. But, it is the destructive affliction HIV/AIDS, which we will discuss later in this chapter, that changed women's social and economic roles. Exhausted from fighting poverty, children, women, and their brothers and fathers who remain are criticized by a government for fostering laziness and irresponsibility.

Within this social rubric, schools' problems are discussed throughout Tanzania amid criticism from international organizations such as the World Bank and the British Council. Each, taking its own approach, calls for change, the results of which, they believe, will allow Tanzania entrance into the global market economy. They criticize the school environment and lagging educational standards while admonishing Tanzanian teachers to improve their teaching skills and academic knowledge. On the other hand, schools controlled by international charity organizations, foreign government agencies, or others that act as parallel institutions are hailed as "models of effectiveness." To counteract the decline, the government, prompted by international lobby groups, has called for increased economic infusion, legislating parental participation in funding their children's education. In other words, schools, as we will discuss later in this chapter, now charge parents, many of whom live in poverty, fees to improve their children's instruction.

At the same time, organizations such as the British Council tantalize Tanzanian business executives with opportunities to interact with British entrepreneurs, bringing them together in London or Dar es Salaam to discuss mutual economic opportunities. With this type of encouragement, the British Council has created teacher development programs to assist Tanzanian secondary school teachers learn new classroom teaching techniques and strategies. Of course, the language of instruction the council prefers teachers use is English rather than Swahili, the language of instruction in the primary schools.

Taken as a whole, these criticisms are specifically detailed to force fundamental change in Tanzanian schools and society. Regardless of the absolute need for economic assistance, creating policies in which parents support their children's education through a system of school fees divides Tanzanian society, rich and poor, urban and rural, and male and female. Within the same scope, language further divides people. In this case, young, rich, urban males, wanting to become the nation's elite, mimic European managers, while women, remaining in poverty, represent remnants of the African indigenous.

It is that way with Joseph.[6] He is a taxi driver in Dar es Salaam and is thinking about American movies, MTV, and dancing.

"These Englishmen are really stupid," thought Joseph, as he let them off at the Holiday Inn. Joseph is a sixteen-year-old taxi driver in Dar es Salaam. "They will pay anything you ask. They don't even check to see if the price I told them was too high or too low. They're stupid for not even checking—and they gave me a tip on top of it." Putting a pound note into his pocket, he thanked them and slowly drove away.

"The bloody taxi drivers in this town are really something, don't you think? That one just got out of the bush. I couldn't understand a word he said. I was surprised he even knew how to drive that scrap heap," said one Englishman. The others were laughing at Joseph and mimicking his accent. Joseph heard every word they said—and knew in his heart they were right. Even more than the words, he didn't like their laughter. It stung and made him feel small and unworthy. Worst of all, it made him feel like a colonial.

Even though Joseph was born after independence, he knew what it was like to be a colonial. It was a feeling his parents talked about. He remembered when he was young, watching his father talk to the farm administrator. His father, tall and strong, changed before his eyes—he became like a little child when he talked to the well-dressed administrator, saying "yes sir" or something else—bobbing his head up and down. Those English he let off at the hotel could never experience what he felt. "I am a colonial," Joseph said aloud. "I hate that feeling and they will never let me forget it no matter how hard I try."

"I remember the smell of the English administrator. It was so weak. It was as if there wasn't any smell to him at all. He smelled just like those Englishmen who laughed at me. It was as if they took up no space."

Joseph slowly drove past the hotels by the Holiday Inn. He was looking for fares, but knew it was too late in the evening for Europeans to go out, so he turned to the north. He was tired and wanted to go to bed. Maybe he would watch some television before he went to sleep, or better yet, watch some of the video cam recorder tapes he got from his friends. "I can watch Garth Brooks—he plays a guitar. I would like to have a guitar to play if I could afford it. The way those American kids dance makes you feel excited." Turning a corner, Joseph saw what he was looking for. It was a European man by himself. Stopping his taxi, he knew how he could earn some money to buy a guitar. "I hope he doesn't have the Western disease that some of them do," thought Joseph as he walked toward the stranger. "Before we do anything maybe I'll ask."

In most ways Joseph reflects postcolonialism's struggle to join the global market economy. At age sixteen, he is young but probably is not aware that he has lived about half his life.[7] Joseph understands postcolonialism as a lived, visceral issue because he sees his world through the lens of global economic divisions. Moving to an urban setting, surrounded by new and unique manners of living, Joseph meets life's changes. Leaving a family and village in which he is part of a stream of life, Joseph now is independent. He lives in a small room with other young men/boys he knows little about. It is not that he is wary of his colleagues, for they came to Dar es Salaam for the same reasons as he, but he feels separate from them and their village histories.

Joseph recognizes that his life is changing in the smallest and largest ways possible. He that knows if you are wealthy and live in the city, your home is controlled by electricity. Electricity makes life easier. Just imagine pushing a button and having the lights come on! Cleaning clothes with machines and cooling food in refrigerators are new experiences for him. Joseph sees the effects of electricity in his boardinghouse, hotels, and homes of the wealthy. He wonders what his mother, who lives in a world lit by candles and lamps, would say if she had a refrigerator and electricity. Learning how to drive a car was a small matter for Joseph. He thought he knew all about cars from seeing Americans drive on television. But understanding the "rules of the road" is nonsense to him when all he has to do is watch where he is going, look where other cars are, and communicate with them with his horn.

But it was the wonders of the video cam recorder that were momentous to Joseph. It is a machine that connected him to the world and his dreams. He is not entertained watching government television programs in which political leaders talk about national agricultural and industrial issues. These are meaningless to Joseph. Now, he can watch prerecorded MTV programs. The music is so different. Its beat is enthralling and the dancing sensual. Watching and listening to Garth Brooks, or other stars he tries to mimic, presents him with different perspectives about his life. "What a perfect life they live," he thinks as he and his friends watch taped American movies. "I want to be like that, and dress like that, and talk like that."

Joseph is in the process of evaluating his culture based on his television viewing experiences. Yet, there are disturbing elements about what he sees and feels. Mixed with the wealth and excitement spawned by the staged entertainment, there is something missing. It seems that everyone he watches through the eye of his television are friends, living exciting lives. The characters seem somehow shallow to Joseph. They appear self-centered and only allow themselves to be part of others' lives on a superficial level. Even in the movies, he sees few examples of family life, and when he does, there is much dissension between children and parents. Life seems transient, and wealth doesn't make them happy, as he knows he would be.

The cultures that entrance Joseph on television are causing him to think of himself and his life history differently. There is an undercurrent of loneliness in the movies and music he watches. He is becoming aware of the schism between the lives lived by those who think of themselves as "I," as opposed to others, like himself, who think of themselves as part of communities who speak of "we." The new culture he is watching begs him to become part of the capitalist elite. And, while Joseph wants that, he values his life within his village and family.

For Joseph, postcolonialism is more than economics and the global marketplace. Much like Tanzania, he is at a crossroads in his life. To enjoy a life in which health and wealth are the expected inheritance, the costs of elitism are high. In part, Joseph was born into two worlds. One world is the village of his parents, where his life history was within the reaches of those he knew, loved, and respected. In childhood, he experienced the totality of life in what he learned from his parents, family, and villagers. He was part of an inseparable whole. There was no dividing line between who he was, what he learned, and how he worked. Even primary school supported his personal history. Much of the time he learned with others in the shade of a grove of trees if it was too hot in the classroom. It seemed so natural to be outside listening to the teacher. He could understand what the teacher was saying. The teacher spoke Swahili, just like Joseph. Joseph knew Swahili was not the teacher's native language, but it was understandable when he spoke it, and that meant learning was fun and easy.

Yet there were changes. When he first went to school, it was simple. He simply walked into the classroom as if he was returning to his family's home.

Now, teachers make students feel uncomfortable. Teachers require students to line up to enter the school building and to run in formation with classmates when it is time to exercise. Now, primary school causes students confusion because they teach new European values such as promptness. The teachers tell students tardiness is wrong, to be the last student to sit in a desk is disrespectful, and to hand in your homework late is bad.

All this anticipated his experiences in secondary school.[8] The teachers there seemed so distant. They were rude and self-important because of the European knowledge they possessed. It was as if they felt themselves special because they knew which of the village's traditions were baseless. In many ways, teachers were the personification of the curriculum that taught students a knowledge which was not suitable for village living. While this was obvious in the science and social sciences curricula, the best example was the use of English as the classroom language of instruction. Students and teachers, having a superficial understanding of the language, found it difficult to learn and teach. It was these features that caused rural students like Joseph to fail the national examinations. Still, failure seemed to have little impact, for passing the examinations gave no immediate advantage to those who succeeded.

We will meet Joseph again, as his life and education symbolize the conflict between indigenous societies and the global marketplace.

Russia: The Education of a Capitalist

The collapse of the Soviet utopia had a different effect on Russian education than it did on education in postcolonial societies. Just as Tanzania's experiments with rural socialism were diminished in the face of the global market economy, the Russian entrance into the capitalistic economic structure redirected schools. Perhaps because of its shadowy twentieth-century existence as a global military power, or its pre-Makarenko golden-age educational philosophies, Russian schools have been much more able to adjust to a European-dominated global society.[9] In the new Russia, schools are becoming competitive institutions in which students learn how to participate in a competitive global market economy. Like Tanzania's secondary schools, Russian education, including its universities, define students in economic terms.

So that we may more fully discuss this issue later in the chapter, let us first look at Yuri Gorbunov, a foreign-language undergraduate at Moscow State University.[10] He is preparing to live and work in a global market economy. Unlike Joseph, whom we read about earlier, Yuri does not have the option of failing a national examination. As a consequence, education and schools affect different spheres of his life.

Yuri loves Moscow. He loves everything about it. Moscow is becoming an exciting city with new restaurants, clubs, and cafés that play Western music. He enjoys wearing jeans and Nikes. The clothing styles for college students are, in his mind, awesome. Even the traffic with all of its pollution, Yuri thinks, is a sign of progress. There are so many more cars now that capitalism has replaced socialism as Russia's economic policy. The rental cars in the Marriott's Moscow Royal Hotel parking lot are gorgeous. Most of them are foreign, although he sees an occasional Skoda. "The Western and Japanese cars are so much better," he thinks. The Skoda's engine is small and it isn't always air-conditioned like the Nissans and Subarus. Those are his favorite cars.

Walking along Petrovka Boulevard is fun. Yuri watches the Western and Russian executives come and go. "You can always tell who is European or American," he reasons. "Their shoes and suits are so much more colorful and fit better than the Russian. Americans even have different hair styles that make them look younger and more handsome."

"So this is capitalism," thought Yuri. "Why did it take so long for Russia to figure it out?"

Yuri is an undergraduate student in the Faculty of Foreign Languages at Moscow State University. He has always enjoyed learning foreign languages. The way sentences are constructed and the way words are used fascinate him. He knows languages are teaching him about different cultures and peoples and, at the same time, how others think. He enjoyed his Latin and the World of the English Language courses, but he didn't like the science and computer studies courses he took last term. They were very difficult. He had to spend so much more time on them than his language classes.

Of all the languages Yuri has studied, English is the most tantalizing. It seems the only rule the English language has is that there are no rules to follow. "How can you speak a language that has a rule that says there are exceptions to the rule?" he used to say. He had never considered that the English language had dialects. Of course, he knew the language of England was basic, but the Canadians, Australians, and New Zealanders had some variations.

The American dialects, with their formal and informal street languages are confusing and fascinating to Yuri. His class roared with delight when his professor, to illustrate the various ways Americans used words, told a story about a trip he had taken to the U.S. state of Mississippi. Knowing that he wanted to see an American baseball game, his host, who was also going, invited the professor to join him. Said his host, "I'll carry you to the baseball game early so we can find some good seats." The question the professor asked the class still puzzled Yuri. "Why would anyone use the word 'carry' to mean 'take' when that was the appropriate word?" Yuri remembered his professor's story whenever he listened to Americans speak.

By accident one morning as he was walking to class (his university building was in the center of Moscow, not in the Lenin Hills where the Faculties of Science were located), Yuri stumbled on a curb. Falling, he hurt his ankle. A Subaru stopped and an English voice asked, "May I help you? You took quite a fall." The Westerner was just like the ones he had seen at the Marriott on Petrovka Boulevard. "Are you going somewhere? Can I give you a lift?" asked the man.

Using the best English Yuri could muster, he said, "Yes, I am going to Moscow State University." Pointing, he said, "It is over there." During the short ride, Yuri had a chance to talk with a Westerner from the U.S. state of Nebraska. He was surprised the American spoke so clearly with complete sentences. It was easy for him to follow the conversation. "Thank you for giving me a 'lift,'" said Yuri as he carefully got out of the car. "My pleasure," replied the Nebraskan as he drove away.

"Why did I say 'lift'?" Yuri quizzed himself as he carefully walked away. I should have used the more appropriate word "ride" or perhaps "assistance," or something else. "No, 'lift' was the right word in this case, in fact," laughed Yuri. "I could have used the word 'carry' because it now makes sense."

Yuri's brief encounter with the Nebraskan in the Subaru illustrates the authority language plays in the global market economy. It is significant that, when Yuri and the Nebraskan met, the language of choice in this bilingual situation was English. Both understood their conversation was a representation of social, cultural, and economic power. In Yuri's case, he learned that speaking Russian in Moscow with a representative of a Western nation was unlikely to occur because the English language framed the economic relationship between capitalist and developing countries. It was not that the Nebraskan was disinterested in languages; rather, it was Yuri's responsibility to speak a foreign language, not the Nebraskan's. In other words, the Nebraskan's inability to speak Russian was not viewed by either as an educational handicap, but as recognition of his country's central placement in the economic globe.

These are the same views the English passengers expressed to Joseph in his taxi, except it was clear his elementary knowledge of the language was not acceptable to them. They derided his accent, even the paucity of his vocabulary. While Yuri did not experience this, it implies that even though capitalists value other societies using their languages, social acceptance is not an immediate reward.

Mexico: Living Next to "El Norte"

Nor was social acceptance and language the case for Ester, whom we will meet next. Ester's English-speaking ability in the United States was credible because it was required of her as an interpreter in an American health clinic and later as an elementary school teacher. She and Hector, whom we will also meet later in this section, represent other relationships shared by developing and capitalist societies. Becoming part of a global emigration movement from postcolonial societies to capitalist countries, both Ester and Hector have their own personal reasons for leaving Mexico. While language is important to their quest for a life within the bounds of capitalism, Hector and Ester appreciate the economic and social power represented by the English language. Ester will use English as an interpreter in El Paso and as her language of instruction in a New Mexico elementary school. Hector will, although less reliant on it, use the dominant language to interact with U.S. employers.

Even though English plays a significant role for Ester,[11] she also knows being a woman in the global market economy places her in a different niche in which, if she wants to survive, is expected to compete with both men and women.

It really didn't make much difference. Each day seemed to Ester like the one before. Her life was in shambles. Ester was in a hospital room in El Paso, Texas. She and her mother had been in an automobile accident. The doctors told her one leg was broken and she had sustained multiple minor injuries and bruises. Thank goodness she was wearing a safety belt, thought Ester. Her mother insisted she wear it that day. "You don't know traffic in this country," she was told. Her mother had muttered, "Just because you drive a pickup in Santa Anita doesn't give you license to take chances on El Paso roads—these *Norteamericanos* drive crazy." Ester smiled as she thought of that conversation. Thank goodness her mother was fine. "I don't know what I would have done if she had been hurt," she thought.

Ester and her mother were in El Paso visiting Alberto, her mother's brother. She enjoyed Alberto, and she knew he wanted to keep in close family contact. Ester used her visit to practice her English. "You are getting really good, Ester," Alberto told her. They had spoken English together that week. Several times, they had talked about Ester and her mother moving to El Paso. Alberto told Ester, "You know Santa Anita doesn't have lots of opportunities for young people any more—not even for women like you." Ester was a waitress, and she knew the money she made was not enough to support her and her mother. The truth of the matter was, to make ends meet, Alberto sent them one hundred U.S. dollars every month.

Ester knew Alberto was right when he described her life as having few choices. She also knew he would not want to send money after her mother passed away. And, even though, God help us, that was a long way from now, her only chance for some security was to marry—but none of the men she knew was wealthy or had prospects. They were like her, perhaps with less education and living on *ejidos* or working at odd jobs.

When Ester talked to herself this way, she used those types of words. Wealth did not mean richness to her. It meant living in a house with electricity and running water. Wealth was sending children to school to learn how to read and write. It was eating better food than she and her mother were used to. And, she had to admit to herself, wealth was living like Alberto and his family.

But, it was Estrella, Ester's nurse, that taught her about a different type of wealth. They had become friends and were speaking in both English and Spanish about Hispanic women in El Paso. "You know," Estrella told Ester in Spanish, "there are many women just like you and your mother who can't get into a hospital or even see a doctor when they get sick." Ester didn't know what she meant. This was the first time in her thirty-two years she had needed a doctor—and the first time she realized she had no one to help her if she got sick in Santa Anita. She had only her mother. She shuddered to think what would happen to her mother if she got sick. What would I do? thought Ester. I have always counted on her—I don't know anything about medicine. "Its important you understand, Ester," said Estrella. "You and your mother aren't as healthy as American women. They see doctors even when they aren't sick. There are public health clinics for the poor so women can find out how healthy they are."

"Why are you bothering to tell me all of this?" said Ester in English. "It's all very good for those who live here, but that doesn't help me! And besides, you have to be a citizen." "I came from Mexico years ago when I was your age, Ester," retorted Estrella in English. "I came because I wanted a better life. I went to school and finally became a nurse. I love my husband and children. And mostly we love our lives."

Now, almost as if Ester wanted to argue, in Spanish she said, "Good for you. You became a nurse. I am only a waitress and have little education." Then in a contrite whisper, "I don't have any skills, Estrella, except being a waitress—there is nothing I can do in El Paso. Who would want me?"

Estrella smiled. "I have been watching you the last several days, and I notice you speak English better than many who lived in El Paso for years. Some doctors in this hospital want to encourage more Hispanic women to come to their clinic for health checkups. They are afraid many women may have diabetes or develop breast cancer but will not come because they do not trust people who don't know their ways. What I am trying to tell you, Ester, is we need more translators who speak both English and Spanish in our clinic, and if you want me to help you get a job in the clinic I will talk to the chief medical administrator."

Ester understood. To be a translator would be important work, she thought, and I would get paid to speak English. Besides, this is my chance to help my mother stay healthy, too. She can come in for checkups along with others. Ester was excited. She saw a future before her that she had never seen before. Her life seemed to focus. She knew Alberto would help them come to El Paso.

"Sí!" Then, breaking into English, Ester said, "I mean, yes! Estrella, my mother is visiting me this evening. Alberto is coming, too! I want to tell them what you told me. I want my mother to say yes and come with me even though she knows what changes will be made in our lives. Alberto will help us learn how to come to El Paso to work."

Later, waiting for her mother and Alberto she said to herself, "Yes, now I
have a chance to be wealthy."

During the years that followed, Ester became a citizen and worked as a
translator with Estrella in the clinic. She and her mother lived with Alberto
and his family. Ester resumed her education and later, with a scholarship,
graduated from the local college. It was during her college experiences she
discovered another wealth. Not only could she live in a house with water
and electricity, but she could be what she had secretly wanted to be—an
elementary school teacher. After her mother's death, she and her husband,
Jorge, moved to a small town near Albuquerque where he is an office manager and she teaches third grade.

On reflection, even though Ester's and Joseph's lives are worlds apart, in
many ways, they are strikingly similar. They are symbolic of indigenous rural poor who, living within the parameters of family and village, are faced
with revolutionary social change produced by the global market economy.
Joseph discovered that social change was represented in his life as the radical difference between his rural personal history and his new life in Dar es
Salaam. Likewise, Ester recognized social change was represented in her life
as a woman from Mexico now living in El Paso. Like a good daughter, she
worked in rural Mexico as a waitress giving money to her mother. Because
she had not married, Ester was socially and economically vulnerable and
would become more so when her mother died. It was this type of economics Ester and her mother experienced that prompted her to move to El Paso
and live with Alberto and his family.

The impact her Mexican schooling had on Ester is interesting. She probably graduated from primary school. However, her educational experiences
may have simply included the first four years. She learned the same basic
capitalist-influenced curriculum as children in other indigenous societies.
She understood the importance of working hard, obeying instructions, and
on-the-job promptness. She also learned the basics of reading and writing.
Undoubtedly she received enough language knowledge to sign her name
and read the most elementary newspaper, although her foreign-language fa-
cility was learned outside the classroom. She also learned arithmetic sufficiently to add and subtract. But, if Ester left school after the second year, she
would not have learned how to multiply and divide.

Ester's primary school classroom was crowded with as many students as
it could hold. Her teacher spent very little time with her simply because of
the number of children who needed individual attention. The books she
used were few, old, and outdated. She could not take them home because
she shared them with other students. Beyond reading and writing, much of
her learning was oral. She learned through such teaching techniques as
memorization and reciting.

Ester's life dramatically changed when she and her mother left Mexico to live with her brother's family. Legally crossing the border at El Paso, she was presented with a multitude of opportunities from which to select. In her case, she worked as a translator and continued her education, deciding eventually to attend a local college and become an elementary school teacher. She became a U.S. citizen. In fact, American capitalist formal schools revolutionized Ester's life. She fulfilled her dreams while living in an Hispanic cultural enclave. Living her culture, Ester was able to filter various social and economic differences presented to her through work, entertainment, and daily living. The Hispanic filtering agent was represented by her family, friends, Spanish language television, and other parts of her life. Although Ester is an immigrant in the United States, she had little need to change her indigenous culture, for it is not threatened. In this regard, Ester is special. While immigrants from other indigenous societies are required to culturally disrobe, she was not.

However, Ester represents only one type of education and life experience Mexican children received during the later part of the twentieth century. Hector Fuenta[12] represents another type experienced in Mexico and the United States.

Hector moved to Ciudad Juárez three years ago when he was twelve years old. He is fifteen now and thinks of himself as a man able to take care of himself, his mother, father, and three younger sisters. He was born in Chiapas and is dimly aware of what his life was like there. But he is not certain if he really remembers Chiapas or just the stories of hunger, revolutionaries, and turmoil his mother and father talk about. He remembers his father working on a coffee plantation before the family moved to San Cristóbal de las Casas. His father thought he could make more money there selling artifacts and trinkets to tourists, but the revolutions changed all that when the tourists stopped coming. His family moved many times, first to Mexico City and finally to Ciudad Juárez.

Hector remembers the first time he saw Ciudad Juárez. Actually, it was America he saw first. They had arrived in the hills south of Ciudad Juárez late at night when he was asleep. In the morning when he awoke to eat breakfast with his mother and sisters, there in the north and east was something spellbinding. He saw tall buildings, houses, streets, green grass, and cement highways with cars speeding along them. He had seen all of these things before in Mexico City and other places they lived, but here was a difference. Perhaps, it was the morning sun, but what Hector saw was cleanliness. Here in the desert was a city without dirt and dust! He compared El Paso's cleanliness to Ciudad Juárez's and knew he was right. It wasn't the morning sun or the crispness of the air that made El Paso shine. What he saw was real.

The city seemed so close to him. It was simply across a river (he learned later the river was the Rio Grande, its riverbed cemented so it did not shift according to the seasons). How easy it will be to visit there! And in fact, it *was* easy to visit El Paso. Later that month he and his mother walked through Ciudad Juárez to the bridge that separated Mexico from the United States. It was a free bridge, he learned. He didn't have to pay like the Americans. His day was a marvel. He saw things he had seen only in movies and television. They were real. He and his mother walked through department stores looking at clothes. Hector watched his mother. He saw her smile. They were long smiles. She is smiling to herself, Hector realized. Clerks offered their assistance. They spoke kindly to them in Spanish. Hector, just for the sport of it, tried on a shirt in a store close to the border. He wanted his mother to see him in something new. The shirt felt so good, but when he looked in the mirror he saw himself not as he was, but as he wanted to be—a person living in El Paso.

Hector quickly learned that realizing his dream of living in El Paso was more complicated than he thought. He didn't have a social security card or a driver's license or any type of paper that said he was an American. Worst of all, he didn't know anyone in El Paso who would let him live there or help him get a job. Besides, he wanted his family to come with him. It was then he learned about the coyote.

The coyote Hector was introduced to walked on two legs and was named Oscar. Oscar was old, but Hector saw him through the eyes of youth and thought him ageless. "Because you are young and do not want to go to Seattle to work the orchards, I will charge you less," said Oscar. "For five hundred American dollars, I will take you to El Paso and get you a Texas driver's license and a fake social security card." Oscar, shrugging his shoulders in a fit of seldom expressed honesty said, "I don't know why you want those papers. The police don't check them. The people you work for will not ask for them. They don't care if you are legal or not—they just want you to work at jobs the fat Norteamericano teenagers think are beneath them."

That evening, Hector climbed into an aged, rattling, enclosed pickup with a dozen other men, young and old. Heading into the desert, the coyote drove through the night. Hector could not see what was happening, but the coyote had left the roads of Ciudad Juárez hours ago. First, traveling south into the desert mountains and then west and north into valleys and arroyos, the pickup finally stopped. "Get out and be quiet," whispered the coyote. "Stay smart and run to the north. Stay low to the ground or the patrol will see you." With that said, Oscar the coyote got into his pickup and drove south.

Hector didn't know what to do except follow the coyote's instructions. Leaving the others, running quietly with his back bent low so as not to be seen, Hector ran for what he thought was forever. The sun was coming up in the east, and while he expected to see El Paso in the distance, he saw instead a truck—a Land Rover with uniformed men in it. They were armed and spoke English. They spoke many words Hector did not understand, but he knew they wanted him to stop. Straightening his back and placing his hands in the air, Hector was taken into custody by the Immigration Service.

The part of El Paso Hector had not expected to see was the inside of a jail. Looking around him, he saw many of the laborers who had been with him in the coyote's pickup. "We have all been caught," thought Hector. "None of us made it through." He felt sad and disappointed. Mostly though, he was disgusted with himself. His dreams were shattered. Without thinking or paying attention, Hector went through the process of police identification. Cleared, he and many others were taken in a van to the border—to the same free bridge he and his mother had crossed the month before. Passed by the officials to Mexican police, Hector was taken into Ciudad Juárez. Later freed, walking home, Hector recognized the coyote. "Hey," laughed Oscar, "back so soon from your travels?"

"Yes," replied Hector. "My travels are teaching me how to live a new kind of life."

Like Joseph and Ester, whom we have already met in this chapter, Hector recognizes that he too is learning how to live a new kind of life. His first reactions to capitalist wealth personalized for Hector, as it had for Ester and Joseph, the economic gaps that exist between indigenous and capitalist nations. Unlike Joseph's response, in which wealth was seen through the eye of a television set, Hector's reaction was immediate and twofold: first, the beauty and wealth created in the form of El Paso's cleanliness; second, the retail markets he and his mother visited were framed in recognizable cultural detail of language and courtesy. It is this that formed the edifice of his schooling.

Hector's new school curriculum was a continuation of that which he and his sisters already possessed. Hector understood this new curriculum, for his life existed in the Mexican economy's informal sector. He knew he would not be offered a job in El Paso from which he would receive a regular paycheck and fringe benefits. At best, he hoped he would work as a gardener or in a small shop owned by someone he knew. Again, he expected his pay to be less than minimum wage and without fringe benefits. Like most of his friends and all of his family, Hector was bound to the economics of the small-time entrepreneur, sometimes selling his services in markets he recognized. To put it another way, Hector's life education was to find jobs that existed on the street. Selling gum, shining shoes, watching cars for tourists—all were jobs of the moment. If Hector was musically talented, he could also wander the streets singing in a mariachi band or become a professional beggar. In the latter case, there was a certain amount of economic security given him not found in other jobs. He could either rent or be assigned a street corner by a self-appointed manager, who would, for a share of his profits, protect him and perhaps help him increase his customer base.

His curriculum was also social. Like many others from Chiapas and elsewhere, Hector's family was very poor. In fact, Hector assumed, by the age of fifteen, he would always build the homes he lived in from scrap sheet metal, lumber, and cardboard, just like his father. He also experienced the small rural entrepreneuralism of raising crops in which only the surplus is sold or bargained to others. He is presently experiencing the human interactions of transient laborers looking for work regardless of geography or season. Yet, Hector did not think his social education placed him at a disadvantage or in a specific class, because his relationships with his family and extended family was life-encompassing.

However, his life experiences were sufficiently sophisticated for him to recognize that others, even in Mexico, lived different kinds of lives. Both Mexican and American television were creating an awareness that how people lived had some relationship with the color of one's skin. It was not that skin color defined a person's class, as in the United States, for in Mexico it was within the rubric of social interaction that some persons' skin could be lighter or darker than others'. But Hector's social education gave him the parameters to know that lighter skin was more admired than darker skin. On television, those whose hair was blonde or who were light skinned seemed to be younger, more talented, and more energetic than darker-skinned people.

Supporting this, it seemed to Hector that those whose complexions were darker appeared less talented and more dirty. While not putting his thoughts into words, Hector was developing a social assumption that darker skin equated to an older generation who lived a life of labor, while lighter-skinned people seemed to enjoy the fruits of life. For this reason, Hector—but not Ester—was attracted to El Paso. While he was not light skinned, he wanted to live on the fringe of that type of capitalist society.

Hector understood that living in the United States was complicated and chose to remain in Ciudad Juárez. Beyond economics and language, he experienced the significance of social meanings of such outward differences as skin color. Hector represents the clash between capitalist and indigenous social descriptions of race, culture, and economics. But he also recognizes that elite social descriptions permeate his society. He appreciates, for example, Mexico's tri-cultural history in which both Indian and Spanish are creating a new race.[13] But, Hector is confused by television programs beamed from Ciudad Juárez or Miami that present media personalities who change their hair color, flaunt their light skin tones, and mimic an elite American culture.

India: Education, Castes and Emigration

Nevertheless, capitalist social values defining skin color as representations of indigenous societies are erratic. To illustrate, while Hector's personal history required him to adapt his life to this value, others like Jay, whom we will meet next, did not. One reason, perhaps, is that Jay's personal history represents an acknowledged European (British) positive regard of India's cultural and educational history. Another reason, possibly more accurate in

Jay's case, is the unbiased academic environment that protected him, first as a student and later as a professor. Representing an elite caste within his own Indian society and demonstrating intellectual abilities in a capitalist society allowed Jay to discover other relationships that separated indigenous people from capitalist groups.

To most, Jay, perhaps five feet and a couple inches, is a small person.[14] He had come from New Delhi (he calls it simply Delhi) over three decades ago to go to university in the United States. He already had bachelor's and master's degrees, but they were from universities in India, and he knew they would not be acceptable to American employers—and he wanted so much to live in either Europe or the United States. Intellectual life was fascinating and fast paced in those countries, and he wanted to be part of that. It seemed to him India was in the "intellectual backwoods," as he called it.

Jay's full name was Yashal Jayaprakash, but he became "Jay" the first day of class. The professor tried his best to pronounce all of his name, but in desperation finally said, "Sorry, young man, but in this class your name will be Jay." It seemed like yesterday he was baptized with an American name, but during his life journey in the United States, he had accumulated two advanced degrees, an Indian wife from Delhi, three children (now, thankfully, all graduated from good colleges), a beautiful home in the suburbs, and a challenging research professorship at a major university. And, today was his last day in the labs with his graduate students. The semester was over and he was retiring.

Jay was in a reflective mood. He knew he did not have a lifetime of things to do during his retirement because he had focused so much of his life on his work and family. In fact, once he had taken up golf to prepare for retirement, only to give it up. He found it boring. Keeping a lawn trimmed and green like his neighbors was fine, but others could do that for him. Besides, lawn work was work to Jay. It was not relaxing. He had difficulty with the suburban values of the weekend warrior-gardeners.

Jay had an abundance of friends in the university's Indian community. In some ways, though, interacting in the Indian community was like living in a ghetto in which values that could not be understood beyond the community imprisoned those within. Some of his friendships were formed at conferences he attended as a consequence of his research. Other friendships were a continuation of social interactions he and his wife established with parents of his children's friends. But, to be honest, most of the people he knew fell into that great mass of what Jay called "acquaintances." He knew none of his friends or acquaintances could give him a feeling of meaningful fulfillment in his retirement years.

Jay understood his feelings. The United States was too free for him in some ways. While he recognized the evils of racial tensions he had seen, there was little respect for social status. His early life in India was framed as a Brahman, and he missed having others in the United States recognize his social stature. He knew he received respect from students as a professor, but as a retired person, he would lose that. He prided himself on his graduate degrees and knew he would receive additional respect for these accomplishments only if he retired in India. In the United States, little public acknowledgment was made of his successes. Even his children seemed not to acclaim their education. Their lives were so different than his had been when he moved to the United States. While he was driven to succeed at his studies, first as a student and then as a professor, his children were comfortable with their lives as they lived them. It was not, he knew, that they were lazy or disinterested; it was they were so relaxed in their efforts to become what they felt to be their futures.

Jay has yet to understand who he really is. First, labeled with a shortened American version of his name by a professor who was unable to cross cultures, he had become someone other than Yashal Jayaprakash, whose personal history was centered in India. By allowing that to happen, it was if he had denied himself part of his life. He still was Yashal Jayaprakash, and it was he who had yet to come to terms with the culture in which he had lived during the last thirty years.

Jay's life, as seen from India and the United States, obviously was viewed differently. In both cultures he exhibited the hallmarks of professional and social success. For example, the awarding of two respected American graduate degrees was considered a signal accomplishment in India. And those in his family who visited him in his academic environment or saw pictures of his suburban home and family also recognized these as hallmarks of success. Even for the Americans, Jay was a success. Professional position and social statements of affluence led many at his university and elsewhere to accept him. His career was rewarding, and he wanted his retirement to be his reward.

Of course, Jay found his career rewarding because he was able to immerse himself in a research regime from which he could control his social environment. Working with others who were researching the same intellectual issues allowed him to participate with the outside world on his terms. It was not, however, until his pending retirement that Jay, now about to be stripped of his positions and accomplishments, was able to see his social environment in more critical detail.

Unlike Hector and Ester, whom we have already met, Jay, because of the cultural protection the university afforded him, did not want the biosocial experience of working in the American capitalist culture while living in his cultural ghetto. To be clear, while Hector and Ester experienced the U.S. culture and economy, both were able to successfully position themselves within the grasp of Mexican society. For example, Ester elected to remain in the United States so she could pursue her dream of teaching while living in Hispanic Texas. Hector has learned a new kind of life, as he admits in his last comment. His travels have taught him how to get over the border without being caught—just like millions of others who pass from Mexico to the United States daily. He works for less, without benefits, for money that he could not earn in Mexico. He continues to send money home and return to Ciudad Juárez when he cannot find work on the other side of the Rio Grande.

Jay also shared with Joseph some feelings about the perceived capitalist culture's artificiality or shallowness. Joseph experienced these feelings while watching MTV programs. Jay felt them when he observed his children's relaxed attitudes about their lives. That is, both experienced the capitalist culture through the artificial filters of media and academics.

LIVING IN TWO CULTURES:
THE PRICE OF A CAPITALIST EDUCATION

Boy (with picture of Columbus)—
More than four hundred years ago
Columbus lived, as all school-boys know;
He was born in the city of Genoa
Which lies upon fair Italy's shore.
Girl (with map of West Indies)—
On October twelfth, fourteen ninety-two,
Some fair green islands came into view;
"Asia!" he cried, but we know, today
Not Asia, but the West Indies were they.
Boy (with picture of Indians)—
The people who dwelt on these islands fair
Had tawny skins and straight black hair,
They were childlike and simple, and, in their eyes,
The white men were gods come down from the skies.[15]

Virginia Baker's poem "A Columbus Day Exercise," acted out in American elementary schools during the beginning years of the twentieth century, describes in lyrical fashion the relationship between postcolonial societies and elite capitalism. It is this relationship that was a dilemma each person in this chapter addressed. Confronted with differing definitions of the individual, such as those Baker uses, each person we described, like the societies they represented, was overwhelmed with capitalist European cultural artifacts. They were confronted with the meaning-making of the artifacts and responsible for placing them within their personal histories. At the same time, each person was faced with recasting himself or herself as an economic entity within the global market economy. Capitalism had taken from each of those we discussed the traditional education of an indigenous society. And nowhere was this more noticed than when each person responded to the global marketplace. Now that we have been introduced to their lives and understand the dilemmas they experienced, let us look at the education each person received so we can better understand the global market economy's impact on postcolonial schools.

Joseph: Stuffy Teachers versus Village Life

In many ways, Joseph's life in Tanzania is emblematic of the cultural conflict created by the global market economy and experienced in postcolonial societies. No longer considered discrete political units by capitalists, postcolonial societies experienced the diminished appeal of their traditional educational objectives.

What Joseph learned in his formal schools, at first glance, appears disconnected from his rural life. Yet, this was the purpose of the school. It was acting as a change agent of the free-market economy. Teachers were encouraging Tanzanian students to think less of their lives as continuations of those represented by their parents and villagers and more as valued workers in urban Tanzania. These school curricula were purposely designed so students learned values other than those parents and villages taught. Students experienced the capitalist, value-laden primary school curriculum. It taught the social values of individualism and the economic values of worker responsibility. Standing in lines, running in unison, and speaking English gave students experiences of being responsible to others who might be their future managers or employers.

In the same regard, secondary school teachers taught students more complex economic values to make them even more desirable laborers. Acting like managers, teachers yelled at students, gave them orders, and degraded them if their school assignments were less than expected. Teachers were teaching students that taking orders from managers in return for wages was morally superior to idly developing social relationships. It was money, not personal interactions, that was the reward for a well-ordered life. Or, to be more clear, students were learning how to work for wages paid them by those who are investing for profit. The classroom learning experience taught students that capitalism improved their quality of life by increasing the quantity of their possessions. Those who listened and watched themselves learn in the postcolonial formal school discovered the capitalist definition of life's quality was much the same as the colonial definition in earlier years.

Students were also learning a social curriculum. Becoming acquainted with dominant cultural artifacts such as television, cassette recorders, DVDs, and other devices reinforced the attraction of Western mass culture to young workers. Many of the devices were central to their lives because they gave them a glimpse of capitalist popular culture through movies, programs, music, and dance. Perhaps without really understanding the social reinforcement of capitalism, young workers responded to popular culture positively by learning English, the language of capitalism.

On the family level, it was this capitalist social education that confronted traditional schools. Coupled with the formal school curriculum, it was the expected next step for young adults to question the traditional education they learned from their parents, relatives, and other adults in the village. The fulcrum upon which this was based was that, if there was something to know, someone in the village would teach them. The teaching of values was everyone's business, for every adult in the village was obligated to interact with every child, regardless of parentage. In sum, the dilemma presented to young postcolonial laborers who are products of both traditional and formal curricula is, How can you live in a world in which you share responsibilities with others, while working in a global market economy that assigns each worker different responsibilities?

Yuri Gorbunov: The Price of the Entertainment

The conflict between the newly formed Russia and capitalism is a product of a history of political and military dissidence sparked by early twentieth-century Soviet social experimentation in state-sponsored collectivism. While some may compare Soviet collectivism, in the broadest sense, to indigenous village life, the difference rests in the social and intellectual gardens from which they sprung. Indigenous village society was based on mutuality in which persons participated jointly. Soviet collectivism sprung from the pen of Anton Makarenko, an educational philosopher much admired by Joseph Stalin. Consequently, dissonance between an intolerant Russian society and capitalism was not centered on the *I–we* conflict experienced by many postcolonial societies, even though each had immediate past histories of groupism.[16]

Yet, Russia, like other postcolonial societies, experienced the educational consequences of globalization. The educational theory of manual labor propounded by Lunacharsky, Blonsky, Shatsky, and others in the golden age of the 1920s, for example, was easy to transfigure into the capitalist's educational philosophy. Therefore, the study of foreign language is an important laborers' curriculum because of its economic outcomes. Within this sense, Russian schools embracing capitalism reflect a society learning to be sympathetic to renewal. As a counterpoint, Tanzania's formal school teachers' poor command of English may be viewed as an expressed fear of the global market economy.

Ester Cardenas, Hector Fuenta, and the Coyote: Tri-culturalism in a Bi-social World

While the Mexican school system experienced the same educational issues created by the global market economy as other developing nations, its educational reactions were different. Framing that difference is Mexico's proximity to the United States and its reactive history to American cultural, economic, military, and political incursions. As a consequence, the global market economy, as expressed by the United States, has presented itself to Mexico's schools in more muted terms, mutually understood by both societies. It is the eerie voices of the prerevolutionary educational reformers Palavicini and Sierra, speaking their capitalistic educational theories about children becoming Mexico's economic assets, that are now heard. These voices, countered by Vasconcelos's postrevolutionary thoughts of encouraging schools to become partners for social change in the creation of a tri-cultural Mexico, are the philosophical platforms upon which Mexico's school reformers discuss education's cross-purposes within the rubric of the global market economy.

Similarly, the global market economy's social education projects a bisocial curriculum, teaching Mexico's emigrant labor core an accommodation that capitalist and indigenous societies require to exist side by side. This is the education of living on the knife edge of two societies. Accepting the roles forced upon them by the global market economy, the bisocial curriculum teaches its students how to become economic and social entrepreneurs. As graduates of this education, each lives within and without the global market economy. In the future, the education of Mexico's emigrant labor core may be institutionalized in formal schools in which the dynamics of the global market economy will educate docile students, now managed by the elite, to become contentious.

Jay's Retirement: What's in a Name?

We were concerned in this chapter about the educational impacts the global market economy placed on school systems and how they were reflected in individuals' lives. We wanted to understand how indigenous or developing countries such as Tanzania, India, Russia, and Mexico accommodated, accepted, or rejected capitalist undertakings within the confines of the global market economy. But we have yet to understand the impact of the global market economy on indigenous peoples who for very personal reasons, perhaps beyond those of economics, chose to move from their country to a capitalist society. Yet, the global market economy is universal in its outreach, so these indigenous sojourners have also experienced the conflict between their life histories and the capitalist societies in which they live.[17] It is for that reason Jay is important to us.

Jay acts as a summation of the capitalist school's influences on the postcolonial or indigenous persons we have discussed. Beyond the social conflict created by formal and traditional schools in indigenous societies, he is the representation of the millions of indigenous university students who, for a brief period of their lives, live in capitalist societies, studying in universities and institutes. He is also representative of those sojourners and settlers, who for unaccounted reasons, leave homes of their birth to live in societies far removed. These students and sojourners are bisocial; they emigrated from a concentration of labor and resources to a concentration of wealth. They are double schooled because they understand equally well the social conflict created by the global market economy's education of laborers and managers.

It is this that serves to explain the costs indigenous societies pay as they interact with dominant, elitist, capitalist cultures. It is the economic relationship, in which capitalists position concentrations of labor and resources in transparent school connections, that respond to the global market economy. The costs of maintaining these educational connections differ. For example, seen through the eyes of an emigrant labor core, Mexico's educational costs have been in the curriculum of accommodation. Russian educational response has shown itself to be positive as it repositioned its role within a global economic economy. Tanzania, on the other hand, like other indigenous societies, has paid the cost of despair, reforming its indigenous society into a social disjoint. It is all of this that Jay summarizes for us.

Like indigenous students and sojourners who live within concentrations of wealth, Jay paid his price early. As we learned earlier in the chapter, Yashal Jayaprakash's American professor verbally expressed difficulty pronouncing his name during the first class of the semester, so he summarily changed it to Jay. On a personal level, it was apparent the professor was not interested in harming Jayaprakash. After all, it was simply, in his eyes, an act of convenience. But, the act of labeling Jayaprakash "Jay" for the convenience of a dominant society (in this case, a university professor) illustrated to him that, regardless of his Brahman elitism, he remained an indigenous, interacting in a capitalist society only because he was in an approved position. In fact, that happened to him as a professor—Jayaprakash remained what he was as a student. As a metaphor, the labeling of Jayaprakash is the transparent school connection through which wealth educates labor and resources. That said, capitalists remain unchanged. They are like Christopher Columbus, labeling the indigenous to suit the world he thought he knew, forcing those who have "tawny skins and straight black hair, . . . childlike and simple, and in their eyes, / The white men were gods come down from the skies"[18] to remain powerless.

LIVING IN TWO CULTURES:
SCHOOLS AND THE GLOBAL MARKET ECONOMY

In this chapter we met five people, each of whom gives us, through his or her personal history, glimpses of various postcolonial responses to the global market economy. Although each individual is different, a uniting sameness exists among them. Collectively, they show us that concentrations of wealth continue to manage indigenous concentrations of resources and labor. Even through the resulting social conflict, their formal schooling drew them together as they learned the values and skills purposely designed to enhance their worker abilities to compete in a global market economy.

Schools and Social Disruption

Beyond the social sameness among them, there are striking differences between our five individuals and the family members and villagers with whom they grew up. Competing with traditional schools and family orthodoxies, formal schools created values and gender controversies that are still debated in families and villages. Amy Stambach talks about how secondary schools and East African initiation rituals create social clashes between parents and children and males and females.[19] Many adults, she says, are troubled that secondary schools are ruining children by educating them to become little Europeans rather than East Africans (in this case, Tanzanians). As a consequence, boys and girls who are receiving a formal education are redefining their social roles, moving to urban areas, and living, say their parents, immoral lives.

The crux of the parents' argument is that they understand the evil influence formal schools have on children and are voicing their fear that the future society their children live in will deviate from the traditional society the older generation understands. They worry that formal education limits their children's opportunities to live in the village. On the other hand, children learn that the promised life of labor, with affluence as its rewards, is better than living without electricity in villages. It creates conflict in mothers' minds if their daughters should graduate to womanhood through female circumcision or live an urban life of prostitution.

But, the controversy about educational disruption in many postcolonial villages can best be understood through HIV/AIDS, for that is the anvil upon which educational issues are argued. For example, the World Summit for Sustainable Development describes a sub-Saharan Africa plagued with approximately twenty-eight million HIV/AIDS patients. Affecting everyone regardless of age, gender, or social status, the disease strikes working men and women at disproportionate levels.

In urban areas, labor costs continue to rise because of absenteeism, worker deaths, and required subsequent training of replacement workers. In rural areas, agricultural costs continue to increase because fewer workers are able to tend the crops. While HIV/AIDS is deepening a continued food crisis, its impact is felt by an estimated thirteen million people who have little to eat. In some postcolonial sub-Saharan societies, it is estimated that perhaps more than one in every five persons is infected with the disease. For example, Zambian officials report that one of every two hospital beds is filled with an HIV/AIDS victim. Regarding the catastrophe's human toll, its impact on school-age children is devastating, as the quality of their educational experiences is touched by expanded teacher shortages heightened by infected HIV/AIDS teachers.

Further, the HIV/AIDS impact on schools is experienced through family dislocation and is immediately felt as husbands and wives, fathers and mothers, and sisters and brothers succumb to the disease. Destroying families, women discover they are also susceptible to its ravages. Regardless, they continue as caregivers, while assuming family roles as mothers to their brothers' children and grandmothers to their deceased children's children. They are now mothers and grandmothers of village children. As families perish, many women take on responsibilities to raise orphans as if they are their own issue.

Not only is social disruption experienced externally as the World Summit for Sustainable Development and Stambach's study report, but there is disruption within the school as well. In this case, internal conflict is focused on educational finance and assessment issues. As noted earlier in this chapter, postcolonial educational policies, reacting to increased budget demands (such as interest payments to international banking agencies or domestic issues including HIV/AIDS) are now expanding their monetary base by requiring parents to financially contribute to their children's schooling. Although governments in some cases have attempted to lessen the economic impact on family budgets, school fees are divisive tools that have built social and economic barriers between the poor and the less poor. The result of these funding policies is that the formal school is actively helping to create an uneducated underclass to live in greater poverty in their own economically crushed societies.

Beyond the internal conflict of school fees, student assessment has created additional internal conflicts among those who have classroom experiences. Especially, in the formal schools, which teach capitalist curricula, students are tested on nonlived knowledge. Failure rates continually remain high among students who attend schools that have few facilities, textbooks, and supplies. Of course, this is compounded with teacher shortages and issues of language competence.

Schools and What Students Learn

Just as external and internal conflicts are the environments in which postcolonial schools react to issues beyond their control, student learning still exists in the classroom and is within the schools' control. Teaching expected worker values and skills, classroom teachers extol the significance of manual work, use of expensive technology, and worker–manager relations in a school environment that disrespects manual work, has nonexistent technology, and formalizes student–teacher relations.

Perhaps the most significant instruction students learn in the formal school is foreign languages. Learning the languages of capitalist societies, teachers tell students, allows greater economic opportunities in the global market economy. Hidden within the teaching is the inferred value that, because indigenous languages are less valued by capitalist organizations, those who speak them are also less valued. Therefore, the foreign languages students learn are those spoken by foreign entrepreneurs, corporate managers, or their previous colonizers. However, postcolonial youths' social acceptance of English as a language of the schoolroom and the street is appreciated by teachers because of U.S. dominance within the global market economy. Of course, part of the reason for postcolonial youths' acceptance of English as a language of instruction is because of the exportation of American movies, music, dress, and other aspects of popular culture.

Similar to the parental reaction of external conflict noted above, foreign-language issues also create family conflict between children and parents. Understanding new definitions of labor, technology, and human relations expressed in a language parents do not understand gives children a power independent of parents and the village. Unable to understand, parents reinforce their children's power of independent decision making by offering them unwanted social and economic alternatives that will lock them within the fold of the family and village. Because children learn from their teachers that worker values are incompatible with village life, they leave for urban centers, forcing parents and villages to adjust to unwanted new ways.

In the next chapter, we will continue the theme that schools are competitive entities in the global market economy. Just as indigenous children are taught to labor in the global market economy, chapter 6 questions why some children in developed societies are taught to devote their life to labor, while others, more privileged, become managers. Let us turn our attention in the next chapter to five individuals who are in the process of learning how to live in the global market economy.

NOTES

1. The term "little Europeans" is a derogatory phrase to describe students who attend formal schools. For a better discussion of this, see Amy Stambach, *Lessons from Mount Kilimanjaro: Schooling, Community, and Gender in East Africa* (New York: Routledge, 2000), esp. chapters 2 and 6.

2. George Foster, *Culture and Conquest: America's Spanish Heritage* (Chicago: Wenner-Gren Foundation for Anthropological Research, 1960), quoted in David J. Weber, *The Spanish Frontier in North America* (New Haven, CT: Yale University Press, 1992), 14.

3. Weber discusses this topic in his introductory chapter in *The Spanish Frontier.*

4. Ambassador Vural's governmental responsibility at the turn of the twenty-first century was to revamp Turkey's economic, social, and political institutions to meet the European Union's standards. See Georgie Anne Geyer, "Turkey working hard to 'Europeanize' itself," editorial, *Tulsa Tribune*, June 18, 2002.

5. Geyer, "Turkey working hard."

6. Joseph is a composite of interviews by the author with selected sub-Saharan students attending universities in the United States. Students were asked to reflect on their personal histories and that of their parents and friends.

7. In many sub-Saharan nations, life expectancy has retreated to pre-twentieth-century levels (approximately forty years). Causes for the decline include poor health, war, famine, and HIV/AIDS.

8. Stambach, in *Lessons from Mount Kilimanjaro*, discusses her experiences as a teacher in a Tanzanian formal school.

9. Late twentieth-century Russian educational reformers, in an attempt to modernize schools and because of financial problems, have modified the direction of schools so that they are more able to respond to social and economic demands. For a more complete discussion, see Stephan L. Weber, *Society in the New Russia* (New York: Palgrave Macmillan, 1999).

10. Yuri Gorbunov is a compilation of young Eastern European university students studying in the United States.

11. Ester and the others in this illustration are fictional characters, although the locations exist.

12. Hector Fuenta is not a real person. He is a compilation of the life histories of some laborers whose life histories included coming to the United States illegally. Oscar the coyote is fictitious and is painted in a positive light. Most coyotes are not like Oscar. See Steven Zahniser, *Mexican Migration to the United States: The Role of Migration Networks and Human Capital Accumulation* (New York: Garland Press, 1999).

13. Mexico is a pluralist society. Its cultures are defined variously, but generally Aztec, Spanish, Indian, and Mestizo are the basics for Mexicans. It is still changing because of different cultures moving into the country. I also include French because of that country's profound impact on the government, education, and values of the people.

14. Jay is not a real person. He is a compilation of selected students who came to the United States to study as young men. Many, becoming citizens, stayed. They

usually married within their culture and are now grandfathers and retired. The author chose to present them as successful university professors.

15. Virginia Baker, "A Columbus Day Exercise," verses 1, 4, and 5, in Grace B. Faxon, *Practical Selections from Twenty Years of Normal Instructor and Primary Plans* (Dansville, NY: F. A. Owen, 1912), 241.

16. The complexity of this position is illustrated in Girard's study of twentieth-century Soviet and seventeenth-century Puritan schools. The overarching commonality she identified was that both societies were moralists, purposely isolating themselves from others in order to develop a utopia. See Sundra Kaye Girard, "The Puritan and Soviet Schools: A Comparative Study" (Ed.D. diss., Oklahoma State University, 1993), 132.

17. Sowell defines sojourners as those who are journeying through a foreign land in the same way a transient worker or a vacationer might. A sojourner who stays, says Sowell, is a settler. For a fuller understanding, see Thomas Sowell, *Migrations and Cultures: A World View* (New York: Basic Books, 1996).

18. Baker, "A Columbus Day Exercise," verse 5.

19. One of the ways Stambach discusses the impact of social disruption is by pointing out the strong connection between rural values that outline the evils of formal schools (leading young women to urban prostitution) and formal schools' dismissal of female circumcision as an uncivilized action performed on women under the guise of an initiation ritual. See Stambach, *Lessons from Mount Kilimanjaro*, 72–79.

6

The Education of Mean Middle Managers

In chapter 5, we put faces on the free-market economy to better understand the complexity and totality of globalization's impact on indigenous societies and developing countries. By viewing individuals, we were able to comprehend how formal or elite schools, curricula, and teachers are creating social and economic revolutions that are constructing the *global village*.[1] These revolutions are fought on many levels, but nowhere are they argued more vehemently than in schools in which generational and gender differences are exposed. Captured within these differences are social convulsions caused by new ways of living, different forms of illnesses, and variant languages that do not represent indigenous social histories. Unable to frame these convulsions within a common vocabulary, none of the individuals we studied in the previous chapter was able to understand the commonness of the educational experiences in which each reacted to capitalist economic and social incursions. Within the extremes of acceptance or rejection, none of the individuals we viewed in chapter 5 was given the choice of not reacting. That is, capitalism did not allow them the option of *whether* to live in a global village, just *how* to live in it.

Yet the global village includes much more than indigenous concentrations of labor and resources. Commanding much of the global village's economic landscape are dominant countries, international economic enterprises, and financial organizations. These, resting on capitalist platforms, are operated by middle managers who are themselves products of educational revolutions in which formal, elitist schools, curricula, and teachers have created conflicts with progressive, democratic educations espoused by such philosophers as John Dewey. Confronting comparable economic and social issues framed by entrance into the global village, as are the indigenous societies, dominant nations also are experiencing educational revolutions. Similarly, these revolutions are being discussed in ways familiar to indigenous societies. Unlike indigenous societies, however, these conversations are constructed within reform agitations prompted by creative destruction, knowledge creation, and conflicting definitions of community or individual opportunity. In this chapter, we will follow the lives of six individuals who, in varying degrees, have been influenced by neoliberal education in the global village.

NOT ALL MEAN MIDDLE MANAGERS ARE THE SAME

In the final years of the twentieth century, Eric Hobsbawm, summing up that tumultuous period, notes that in absolute terms such as Nobel laureates, developed nations or concentrations of wealth have been intellectual centers of learning. In fact, he is quick to point out that in the twentieth century very few Nobel laureates have come from sub-Saharan Africa or Latin America. Even Japan and India have produced few Nobel laureates in relation to their populations. Further, he points out that during the last century, Nobel laureate numbers have decreased in European countries because researchers are moving to the United States.

> It is a striking fact that (at least) a third of the Asian Laureates do not appear under their own country of origin, but as US scientists. (Indeed, of the US laureates twenty-seven are first-generation immigrants).[2]

The reason for the intellectuals' emigration, according to Hobsbawm, is simply a matter of economics.[3] That is, intellectuals respond to national research budgets in the same way corporate managers respond to national budgets that grant tax cuts to the wealthy. To state the point otherwise: Reacting to the economics of research is a one-dimensional response of intellectuals. Regardless of their cultural histories or nationalities, their choice to remain or leave an economic environment is based on its commitment to their intellectual priorities.

This is the context in which neoliberalism has constructed its definition of education. Education is intellectualism's and entrepreneuralism's offspring, and the school is the agency that teaches and appraises students as they become more recognizable economic assets. It is, says Francis Fukuyama, the agency which is multigenerational, for student success can be financially rewarded, but failure "can be laid at the door of families that were disrupted . . . or in other ways less able to pass on skills and knowledge."[4] In other words, education is the voice of capitalism, and school is the scale upon which the quality of its managerial products is weighed.

Infant Health Care: Making Money the Old-Fashioned Way

Thomas Friedman, in his text *The Lexus and the Olive Tree*, defines globalization or the free-market economy variously.[5] One definition he presents his readers is Joseph Schumpeter's idea that the economics of globalization are different than in the past because, unlike industrialization, capitalism has been freed from government restrictions. Pure capitalism or neoliberalism, says Schumpeter, has the power to tear down the inefficiency and ineffectiveness of the past-present. The present, now also a part of the future, Schumpeter implies, is that economic stage in which efficiency and effectiveness are created, only to be torn down again for more advanced efficiency and effectiveness. Capitalism, he says, is "creative destruction."[6] This, responds Friedman, is the thoughtful base upon which Andrew Grove, who presents the other of Friedman's definitions, advances his views that the present-future replaces the past-present because of capitalism's inclusion of technology and intellectualism.[7]

In reality, the two definitions of globalization Friedman gives us do not conflict. He recognizes that both Schumpeter and Grove speak of the future joined to the present even though each is separated from the past-present. Globalization, says Friedman, replaces industrialization, that social and economic period which defined itself through its own stagnating grandeur resting on stylized traditions. Globalization is without grandeur and traditions because it is always creating new beginnings. Spurning stagnating grandeur and traditions, globalization is the continuous task of repeatedly reinventing products that immediately become obsolete and beg to be reinvented. Globalization is industrialization's replacement, or to put it another way, globalization is neoliberalism or pure capitalism freed from social restraint. Thus freed, capitalism's purpose, says Jacob Frankel, is to "study the global framework within which we operate and then decide what to produce."[8]

And it is this freed capitalism that Kevin, a junior executive, whom we will meet next represents. He and Charles Browning, president of Fenders Chocolate International, want to reinvent their company's infant formula product that has lost market share.[9] They have studied a market within the global framework and are in the process of deciding how to increase sales by producing greater customer acceptance of their product.

"I don't believe it! That's what got Nestlé's in trouble in the 1970s, and you want us to export baby formula to Malawi?" It was Charles Browning, president of Fenders Chocolate International, talking with his vice presidents about lagging sales. "We don't look good on Wall Street," he had said, when Kevin, a young executive, mentioned selling infant formula to Malawian mothers.

"Obviously he is too young to remember," thought Browning. "These big league schools don't put out quality M.B.A. graduates like they used to," he mused.

"Look," interrupted Kevin, "the Nestlé's thing is in the past. If you read their stuff on the Web they tell you they only ship infant formula to working mothers in developing countries who don't have time to breast-feed. They even tell you they don't advertise or anything to encourage poor rural area mothers in developing nations to use infant formula. All of that which gave Nestlé's a bad name in Africa happened before the AIDS crisis."[10]

Kevin continued, "There are lots of reports coming out of Africa that mothers with AIDS are inadvertently killing their babies through breast-feeding. In fact, mothers aren't even told they can use infant formula to protect their children from AIDS."

Browning was impressed and listened carefully. "Let's look into this and see if there is something that will help us look better to investors. We need to increase our market share in infant formula."[11]

What the executives were talking about was generally true. In fact, after their legal department investigated the circumstance, they learned that in the 1970s the infant formula industry had been accused of abusive marketing practices in merchandising their products to developing nations' mothers. Receiving free infant formula samples from local health care professionals, who had themselves received the products from manufacturers, mothers often mixed the formula with water. While the mothers' immune systems allowed them to drink the contaminated water, their babies, who did not yet have that protection, were prey to gastrointestinal diseases from which their systems could not protect them. Eventually, learning that additional supplies would cost them and their families large amounts of money, many mothers attempted to return to breast-feeding, only to discover their breasts had dried up. To stave off the inevitable, many mothers returned to using the diluted formula. What happened was predictably catastrophic. Because the instructions were printed only in English, mothers did not know feeding their babies less formula would cause malnutrition and death.

"That's why I think this 'ethical thing' is all in the past," said President Browning. "Since that time in the eighties when the World Health Organization and UNICEF developed a voluntary marketing code that restricts advertising and giving away infant formula samples, AIDS has become a hot topic."

"It would seem to me that an AIDS-infected mother who breast-fed her child would pass along her AIDS disease," said Kevin, the young executive.[12] "And, now that we know there is some research that supports this case, we have an advertising tool to sell our products."

In fact, Fenders Chocolate International's advertising campaign was a tremendous success. Using color pictures and recognizable words (not sentences) on billboards, the advertising campaign showed happy mothers bottle-feeding their newborn children. The pictures showed mothers who were portrayed as Western, progressive, and busy with their lives, actively aware of the inconvenience of breast-feeding. Never mentioning AIDS as a disease contracted by a child from an infected mother, the billboards signaled mothers that their children would start life healthy if they were formula fed. Therefore, the most important part of the advertising campaign was educating African mothers about the European values of bottle-feeding. The mammary gland, once thought of as that with which mothers suckled their children, was now Europeanized to be a female's sexual body part, clothed and out of sight as if it was unclean. Supporting the education of these European values, family and friends were admonished to honor her private time when she fed her baby. These curricula that educated the family and community to Western values, in fact, helped mothers with AIDS bottle-feed their children without others knowing their real fears.

Kevin was delighted with the financial report produced by the accounting division of Fenders Chocolate. He knew Mr. Browning was pleased with his work and planned on giving him a midyear raise.

"You deserve it," said Browning, "It's always good news for the stockholders when they read the financial sections in the papers to see their stock has gone up."

"That's right," thought Kevin, "and now, with my wife Marg pregnant, I will really need the money to give Sarah (they already knew their baby was a girl, and both loved her new name) a good life. She will have the best obstetrician and pediatricians. I want Marg to stay home with Sarah until it's time for her to go to school. And then, I want her to attend the best private school in the state."

Yet, he was confused. Marg, his wife, insisted that she would breast-feed Sarah after she was born. "I don't understand women sometimes," thought Kevin. "Where did she ever get the old-fashioned idea that breast-feeding was better for Sarah than bottle-feeding?"

Kevin's difficulty in understanding why his wife wanted to breast-feed their new daughter was not so much based on his personal history as it was on his education. It did not enter his mind to question whether he or his wife as infants had been breast-fed. Rather, Kevin's consideration was based on the European stereotype that breast-feeding was an old-fashioned form of giving new babies nourishment. Obviously, non-European women who represented differing cultures and ethnicities seen in *National Geographic* could accept the stagnant traditions upon which breast-feeding rested, simply because they were illiterate and uneducated. But, Kevin's life was not based on stagnant traditions. It was his responsibility to market new and better products that obviously, he thought, culminated into new and better ways of living. That was the reason he wanted to help new African mothers feed their children. It had to be better, thought Kevin, to feed a baby cow's milk than milk from a sick mother. He could understand why indigenous African mothers were limited in their choices of feeding their children, but why would his wife Marg want to do the same thing?

Escaping the Empire Period: Managing the Professorate

Hobsbawm's sweeping evaluation of the globalization of intellectual resources is interesting in the manner in which he traces the geographic locations of Nobel laureates during the last century. Yet, the explanation of the borderless world in which intellectuals live and think, as he describes it, is also situated in earlier periods of the twentieth century. As early as the 1950s and 1960s, scholars, including Robert Maynard Hutchins, argued that intellectualism had passed beyond the limits of national politics and language to enter into a universality of research.[13] He painted a picture in which mid-twentieth-century American higher education institutions—he calls these "multiversities"—were creating new and unique knowledge departments. These departments, using the language of research—which Hutchins referred to as "jargon"—artificially separated types of knowledge from others.

To explain his point, Hutchins gave the reader the example of two physicists, one American and the other Russian (Russia at that time was part of the Soviet Union, the archenemy of the United States), discussing knowledge common to both in a jargon each understood. Ironically, says Hutchins, the American physicist would have more difficulty discussing another type of knowledge with his next-door neighbor, who might be a professor of education, because the two do not have a common jargon. Of course, we now understand Hutchins was aware of the internationalization of knowledge creation that formatted globalization and the free-market economy. Without using his terms, he was becoming aware of the impending educational consequence of the jargon or knowledge languages created by capitalist higher educational systems.

While Hutchins chose to complete his criticism of American higher education by calling for the restructuring of *multiversities* into *universities* that encouraged students to learn the interdisciplinary nature of knowledge, the intellectual free marketplace created knowledge concentrations instead and placed them within dominant economic concentrations. The resultant knowledge creation, explained by Hobsbawm's example of Nobel laureates, illustrates that specific knowledge, living independently, creates academicians who become managers of their own research. In short, intellectuals, like their corporate cousins, have become entrepreneurs of their own form of wealth within a free-market economy. It is because of this we meet Edwin.

Edwin just smiled and laughed.[14] He had just received an e-mail from a friend in Canada telling him of an advertisement about a tenure-track position at the University of Saskatchewan. Edwin was in the final stages of completing his Ph.D. and was looking for an assistant professorship. "Send in your credentials, Ed," his friend had e-mailed. "You are really qualified for this position. I know you would be a strong candidate."

The reason for Edwin's laughter was not because he was happy with the news. It was because it brought back bittersweet memories of when he was a seventh-grader in Saskatchewan. Back then, he didn't like school that much because his teachers yelled at students, made them line up, and demanded they learn through memorization. But he enjoyed playing winter sports. His elementary school was named Empire, and his hockey team was called the Canucks. Edwin was the goalie.

At the end of the academic year, like other seventh-graders in the province, Edwin had taken a series of academic tests (called "departmental examinations" in those days). He knew the examinations were important, and if he failed them he would be retained in the same grade and then placed in a trade school. He wanted so much to attend a collegiate, so he could learn algebra, Latin, French, and other subjects. While he could not put his thoughts into words at that time, Edwin knew these subjects were reserved for bright students, and if he didn't learn these, he would be labeled dumb.

At the end of summer vacation, Edwin's dad had called him into the living room and handed him a newspaper. In those days, newspapers published the names of all the seventh-grade students who passed the departmental examinations. Edwin had no difficulty knowing what the paper said because he saw the results on his father's face. His name was not printed in the newspaper. He had failed.

For the next six years, Edwin attended school. First, he retook his seventh grade. Then he completed eighth grade, which was followed by four years in a trade school learning something called "commercial." During this time Edwin learned two things: he hated school and he loved learning. After graduation, using money his father gave him, Edwin packed his clothes and typewriter and moved to the United States. He had no interest in returning to Saskatchewan, and that is why he laughed when he received his friend's e-mail.[15]

For his own reasons, Edwin became part of an international movement of scholars. Beyond his personal history in Canada's Empire period, during which schools vied with each other to see which could best model British educational elitism, Edwin's emigration dramatized Hobsbawm's observations of intellectualism's centralization within concentrations of economic power.[16] Just as Hobsbawm observed European intellectuals' retreat to the United States, so was this happening in other developed countries, including Canada. That is, Edwin's decision not to return to his homeland was based on whether or not his intellectual interests could be best served through a provincialism in which creative learning was thought to be outside accepted academic practice. His decision was based on the assumption that his academic and economic future could only exist in that place where he was able to manage his own learning and research.

Edwin's professional and personal goals coalesced during his graduate studies. Foremost was his wish to become a manager, not in the traditional industrial sense in which he would direct the construction of parts or products in factories. To Edwin, management meant controlling his life so he could work for himself. As his own manager, Edwin was preparing himself to reinvent his academic future through creative destruction. For this, others would pay him. How could that be done? In fact, it was not difficult. Edwin had several higher education interviews. He chose a university in the southwestern United States even though it paid less money than the top-rank schools in the Northeast. His decision was based on several factors, including university research budgets, quality of life, and weather. Mostly though, it was university research policies that attracted him. He was expected to teach several classes each year and involve graduate students in his research, but the rest of his time would be consumed with the management of research that interested him. It was like graduate school, except he was now a tenure-track assistant professor.

Understanding academic management, Edwin knew that other than what students required of him in the classroom, there were but two obligations expected of him by the university. One was that he compete nationally for research grants offered by private and public foundations and governments. From his graduate school days, Edwin knew professors were expected to write proposals to agencies that might help them finance their research. He enjoyed writing the proposals for that purpose. In fact, Edwin discovered that many of the grant applications presented unique, intriguing research problems that piqued his professional curiosity.

Edwin's second obligation was to gain a national or international reputation through his research. The university's academic reward system was geared on that premise, and if he did not succeed, Edwin knew he would not receive tenure. Unlike some of his more timid colleagues, Edwin welcomed this responsibility, for not only would tenure help him in his present position but, through an enhanced national stature, his opportunities for professional advancement to more prestigious universities, think tanks, and foundations would also be made possible. Besides, the university did not expect him to develop feelings of loyalty to the institution. His loyalty focused on his research and the environment in which it was conducted. In short, Edwin has become an academic manager in a free-market economy.

Managing Poverty: How Mitzi Lost Her Future

Kevin and Edwin are in many ways examples of highly educated managers who represent concentrations of wealth. Learning and living in dominant countries, each is a product of the same capitalist curriculum, although each studied different disciplines. Their formal curriculum and Protestant value system acted as a bond in which questions, hypotheses, and the implementation of proposed solutions were the procedures of conducting one's private, intellectual, and economic lives. Both Kevin and Edwin incorporated the scientific method into their personal histories so clearly that they assumed the world could be seen only through that lens. This is the reason Kevin could not understand his wife's wish to breast-feed their child and Edwin had no interest in returning to Saskatchewan. Yet, it is more complicated than the internalization of the scientific method upon which their managerial education focused. It was their participation in the vigorous creative destruction of the past-present and the free-market economy that was important.

But, what happens if you live in a dominant nation, yet are outside the free-market economy? If you have no economic or intellectual tools to protect yourself from the creative destruction of the past-present, what happens to you? Fukuyama introduces the devastating thought that no such curriculum has been devised for these people because they illustrate the active absence of parents who do not "pass on skills and knowledge."[17] He correctly describes the consequence of this active absence as multigenerational. Yet, his explanation lacks the depth of lived despair and social isolation that Jonathan Kozol, for example, observed as he discovered the hidden American underclass living in urban camps where concentrations of individuals and families dwell in friendless exhaustion with drugs, disease, AIDS, prostitution, and victim blame.[18]

Constructing social identities to differentiate themselves from those who blame them for their victimization and refusing to Europeanize themselves to become poor imitations of those who persecute them, the underclass recreate themselves within the tradition of community. Much like those who know they will die together, the underclass creates a human warmth of living together. It is, as David Shipler states, quoting a young black woman, "We have a joking relationship; we have fun with each other. We spend hours on hours just talking shit and busting on each other. . . . People come up and say, 'Oh, look at you—blue, hoo, hoo.'"[19]

"Mitzi, I don't care! You've hurt this family as much as you can! I hate you. I want you out of this house. Go away!" These were the words of Mitzi's mother. "Where is your father?" (There is no father.) "He wanted you to be flushed before birth. Oh, why didn't I do it? I am sick of you!"

"Momma, I'm pregnant—I need your help—stay with me—don't send me out there. Jeremy doesn't love me. He said so. I want to have his baby and he hates me. Please help." Mitzi is fifteen years old and Jeremy is twenty-four. He just got out of jail—drugs, he said. Mitzi loved him for all the things he wasn't—brave, strong, and honest. "Momma, I don't have anything to live for except this baby. It's mine and I want him. I want him to be with me for the rest of my life."

Mitzi is in the ninth grade.[20] Still learning how to read, she attends an alternative school in North Tulsa, across I-244. The interstate highway from the western suburbs cuts through the city like a knife on its way to Joplin. On the south side of the interstate is white Tulsa, confirmed in wealth, Protestantism, and whiteness. On Mitzi's black north side is poverty and a history of white hatred.[21] Joined in the knowledge of whites murdering blacks in the beginning decades of the last century, Mitzi knows her life, regardless of what they say on television, is structured in the poverty of Tulsa's underclass.

She wanted so much to be a hair stylist at a fancy salon in Utica Square. That was the mall so many south Tulsans came to. It had fancy cafés where whites ate outside as if it was a special treat to have lunch on the sidewalk. She knew there were famous department stores there that had expensive hair salons—how she wanted to be an attendant, perhaps to wash rich old ladies' hair. Anything, Mitzi thought, was better than nothing. And now she had something—a baby. Thank God.

Mitzi's life is extraordinary because it represents an underclass capitalists have difficulty describing and therefore is open to different interpretations. For example, Mitzi can be explained by middle managers as an economic encumbrance, representative of social deviants. These deviants, who do not symbolize the capitalist definitions of normal, are placed with those "others" who walk unseen on society's edge. Voicing words capitalists use, Mitzi is an economic parasite. She expects, they say, taxpayers to take care of her and solve her problems.[22] Capitalists, through a Protestant lens of social morality, explain Mitzi away as irrelevant to them and society, although they soundlessly recognize that their refusal to help is opposite to their Christian values.[23]

All of this is to say that Mitzi's schooling is confusing to her. The formal school, with its European focus on learning how to gain economic success, proved to be unimportant to Mitzi. She has discovered that, regardless of what her teachers tell her, she is a member of the underclass, destined to live on the outer reaches of the capitalist society in which she was born. Defined by neoliberals as a social alien, the formal school Mitzi attended seemed dangerous to her. Mitzi recognized the curriculum and especially the white teachers' purpose was to forcefully change her from something she was to something she did not want to be. This was confusing to Mitzi because she didn't know what that something was. Yet, her mind was made up: she didn't want to be it. If Mitzi had had the words to explain what the school was trying to do to her, she might have voiced them through analogies such as these:

> Wealth is to success as white is to: (a) beautiful, (b) good, (c) normal, (d) all of the above.
> Poverty is to laziness as black is to: (a) ugly, (b) evil, (c) deviant, (d) all of the above.

Mitzi's living curriculum was different than the one she received in school. In elementary school, she enjoyed playing and learning with others, but it was difficult for her to accept the values the teachers, who lived in South Tulsa, expected of her. She understood the importance of honesty and integrity the teachers talked about only because her mother told her these were the values she expected her to have. Mitzi could not understand why people were required to have these special values just because of something called the "world of work." It is within this history that Mitzi chose to view her education through a lens other than those her teachers gave her. What she concluded was that her formal school's purpose was to focus her loyal attention on a capitalist society that gave her nothing yet defined her as unequal to others who were presented opportunities. In blunt terms, Mitzi understood the curriculum of a neoliberal education. While she was expected to be honest, those who were given opportunities to be successful were not. At least that is what she saw on TV.

Bicycles Built for You: Managing Transportation in Risky Markets

Eric Hobsbawm, in his text *The Age of Extremes: A History of the World, 1914–1991*, intimates that the economics of the twentieth century were framed by the immaturity of the capitalist system and the primitive nature of communications and transportation technology.[24] The economic consequence of this for colonial or marginal markets was that they could not mass-produce products sufficiently to significantly lower the costs of production.

Because industries, as discussed in chapter 4, were constrained to remain in dominant countries, postcolonial governments opted to impose import duties to increase revenue. This increased revenue was to aid postcolonial manufacturers in mass-producing products for marginal markets. Regardless, industrial production for these markets was never economically consequential, leaving them both rural and agrarian. As agricultural production continued to rise and fall, thereby influencing gyrating government budgets, most marginal manufacturers priced themselves out of the market.

It is during the last thirty years of the previous century, says Hobsbawm, who refers to this period as the "great leap forward," that the capitalist system matured and advanced technology contained communication and transportation expenses. At this point, some postcolonial and marginal markets had selective and limited opportunities to participate in the global village's economic system. That is, they became producers rather than consumers of their own resources and labor. Their goal, like that of others in the free-market economy, was to compete. In comparison to their previous economic history, however, the impact on education was phenomenal.

"Thank you for your kindness to see me. I have an offer for you that you may find interesting," said Mr. Narayan. Mr. Narayan is a field agent for the Bangalore Cycle and Tyre Works in Bangalore, India. He is talking to Munyika and Lindani, partners in a bicycle repair shop in Zomba, Malawi.[25] Munyika and Lindani operated individual bicycle repair shops for some years, but, as costs for European and American spare parts continued to increase, they decided to merge so they could remain in business and do away with the competition between them.

"My offer is very simple," said Narayan. "Bangalore Cycle and Tyre Works is planning an advertising campaign in the Shire Highlands areas outside Zomba to encourage small farmers to buy our bicycles so their children can ride to secondary school in town. Many children walk for hours in the morning and then again in the evening on narrow paths to go to school, when we know a bicycle will get them to school and home faster and safer. We also want to encourage families, especially the mothers, to use our bicycles when their children are not in school. They can visit friends or come to Zomba to shop. While they are here, we want them to know there is a shop to go to if their bicycle needs repair or a new tire is needed. We want to advertise that Bangalore Cycle and Tyre Works has honest dealers in Zomba who will fix their bicycles perfectly and cheaply."

Both Munyika and Lindani immediately understood that Narayan was offering them a business opportunity of a lifetime. They knew European and American bicycle parts were difficult to find and extremely expensive—even the parts on the black market were priced too high. They also knew that Bangalore Cycle and Tyre parts were very good, and the company could give them a steady supply. Both partners understood they were being capitalized to outcompete their competition.

On the downside, neither Munyika or Lindani had business experience dealing with women. Even on those rare occasions when it had been necessary for them to talk to a woman, her husband had always been present. It was accepted custom that if a nonfamily person such as a doctor wanted to ask a wife a question, that person spoke to the husband, who asked his wife, and then gave her answer. "How do you talk to them? When it is time to make a decision to repair a bicycle, how will they get permission from their men to let us? Worse, when it is time to pay, would they, using their own hands, actually place the money into our hands?"

"Listen," said Mr. Narayan, "the world is changing. Do you remember when you were boys and your fathers wanted oxen for farmwork? Today, prices are not what they used to be. Oxen are too expensive these days for farmers to use. They cost up to 150 American dollars now, and the costs of a harness and cart are outlandish. Donkeys are so much cheaper than oxen, so everyone uses donkeys for farmwork these days. They cost only sixty dollars. But, the best thing about donkeys is that women and girls can ride them. Their husbands and fathers would never let them do that with oxen. A Bangalore bicycle costs the same as a donkey. But, it requires no food, they are faster, and women can ride them easier than a donkey.

"These days most men allow their women to leave the farm to shop in town. Some girls even know how to read English and are becoming adventurous. They will enjoy riding a Bangalore bicycle after they learn how. Girls today are not like our sisters who stayed home, drank banana beer, and married the first man who asked our fathers. They now go to school. When the girls finish secondary school, they will want to come to Zomba to find office work if they have a chance. They are smart enough to get permission from their fathers to leave home. Their men will feel they are safe here because there is little traffic. Its not like Lilongwe that has so much traffic and there are many accidents. Besides, their mothers will be happy to visit friends from Balaka or some of the other places south of Zomba when they come here, too."

"If we agree to this, what is it you expect us to do?" asked Munyika.

"Yes, and what is it you propose to do to help us?" asked Lindani.

"The deal is this," said Narayan. "You will repair all Bangalore bicycles for a fixed price. It will be less than the cost of repair of bicycles manufactured in the United States or Europe. To help you make a larger profit, we will sell you bicycle parts for less money and you can charge your customers more. But, you cannot charge your customers more for our parts than those made in the United States and Europe. That way you will attract more customers and we will sell more bicycles.

"As for the Bangalore Cycle and Tyre Works," Narayan continued, "our profits from your repair work will be reasonable, your customers will be happy, and you will cause other repair shops in Zomba to go out of business."

"Ah," said Munyika, "I think this idea of a marketplace economy is not so bad. What do you think, Lindani?"

Mr. Narayan, Lindani, and Munyika represent different stages of learning about the market economy. Unlike Mr. Narayan, Lindani and Munyika occupy many economic positions at the same time simply because they are in a developing market niche. They learned to be entrepreneurs when they merged their individual investments into one single cycle repair shop. Part of the intellectual capital each brought to the cycle repair shop was a worker's knowledge of repairing bicycles. And, as managers of the enterprise, they had the mutual responsibility to operate their business efficiently so they could make a profit.

Yet, neither Munyika or Lindani will be disappointed if they do not immediately garner a profit from their investment. They know that to remain competitive with other bicycle repair shops in Zomba they will be forced to keep their prices as low as possible. As a consequence, both managers are willing to forestall any profit from their investment if they receive the same wages workers who do not own businesses are paid. For Lindani and Munyika, management of the repair shop is a free service because, at this moment, they are still part of Zambia's concentration of labor. While each could have worked in the agricultural sector surrounding Zomba, both knew urban life was socially and economically more attractive. Their minimum economic knowledge was sufficient to allow them to have a business location in Zomba rather than simply having a place to go to work.

Mr. Narayan was different than Lindani and Munyika. Both knew Mr. Narayan was not personally wealthy, but he represented the power of wealth. It is for this reason they referred to him in a formal capacity and were not surprised when he did not reciprocate. But, the title "Mr." meant more to Lindani and Munyika than the capitalists' wealth, for they assumed Mr. Narayan was formally educated in India. It is these assumptions about Mr. Narayan's representations of wealth and his education that defines what it means to be a manager. In fact, Mr. Narayan's educational history was much as Lindani and Munyika assumed. He had grown up in Bangalore during the mid-twentieth century. Even though he and his family were colonials, his parents had an attachment and profited from English colonialism. Carrying the family religious hatred of Muslims with him, he did not question his government or religious teachers who taught him that the sanctity of India would be forever threatened by the evil, aggressive Pakistani Muslims. Never knowing others in Pakistan mirrored their hatred of India with similar stereotyped religious logic, it was to this he dedicated his life. Without question, he also accepted the social and economic costs of maintaining a strong military and expensive atomic research. It was he, an Indian with a British education, who would work for India's economic success by making the Bangalore Cycle and Tyre Works, a wholly owned subsidiary of the British Bentley Bicycle Company of Liverpool, profitable.

For Mr. Narayan's parents, learning a formal curriculum was, in their minds, an extension of England's economic power. It was with quiet pride they sent their child to a private school where he studied European history, literature, mathematics, and the sciences. Their child knew that students just like him in England were using the same textbooks as he and learning the same curriculum in the same types of schools. In some ways, Mr. Narayan felt superior to them because he learned his studies in English even though his native language was Telugu. Yet, he sometimes thought his accent betrayed his colonialism. He memorized the lists of English kings and queens, memorized Shakespeare, and quoted long passages of Greek epic poetry. He found European science fascinating because it caused him to think differently, and therefore he retained a suspicion of it, thinking it smacked of Christianity. The ideas of problem solving, experimentation, and discovery were new to him yet enticing, because these were the reasons for Europe's economic dominance. Mostly though, he enjoyed the study of the English language. It was a vehicle for him to meet others like Lindani and Munyika. As the Bangalore Cycle and Tyre representative, it was of no consequence to him they were Muslims.

Interestingly, Lindani and Munyika's conversation with Mr. Narayan about who their potential customers might be illustrates they are becoming aware of a different world, controlled by an aggressive form of economics that is impinging on their environment and life values. They are experiencing the economic power of those who receive formal schooling, as opposed to those, like themselves, who do not. At the same time, their new education is introducing them to new ways of relating to new customers who are more demanding than those in the past. Lindani and Munyika recognize they too are part of a different, foreign educational process. While both experienced a traditional education like Joseph in chapter 5, in which parents and villagers helped them learn a village life curriculum, their experiences in Zomba taught them they were not prepared for their urban existence or the free-market economy. Lindani and Munyika's elementary education in globalization has forced them to look beyond themselves to a world in which they are only a small part. But it did not give them the peace of community they thought would be theirs after they discovered the dark underside the power the free-market economy represented.

THE EDUCATION OF MEAN MIDDLE MANAGERS

Quite the contrary, the new issues are to a large extent the product of the solutions to these problems, achieved by a combination of economic growth and the successes of the reforms advocated by the Social Gospelers, their allies, and their successors.[26]

This quote describes Robert William Fogel's position that, except for the final decades of the twentieth century, the U.S. industrial period was a national experience. Even so, he says, the history of that period, especially that which began during the Great Depression, catalogues a roster of social, political, and educational successes, all of which are embedded in the national consciousness. Within this context, Fogel advances the theory that globalism's present-future need is to reinvent that which represents the successes of the industrial era's past-present. He, like Schumpeter, is positioning the reader to rethink these industrial successes such as Social Security,   · begun in the Roosevelt administration, as neoliberal stepping-stones to new beginnings.

While we will speak of Fogel in greater detail in another chapter, it is fundamental that we understand why he believes the industrial period's successes could, all of a sudden, become causes for new beginnings. What are the successes Fogel identifies, and why is there something wrong with them now? To this, he answers that the industrial period—he identifies several in U.S. economic history, but we are concerned with that of the twentieth century—was presented with social issues created by big business and industrial concentrations. The genius of that period, Fogel implies, is that it learned industrial, social, and economic problems could not be solved by institutions created for an agrarian society. The birthing of an urban industrial period, with large federal government bureaucracies, was essential if it wanted to grapple with these issues. This created the federal government's vital social force in the capitalist life of the nation. The problem with this success, says Fogel, is that the industrial period became institutionalized in big government. Fogel, like Schumpeter before him, advances the theory that the industrial age, with the aid of big government, now hinders the nation's capitalist economic system. Enforcing tradition and misunderstanding and spurning change, Fogel says, will not allow an egalitarian society to emerge.

What is an egalitarian society? Understandably, social issues such as civil rights, health care, and others (Fogel's list includes female franchise, prohibition, and universal primary education) are significant. Yet, says he, each represents a specific government bureaucracy in which citizens, through a democratic voting process, mandate their political location or position. This traditional democratic collectivism is in the past-present. The necessary creative destruction required by neoliberals to reinvent an egalitarian society for the present-future, he says, is defined economically, not politically. Here, people acting in their self-interest, rather than communities, live their particular lives. Simply put, the industrial period was concerned with the *community's equality of condition*, whereas the postindustrial or neoliberal period, framed within the free-market economy, is concerned with the *individual's equality of opportunity*. Let us assess each of the individuals we met in the first section of this chapter against this neoliberal benchmark.

Kevin and Edwin: Education for Different Managerial Labels, Same Product

Although Kevin and Edwin seem so different in what they planned for their lives, their sameness is much more pronounced than their differences. Both were vitally interested in capturing opportunities to fulfill their individual potentialities. Each had a strong sense of purpose, both focused their futures on themselves and their families.

Fogel labels these types of neoliberal personal characteristics "spiritual resources." Regardless, both Kevin and Edwin grasp the essence of living in the free-market economy and have attuned their personal lives to that end. It is to them a code of conduct or a field upon which they actively play out their lives. They exemplify neoliberal education in its purest form. Unfettered by policies or customs, oblivious to traditions and uncommitted to community, their education is supportive of their lives and dreams. While laborers are taught how to work and retrain themselves for jobs yet to be invented, these young professionals are educated to connect their present to the future.

Living thus, this is Edwin's intellectual platform for managing his research. To look at *that* which is, to understand all that forces *that* to remain the same, to dream of what *that* could be, and to create the procedure to activate the reality—is Edwin's life. That is the education of the raw, unfettered neoliberal who can visualize the future and then create it through a free-market economy. While research was Edwin's currency in the free-market economy, Kevin's was selling infant formula to African mothers.

Mitzi: The Education of a Deviant

Mitzi is the antithesis of Kevin and Edwin. She would eventually realize she had no currency to spend in a neoliberal society committed to the free-market economy. It wasn't that Mitzi was born without currency, for she was told by her teachers the purpose of the school was to educate her so she could have the same economic opportunities as Kevin and Edwin. She knew the school was in some ways foreign to her, because her mother, while talking about her own school experience, seldom praised the teachers she remembered. It could have been her mother's attitude about school Mitzi remembered, or perhaps she had created that attitude on her own.

Either way, Mitzi's educational experiences were much like other children's in her neighborhood. As an elementary student, she learned basic communication and arithmetic skills. Teachers read books to her and talked to her and other students about how they should behave. She enjoyed playing and learning, but the academic structure of the curriculum and the social differences the teachers represented had confirmed her judgment that she did not want to be part of its purpose. It was not that her teachers were unsupportive of her or that the curriculum was difficult. They were interested in introducing Mitzi to a world that was beyond her field of experiences. But, as she traveled through her education, grade by grade, there were so many things she did not know or which seemed nonsensical that the opportunities the teachers once talked to her about seemed to vanish. Or at least that is what her teachers assumed.

Mitzi evaluated her school experiences in much harsher terms than her teachers did. They had, she knew, presented her a curriculum that allowed only two choices. It was not that the choices were so different, it was mostly their consequences that illustrated the difference. For example, the first choice reflected capitalist suburban values. Its goal was to direct Mitzi away from her personal history to accept economic and social value structures she did not understand or appreciate. To illustrate, in her ninth-grade math class, her teacher's visible frustration was humorous. She had spent all period teaching the students a math unit about writing checks and balancing their personal bank accounts. Mitzi felt sorry for her teacher. She wanted to tell her neither she, her mother, or anyone else in the class needed to know about writing checks because they didn't make enough money to have a bank account. And, if they did, Mitzi wanted to tell the teacher, there were no banks in their neighborhood in which to deposit the money.

As a girl of color living in poverty, Mitzi knew this capitalist suburban curriculum was not intended to help her accomplish that which her teachers taught her. If it had been, the Tulsa school board would have allowed her to attend school in South Tulsa where better facilities, smaller student–teacher ratios, and more advanced courses were taught by teachers with advanced academic degrees. Given Mitzi's educational environment, the second choice was more realistic. Already she was learning laborers' values. It wasn't that her curriculum taught her how or what she should do as a worker. It was more subtle than that. It taught her she was supposed to be a worker, and in that situation, she should learn how to be docile.

Mitzi chose not to accept either of the choices presented to her by her teachers, the curriculum, and the school. Thereby, she entered a parallel society unseen by her teachers and misunderstood by the school system. Living outside the capitalist mainstream, Mitzi discovered many of the things she needed were now beyond her reach. She learned the real feelings of powerlessness a person such as she owned. Unable to enter the capitalist mainstream, she retreated into a community of others like her in which acceptance and love were the currencies of life. And, she like them, marginalized into otherness, became invisible and lost her future.

Mr. Narayan: The Education of the Lumpenbourgeoisie

Mr. Narayan did not think of himself as a manager, and if he knew what a middle manager was, he would have insisted he was not one of those, either. But he would have believed what Friedman said about globalization, that it "emerges from below, from street level, from people's very souls and from their deepest aspirations,"[27] although he might not have used that word. To understand Mr. Narayan's education, it is important to remember he is a product of his Indian colonial personal history. Like Edwin from Saskatchewan, Mr. Narayan's colonial experience is not firsthand, even though the vestiges of British colonialism are much more harsh for him than for Edwin. For Mr. Narayan, British colonialism's exhibition of cultural, social, religious, and educational differences was blatant. It was framed within Protestant structures of religion, government, economics, and education.

Therefore, Mr. Narayan's remembrance of his British education in Bangalore was much more restrictive than Edwin's. Within this education context, Mr. Narayan's study was stylized. It did not allow him the opportunities to use different learning systems. He learned a curriculum in which mathematics and science were presented as theoretical information, not examples of different logics and languages used to draw conclusions. He was also directed away from learning subjects such as business management and accounting, because mid-twentieth-century British educational philosophy considered them inferior to classics such as Latin and Greek. While Mr. Narayan may have excelled in his British education, he could not have been expected to understand the internal logics and philosophies the curriculum represented. And without his active involvement in school support systems that encouraged creative destruction, his intellectual exertions would have been Herculean.

Nevertheless, it is for these reasons that Mr. Narayan would have appreciated Friedman's justification of globalization. But, his education will keep him at that economic moment in which he will forever live. Contentedly remaining with the Bangalore Cycle and Tyre Works, never reinventing the past-present, not becoming a decision maker, his economic task is to represent but not create. He is part of the labor elite, loyal to his Indian and British capitalist employers, managing their economic enterprises in the free-market economy. He is, as Andre Gunder Frank would say, part of the *Lumpenbourgeoisie*.[28]

Munyika and Lindani: Education for Cultural Survival

Munyika and Lindani were purposely left to the end of this section because they illustrate some of the indigenous reactions to the education of managers within the free-market economy. They are those who have glimpsed and experienced management from other vantage points. Unlike Edwin and Kevin, who received neoliberal educations and quickly moved into management, Munyika and Lindani are receiving theirs as lifelong students of the free-market economy. As they became more acquainted with globalization through their business dealings with the Bangalore Cycle and Tyre Works, they became managers and reluctant participant-observers of the creative destruction of their society.

It is assumed they had a sometimes profitable relationship with the Bangalore Cycle and Tyre Works and that they discovered the fundamental economic and social differences between profit taking and wage earning. Like Kevin's M.B.A., Munyika and Lindani's curriculum included such ongoing subjects as principles of office management, personnel management, accounting, inventory control, advertising, international currency exchange, and many others. But the most important information Munyika and Lindani learned in their *marketplace economy* curriculum was that it did not favor all managers equally. Their profits were marginally sufficient to continue their cycle repair enterprise. Yet, Bangalore Cycle and Tyre Works' profits far exceeded Munyika and Lindani's expectations. Because of the lack of city and national tax codes, or the inability of the government to collect taxes, or a governmental desire to participate in a free-market economy, they saw their customers' wealth leave Zomba. Regardless of the reasons Munyika and Lindani suspected, it was obvious they were not economically and socially better off than before. It was as if Munyika's and Lindani's cycle repair business had unwittingly become part of a global monster whose economic appetite was limitless.

The free-market economy taught Munyika and Lindani other, even more important, curricula. They saw young men attracted to Zomba because of personal reasons such as companionship with those their own age. But, mostly Munyika and Lindani knew the youth were attracted to Zomba because of the promise of jobs. From their personal histories, they knew agrarian work was difficult and acknowledged that the young men, while willing to physically work long hours for low wages, wanted some type of life reward other than that offered in the quiet of village life. Worse, the number of jobs available to these young seekers was so few. Munyika and Lindani watched the young men respond to the hard realities of capitalism. Unemployment increased as competition for jobs became more vigorous. For those willing to work at any cost, managers paid them less and increased their work hours. Even though Munyika and Lindani did not understand that social legislation could protect laborers, they sympathized with young workers fired by their managers if they complained about their working conditions. And it took more than just sympathy as they watched managers fire young men hurt on the job who were no longer able to perform their duties.

This young, unemployed workforce, most of whom did not know how to read or write, created Zomba's first crime waves. Wanting productive work, yet needing to fill their days, they wandered the streets, gambling and drinking. Prostitution, previously unheard of as a business, became economically profitable. The spiral of disadvantage continued. Because of the increased crime rate, mothers who were supposed to ride their bicycles to Zomba so they could shop or visit came less often. And when they did, they were protected by their husbands. Within a short period, Munyika and Lindani's business profits fell, which in turn caused them to lay off their workers, thereby increasing unemployment.

What was truly disturbing, however, was not a result of the economics of the free-market economy. They noticed that as young women continued their studies in the formal school in Zomba, their value systems seemed to change. Like the young men coming to Zomba from rural areas looking for jobs, the girls also wanted to remain. Few of them talked about returning to their villages. Most girls, it seemed, wanted to find some form of job in Zomba, as store clerks or secretaries or even primary school teachers. The young girls, unlike the boys when they first came from their villages, were aggressive and flaunted their Western dress. They displayed to everyone their attitudes that they were socially superior to those who had not gone to school. They appeared rude and unwilling to listen to others, especially older men who wanted to instruct them in the requirements of female courtesy. Some adults suspected, as many of their mothers did in their villages, the girls were becoming prostitutes, asking for money so they could continue to live in Zomba. As AIDS became more common, and as more people understood its lethal consequences, and as some suspected single girls were privately feeding their babies infant formula, Munyika and Lindani knew it was their learned independence that had passed on to others the Western values. And, it was they who were threatening the founding theologies of Islam.

One conclusion of Munyika and Lindani's continuing education was the sense that their Islamic core beliefs were being threatened by the free-market economy. They had originally been attracted to the free-market economy; now they suspected its evil side rested in threatening Islam and their quality of life. Saddened, Munyika and Lindani determined they were being recolonized by the same European capitalists who had so recently left, except in this case they discovered the recolonizing methods the Europeans were using no longer included politics and armies. Instead, they were using their formal schools as weapons to educate the young to become economic dependents of capitalists. At this prospect, Munyika and Lindani's lives were filled with terror. How could this encompassing Christian evil, clothed in the free-market economy, be contained?

EDUCATION FOR MANAGERIAL SUCCESS
IN THE FREE-MARKET ECONOMY

Munyika and Lindani's fundamental question—how could the evil free-market economy be contained?—is insightful because they were discovering the relationship between the formal schools and the free-market economy. To understand their question, it is important to first place European capitalist education in perspective. Recalling Dewey's definition of *traditional education* from chapter 2, schools taught an aristocratic curriculum that focused on Protestant economic and class values. During the industrial period, schools became more universal, that is, schooling was extended to young males mostly, where workers were taught the many benefits of physical labor and the blessings of class divisions within the developing capitalist urban centers.[29]

In short, the twin goals of this capitalist curriculum were to educate a select number of students for economic and cultural leadership positions while educating the others to become workers. The educational process through which this was accomplished required workers to discontinue their children's education at the end of elementary school as the elite continued their studies in secondary school. This school model was creatively destroyed during the mid-twentieth century and then reinvented, along with changing university admission requirements, in succeeding decades. In this case, the developing neoliberal school identified academically qualified laboring-class students who were educated to hold managerial positions. Yet, those who succeeded and became managers quickly discovered they had not experienced the traditional rewards of upward social mobility. As managers, they learned, their salaries would be substantially greater than their laboring colleagues, but they would be deprived of participating in the profit motive. This was reserved for the elite.

Of course, this is not a new idea. Managers are seen in many parts of the old industrial economy. In factories they were called "floor managers" or "foremen," as the first among their fellow laborers. Using factories as models, schools identified their managers as superintendents, headmasters, or principals. That is, they were educators who were responsible for those teachers they managed. Therefore, it is understandable that those individuals we discussed in this chapter who had been educated in the neoliberal curriculum are now managers. It is clear both Kevin and Edwin are part of the managerial class. They are loyal to a capitalist elite that controls the economics of business and research. Their absolute opposite is Mitzi. Her educational history demonstrates what happens to a person who refuses to become part of the managerial class or even the laboring class. She was, in fact, dismissed from the dominant capitalist society, left to roam with others like her in shadowy companionship, powerless and futureless.

Although Munyika and Lindani are managers, and are quite unlike Mitzi, they indicate their future might be similar to hers based on their answer to the fundamental question they raised about "this encompassing Christian evil, clothed in the free-market economy." Even though they have not arrived at a conclusion about their fate in the free-market economy, they are grappling with educational ideas about how to defend Islam and their culture. For example, what type of curriculum should be taught to those who would be willing to protect Islam?

It is left to Mr. Narayan to serve as our final example of managerial education. He reflects the ultimate middle manager, uninterested and unable to become part of the capitalist concentrations of wealth. He is proud of his British education even though it is not supportive of his culture. Yet, he is willing to master it for its social rewards. He reflects his family's loyalty to India's politicians and theological elite. In fact, he is even willing to put aside his personal theologies in support of the capitalist elite he has never met. He is an example of the labor-elite. He is the ultimate member of the *Lumpen-bourgeoisie*. He is applauded by capitalists as socially regressive. He is that laborer whose loyalty to their causes his fellow laborers may question. Mr. Narayan is the managerial model neoliberal schools wish to replicate.

In this chapter, we have considered six individuals who have, to various degrees, been impacted by neoliberal schools and the free-market economy. While several have lived experiences in capitalist nations, others have had similar experiences living in indigenous societies. Collectively, they tell us there are varying definitions of managers as well as ranks. In fact, we are also aware it is possible to refuse to join the labor elite, even as we note the costs of rejection. Each person tells us that management, regardless of rank, derives its position from laboring classes only with the approval of the wealthy. At the same time, we have grasped the fundamentals of these labor-elites. They are the prize neoliberals hunger for in their creative destruction of the democratic school. In the next chapter, we will revisit these concerns through an investigation of the American social experiences and the potential for its creative destruction.

NOTES

1. The term "global village" was coined by Marshall McLuhan in *The Gutenberg Galaxy: The Making of the Typographic Man* (Toronto: University of Toronto Press, 1962).

2. Eric Hobsbawm, *The Age of Extremes: A History of the World, 1914–1991* (New York: Pantheon Books, 1994), 524.

3. Hobsbawm notes that scientists are a significant part of international migration, moving from poorer nations to wealthier nations. See Hobsbawm, *The Age of Extremes*, 524.

4. Fukuyama is discussing social disruption as evidenced by student learning. See Francis Fukuyama, *The Great Disruption: Human Nature and the Reconstitution of Social Order* (New York: Free Press, 1999), 115.

5. Thomas L. Friedman, *The Lexus and the Olive Tree* (New York: Farrar, Straus and Giroux, 1999).

6. Friedman is referring to Schumpeter's economic theories of creative destruction. Joseph Alois Schumpeter (1883–1950), an Austrian-American economist, wrote extensively about the role of the entrepreneur in a capitalist society. See Joseph A. Schumpeter, *Capitalism, Socialism, and Democracy*, 3rd ed. (New York: Harper, 1950).

7. Grove was the chief executive officer of Intel Corporation (1987–1998). During this period, Intel demonstrated dramatic leadership in the field of semiconductors and microprocessors. Grove was known for his aggressive leadership and grasp of technology's place in a global society. See Andrew S. Grove, *Only the Paranoid Survive: How to Exploit the Crisis Points That Challenge Every Company and Career* (New York: Bantam Books, 1999).

8. Friedman (*The Lexus and the Olive Tree*, 9) reports that Frankel made this comment during a brief meeting in Israel. Frankel, educated in economics at the University of Chicago, was governor of Israel's Central Bank at the time of their meeting.

9. Kevin and Charles Browning are fictional persons. Fenders Chocolate International is also fictitious. The characters and the company do not represent any persons and companies living or dead.

10. Nestlé's positions concerning the sale of infant formulas to African mothers can be found on its Website, www.babymilk.nestle.com.

11. Contemporary medical research concludes that such illnesses as colds, flu, and diarrhea cannot be passed from mother to child through breast milk. However, it is probable that children of mothers who have contracted AIDS have a 20 percent risk of contracting that disease. To better understand this complicated medical-social issue, see Rebecca D. Williams, "Breast-Feeding Best Bet for Babies," *FDA Consumer Magazine*, October 1995, and Alix M. Freedman and Steve Stecklow, "Bottled Up: As UNICEF Battles Baby-Formula Makers, African Infants Sicken," *Wall Street Journal*, December 5, 2000.

12. UNICEF, the United Nations Children's Fund, contends that more than six million children needlessly die of malnutrition each year because they have been weaned from their mothers either too early or too late. Taking effect before the AIDS crisis, the voluntary "International Code of Marketing of Breast-milk Substitutes" limited global infant formula corporations from exploiting women in developing nations.

13. Hutchins wanted universities to change from the factory model to the learning model, saying that otherwise democracy would suffer. Hutchins was not aware his remarks would be praised in the twenty-first century as a criticism of the globalization of knowledge and scholars becoming knowledge managers. See Robert M. Hutchins, "The University and the Multiversity: Speech at the 317th Convocation of the University of Chicago," *New Republic* 13, no. 3 (April 1, 1967): 15–17.

14. Edwin is a compilation of several secondary school graduates who left Canada because of similar provincial educational policies during the mid-twentieth century. They represent the Canadian worker class. Their primary reason for migrating from Canada was because of economic opportunities.

15. Since Edwin's mid-twentieth-century experiences in Saskatchewan, that province has revolutionized its educational structures. At the time of this writing, the province seems to be less influenced by British colonial educational philosophy.

16. The history of Canadian education is a study of how a British colony gained its independence before it developed a national consensus. Not yet defining who they are, Canadian educators have since that time explained to themselves who they are not. Fearfully, they recognize the increasing similarity between themselves and the United States. This fear is best explained by Brian Mulroney, who as prime minister of Canada during the 1988 free trade debates, answered a reporter's question about anti-American sentiment expressed during the NAFTA debates: "So I had to call an election and I think that election[,] how brutal it was. . . . We were gonna lose our soul, we're gonna lose our languages, we're gonna lose medical care, our regional development, our national identity. . . . Some historians have said that it will rank with the most brutal campaigns in history" (Brian Stewart, "Brian Mulroney: Reflections of a former prime minister," *National Features Online 2002*, www.tv.cbc.ca/national/pgminfo/mulroney, June 2, 2002.

17. Fukuyama, *The Great Disruption*, 115.

18. Jonathan Kozol explains why underclasses create another value system in his *Amazing Grace: The Lives of Children and the Conscience of a Nation* (New York: Crown, 1995).

19. David K. Shipler, *A Country of Strangers: Blacks and Whites in America* (New York: Alfred A. Knopf, 1997), 40. Shipler's thesis is that, regardless of what whites think, schools have never been integrated.

20. Mitzi is a compilation of young single mothers in a small Midwestern state. She is the personification of contemporary feminine poverty.

21. The Tulsa race riot of 1921 was one of a series of white-instigated race riots after World War I. It continues to frame race relations within Oklahoma. See Scott Ellsworth, *Death in a Promised Land: The Tulsa Race Riot of 1921* (Baton Rouge: Louisiana State University Press, 1992).

22. This theory is beautifully defined by Kai T. Erickson in *Wayward Puritans: A Study in the Sociology of Deviants* (New York: Allyn & Bacon, 1966). Placing Mitzi in Erickson's theory of deviancy, she is an outlier who defies social norms.

23. This description of how young single mothers are blamed for their own victimization is explained in Valerie Polakow, *Lives on the Edge: Single Mothers and Their Children in the Other America* (Chicago: University of Chicago Press, 1994).

24. Hobsbawm mentions that the only "small" country that was immediately able to enter the capitalist world during the twentieth century was Japan (*The Age of Extremes*, 206).

25. Mr. Narayan, Munyika, and Lindani are fictitious individuals. They represent globalization in its most elemental form. Mr. Narayan is named after R. K. Narayan, a British novelist born in Madras. Lindani (*lin-da-ni*) is Zulu and means to be patient. Munyika (*u-nyi-kah*) is Shona (Zimbabwe). The Bangalore Cycle and Tyre Works is fictitious.

26. Robert William Fogel, *The Fourth Great Awakening and the Future of Egalitarianism* (Chicago: University of Chicago Press, 2000), 176. Fogel contends that the history of the United States can be divided into four economic time periods. The

fourth, he states, is happening now. Its hallmarks are based on the outgrowths of the old, useless industrial state.

27. Friedman, *The Lexus and the Olive Tree*, 287.

28. Frank defines *Lumpenbourgeoisie* (a Marxist term) as members of the colonial upper caste who believe in the cause of the colonial master. They are conduits, explaining and defending the colonizers' actions to the colonized. See Andre Gunder Frank, *Lumpenbourgeoisie and Lumpendevelopment: Dependence, Class, and Politics in Latin America*, trans. from the Spanish by Marion Davis Berdecio (New York: Monthly Review Press, 1972).

29. Alan DeYoung states that major European educational philosophers, including Jane Addams, Karl Marx, and John Stuart Mill, were primarily economic philosophers. They thought of schools as agents designed for capitalist betterment. See Alan J. DeYoung, *Economics and American Education: A Historical and Critical Overview of the Impact of Economic Theories on Schooling in the United States* (New York: Longman, 1989).

7

Deviants, Nostalgia, and Neoliberal Reformers: The American Social Experience

In chapter 6, we entered the lives of six individuals who, although representing diverse backgrounds, were learning about globalization and how it influences their life dreams. They were placed in educational situations that allowed them the opportunity to choose whether or not they wanted to become active participants in the global economy. For those who chose to become participants, each was given the opportunity to be a decision maker or manager at some level within the economic structure. Through the lives of these people, we traced the different levels and types of managers and observed how they coped with the demands of unfettered global capitalism. For those that did not choose to participate, we observed their reactions to the dark underside of raw capitalism.

The first of these was Kevin, a marketing executive, who identified or created international retail markets in which his company merchandised its products, followed by Edwin, an academic entrepreneur who generated new products that capitalists such as Kevin marketed in the global economy. Mr. Narayan was another type of manager. He interpreted globalization to mean a form of colonialism, economic rather than the political model of his youth. He was willing to participate in the free-market economy as an Indian representative of a British bicycle manufacturing firm. He willingly became part of the *Lumpenbourgeoisie*. Mr. Narayan wanted to satisfy his British investors' hunger for profits but was personally satisfied not to participate in profit sharing if his personal rewards could be met.

However, not all accepted capitalism's choice. Mitzi in some ways shared similar colonial experiences with Mr. Narayan, although they interpreted their school experiences differently. For example, Mr. Narayan's admiration of his colonial heritage would have shocked Mitzi. She, who viewed herself as an African-American colonial in the United States, wanted the opposite of that which satisfied him. Unlike Mr. Narayan's appreciation for his British education, Mitzi feared hers. She believed its purpose was to devalue her life history. She did not want to become an economic unit, whereas Mr. Narayan gladly accepted that role. Her refusal forced Mitzi to experience the consequences of rejecting capitalism. She lost the freedom to value her life history, and for her, the results were worse than if she had continued her education. Mitzi learned she was still marginalized but now her future was shut out. She was becoming a permanent member of the underclass in what neoliberals called a "polluted society."

In the same way, Munyika and Lindani learned the consequences of international entrepreneurism and middle management. They determined they were wrong to assume that, just because capitalism allowed them to buy and sell, they were justified in expecting a profit. Both learned capitalism was not so much a process of competition as it was the economic structure used by capitalists to transfer wealth from indigenous societies to wealthy corporations. Placing their newly learned economic reality within their environment, both Munyika and Lindani reaffirmed and rephrased their understanding of the free-market economy. Interpreting globalization within their cultural heritage, they understood it as Christianity's arrogant use of power over Islam. It rekindled their Islamic faith. They recognized that the twenty-first-century Crusaders' weapons were not the sword and shield of times gone by but the American dollar and British pound.

Yet, the experiences these individuals share with us only represent part of the international social change globalization is causing. Left hidden in American society, which we turn to now, are other issues of the free-market economy. Globalization's questions are new to Americans. They are similar to those traditionally left to indigenous societies to discuss, but distance, time, and lack of communication softened such conversation in those days.[1] In the age of Joseph Schumpeter's creative destruction, American capitalists—or neoliberals, as we will now call them—have watched their society change with the same alarm as others we met in previous chapters.

Like those the Dalai Lama discussed in chapter 1, these capitalists are also questioning the sanctity of their future. Distancing themselves from indigenous societies that complain about neoliberal intrusion, they question the immoral elements in their society. They want to know who the deviants are that hinder the free flow of the free-market economy. They believe they experience the effects of the immorality of large, bureaucratic governments. They contend these issues are the result of a pluralistic, non-Protestant religiosity run amok rather than the social interpretations of inventions Bill Rowley refers to or the schisms within the global village the Dahlia Lama asserts.

In this chapter, we will identify those Americans neoliberals believe are deviant and explain why they are feared. We will also look at neoliberal reaction to their fears and trace how they reformed an institution (in this case, the Southern Baptist Convention) to become a model for educational reform.

NEOLIBERALISM'S FAVORITE DEVIANTS

Americans, according to David Landes, have a love of time.

> Those of us who live under tight time discipline deplore it and flee it when we can. We seek vacations in places where we can put our watches away and let nature wake us and put us to sleep. For others, though, submission to time is the price of modernization, productivity, potential affluence. Who are we to deprecate what we live by and, living, have gotten rich by?[22]

The dividing of seconds into minutes and hours fits well within our social structure. Linear, consistent, and uncomplicated, time measures all things. A cultural voice eloquently regulating its movements as well as humans', it expresses itself as an arbiter of values. Time in America is a community experience. Providing a common centerpiece, it governs lives and gives Americans a sense of living within a stable present leading to a known future. Time in America means profit, and the clock defines that economic goal to mean the future. Reforming America to that state is neoliberals' dream of unfettering raw capitalism from government regulation. It is this aggressive, unregulated future neoliberals harken to as their living place.

But neoliberalism is not monolithic. There are others, as we discussed in chapter 1, who are part of their universe. Coupled with the newly freed capitalists are conservatives who hunger as well for a restored America. They, like their neoliberal cousins, recall that time past when Protestant values were the social commandments voiced in churches, practiced in families, and pleasantly winked at by the white middle class. Conservatives are more than neoliberals' allies. They are, as we discussed earlier, backers of neoliberalism. Believing they live in a society in which the individual is capitalism's ideal, they, like the neoliberals, picture their immediate future to be dominated by deviants who purposely promote impure, anticapitalist values.

Government: The Immorality of the Majority

Americans have traditionally viewed government with a skeptic's eye, say neoliberals, because they recall that their European forefathers were raised in violent, classed societies that were economically, politically, and theologically stifling. And, they contend, even though these issues affected millions of people, the consequences should not be explained away. That is, the various economic and social issues were interpreted by individuals who decided on their own whether they influenced the quality of their lives. That is, emigrants experienced, one by one, a period in their lives in which life's quality was regulated by government. It is these personal reasons, though experienced differently by individuals but replayed over and over again, that caused European emigration.

Here is how these issues presented themselves to individual Europeans. Using Robert William Fogel's description, when European monarchies employed (or assigned) workers to specific labor tasks in the old days, each worker was rated by his or her ability to endure work.[3] To put it another way, the government wanted to know how healthy a worker was so it could estimate how long that laborer would work and how much food was necessary to sustain him or her. During this period, European laborers did not individually control their one economic asset (health) because it was the government that developed agricultural food production policies, not them.

These government policies, which were intended for whole communities, had a direct impact on the amount of work each laborer performed. They influenced each laborer's quality of life. The common sense of this, says Fogel, is that if the government's food production policies were satisfactory and food intake was sufficient for each laborer, then the laborers might have graded their work endurance and quality of life as adequate. However, if governmental food production policies were not satisfactory and food intake was insufficient, then each laborer would have graded his or her work endurance and quality of life as inadequate.

But, say neoliberals, the laborers still would have known that, regardless of which food production policy the government chose to follow, both were wrong because the government continued to exert control over their individual quality of life. In short, it is precisely this action of disallowing individuals to freely choose their own food production policies that is immoral. Individual laborers were forced to accommodate their morality to the majority's.

The neoliberal argument that governments are immoral is best illustrated in a caloric expenditure study Fogel and Roderick Floud conducted in 1999.[4] In this study, the researchers compared the caloric intake of French, English/Welsh, and American male laborers in their twenties and thirties during the years 1700–1980. Fogel and Floud were interested in ascertaining how much body energy was available to male laboring populations after body maintenance needs were met. Their premise was simple: the more calories workers consumed, the greater the worth of their economic asset (health). This would obviously influence their work endurance and the quality of their lives. Data indicate that during the five-year period beginning in 1700, colonial American male laborers consumed 2,313 work calories, while English/Welsh male laborers consumed 720 work calories and the French male laborers only 439.

The data are interesting, say neoliberals, because they illustrate their explanations about the difference between government immorality and moral individuals who are free to create. That is, American colonial laborers, they claim, untethered at that time by government as were their French and English/Welsh cousins, were able to improve their quality of life based on their work endurance. That is, these results occurred because the American colonial laborers controlled their economic asset (health) whereas their European companions did not. This, Fogel and Floud imply, is one reason why the United States experienced a two-hundred-year history of European immigration. Regardless of these considerations, however, neoliberals contend that the Fogel and Floud study supports their assertion that, left to their own opportunities in an unregulated environment, free, moral individuals will succeed, while immoral governments will fail. Massive government, they state, with its multiplicity of rules and bureaucratic layers, becomes capitalism's stumbling block. Completing their argument, neoliberals note that Fogel and Floud's follow-on studies have shown that as late as 1994, French and English/Welsh laborers had yet to equal the colonial Americans' work-calorie consumption rate. This is illustration enough, neoliberals contend, to demonstrate that government, in both the short and long term, inhibits the free individual from creating his or her quality of life.

Neoliberals also contend the Fogel and Floud caloric study may be used as a metaphor to explain their opposition to government using the resources of the few to benefit the many. Through these immoral welfare programs, they say, liberals and progressives encourage those who have little to take ownership of resources earned by the individual efforts of others.[5] Welfare and other programs are social pollutants, they add, creating false expectations for those such as Mitzi, whom we met earlier. They did not participate in the creation of resources. As the Fogel and Floud caloric consumption study demonstrated, the free individual is better able to control his or her quality of life, not government tyrannies.

Social Pluralism: The Browning of America

> Our task is to combine due appreciation of the splendid diversity of the nation with due emphasis on the great unifying Western ideas of individual freedom, political democracy, and human rights. These are the ideas that define the American nationality—and that today empower people of all continents, races, and creeds.[6]

This portrayal of late twentieth-century America, from Arthur Schlesinger Jr., in which he pits the "due appreciation" of a diverse nation with its "due emphasis" on traditional Protestant values, is descriptive of contemporary neoliberalism's dread for the need of such a combination. It is not that diversity in itself is evil, they say—after all, the national narrative has been, with few exceptions, a chronicle of millions of immigrants who, unable to control their quality of life in Europe, chose freely to emigrate to this country. America is portrayed by neoliberals as being more than a nation. It is the economic consequence of free, moral individuals who forsook oppressive governments. It is from this context that Schlesinger speaks.

To voice Schlesinger's neoliberal worry more clearly, it is not this type of free immigration he is discussing. Rather, it is the free choosing of those who do not represent the European experience that he finds threatening. That is, America's recent immigrants do not represent Protestantism's versions of Christianity. Instead, they are the children of others who experienced Protestant's imperialism. America's new immigrants, neoliberals contend, are those who have only recently received civilization's veneer.

In many ways Schlesinger implies that contemporary neoliberalism's portrayal of civilization is much like that of Dr. David Livingstone's discoverer, Henry Morton Stanley. Writing in the 1890s, at the height of British Victorian imperialism and a century before Schlesinger's comment, Stanley expressed his agreement with Livingstone that civilization could be taught to Africans only by Protestant evangelists who were committed to loving charity. But, that did not stop Stanley from later saying that civilization was not an easy subject to learn by those who had no experience with European Christian values. While some might learn through loving charity, he reasoned, most will learn better through cultural mastering.

> May I be selected to succeed him in opening up Africa to the shining light of Christianity! My methods, however, will not be Livingstone's. . . . The selfish and wooden-headed world requires mastering, as well as a loving charity.[7]

These are neoliberalism's great unifying Western ideas to which Schlesinger alludes, as well as the raw power of due emphasis to which he refers.

But we do not want to cast Schlesinger in the negative light of cultural Arianism. Understanding and admiring European values and reflecting the stance of a society threatened by a pluralist future, Schlesinger conveys Protestant, capitalist descriptions of diversity. He judges those who are not like him harshly. Reflective of Stanley and Livingstone, Schlesinger expresses his due appreciation of the other but does not extend his admiration to include their potential educational, political, and theological offerings. In fact, Schlesinger argues that these offerings have the potential power to fragment or disunite American society. This is Schlesinger's worry: If the rising tide of Third World immigrants continues to wash ashore, will European Protestant values disappear in their wake?

While we will discuss Schlesinger's worry in more detail in the next chapter, it is important for us to understand at this point that he is judging those he labels as self-styled multiculturalists to be liberal fifth columnists that are intent on changing American society. In spite of the democratic front they assume, he says, they are opponents of Western values. Their intentions are destructive, and he criticizes those who propagandize that the international appreciation of Western values comes about only because of Western imperialism. Yet, it is strange he includes jazz and rock, outgrowths of American racial colonies, as part of his denunciation: "The popularity of European classical music around the world"—and, one supposes, of American jazz and rock, too—is evidence not of wide appeal but of "the pattern of imperialism, in which the conquered culture adopts that of the conqueror."[8]

It is this balkanized society that neoliberals want to reform. Basic European values expressed through schools, economics, politics, and theology, they argue, are being threatened by values steeped in non-European cultures and logics. It is not that these cultures and logics differ among themselves that is the issue, the neoliberals continue, but that they collectively differ from the European. It is the threatened attack on the free individual by non-European cultures and logics that is the problem. Placing free individuals within the constraining structure of this pluralist society forces them to lose their freedom and morality.

Neoliberals insist that individuals who are freely involved in capitalism's creative destruction of the past-present will be thwarted by the pluralist society representing the *we*. They will succumb and reject capitalist economics and Protestant values. This is why, neoliberals state, a permissive or politically correct pluralistic society, operating through democratic political processes, is immoral.

Schlesinger grasps the price neoliberals must be willing to pay if individuals are to remain free in this society. It is the same price Rudyard Kipling warned Britain it would have to pay to remain an empire.

> Take up the White Man's burden—
> Send forth the best ye breed—
> Go, bind your sons to exile
> To serve your captives' need;
> To wait, in heavy harness,
> On fluttered folk and wild—
> Your anew-caught sullen peoples,
> Half devil and half child.[9]

Libertine Media, Family Values, and Liberalism

> To find out the truth about your true love,
> Look in their eyes, and there will be enough.
> To show you whether it's the truth you've been told,
> Because the eyes in the face are the eyes to the soul.
>
> —Kelly John Rose, "Eyes to the Soul"

For most neoliberals, the media are the eyes to society's soul, and it is through these eyes, they believe, that they will be able to gauge whether society is moral. What neoliberals say they espy is a society becoming more and more permissive, exhibiting pluralistic attitudes and philosophies that bind individuals to conflicting, indigenous, non-European values. Using European family values as benchmarks, neoliberals decry this twenty-first-century libertine society they purposely label "liberal." This society encourages children to become irresponsible, they say. They disparage the liberal society for tolerating children who are pardoned by their submissive parents for their violent bullying of others at school and excusing them for their casual acquaintance with sex. This polluted society, neoliberals say, is influenced by gays and their liberal sympathizers. It is they who are destroying American family values by demanding that society recognize their sinful associations.[10]

Worse, say neoliberals, the media—through which they view this iniquitous society—are themselves guilty of encouraging children to pursue materialism for its own sake. All of this corruption is cultivated by liberal journalists, university professors, and others who, because of their own pluralistic predispositions, represent the libertine world. They are the ones who control television, print, and movies so they can encourage children to accept diverse family values and gender roles.

Who are the media who represent libertine America that the neoliberals label "liberals"? And, why do the neoliberals say liberals are guilty of destroying American family values?

Of all the words neoliberals use to label social evils, *liberalism* perhaps fits their needs best. The label highlights, in raw terms, the difference between neoliberals' moral individuals and their enemy, the immoral majority.

Jeff Cohen captures the character of this dissimilarity after he lists for his lecture audiences examples of right-wing television or radio hosts (such as Pat Buchanan and Pat Robertson). Then, Cohen says, when he asks for examples of left-wingers, or liberals, audiences mention television hosts they believe exist on the edges of society's moral frontiers. "I challenge anyone in the room to name even a handful of partisan, unabashed left-wingers who host or co-host national shows. The names I hear are Jenny Jones, Montel Williams, Geraldo Rivera, Howard Stern."[11] That is, they are representative of a libertine America, who the audience members say are media's deviants. They attack society's core, which neoliberals call "family values."

Yet, to grasp neoliberalism's concern about family values and the importance they play in the polluted society they picture, it is important we first understand that institution within a wider framework. We also want to understand why neoliberals willingly assume "libertine" and "liberal" mean the same thing.

Eric Hobsbawm explains that the global cultural revolution during the last half of the previous century was total in its destruction of the traditional family's social roles.

> The crisis of the family was linked with quite dramatic changes in the public standards governing sexual behaviour, partnership and procreation. These were both official and unofficial, and the major change in both is datable, and coincides with the 1960s and 1970s. Officially this was an extraordinary era of liberalisation both for heterosexuals and homosexuals, as well as for other forms of cultural-sexual dissidence.[12]

Although he describes the "crisis of the family" as sexual, gendered, and generational, he also recognizes its universality. He is quick to point out that the social importance of the family is such because of the depth and scope of its duties. Hobsbawm argues that the primary purpose of the family is to continue the human species, and it is upon this official definition of social-personal relations between and among men, women, and children that neoliberals center their argument.

Beyond that which is sexual, gendered, and generational, they also argue, is the centrality of the family to society's economic core, much of which predates both public and private economic organizations. It is for these reasons they express their fear that even the liberal threat to acknowledge dissimilar kinds of family institutions will pollute society. That is, liberals have within their power the ability to lessen the family's social and economic significance and thereby damage European culture.

The crisis of the family, to use Hobsbawm's coinage, centers around these and related issues. It is because of these issues neoliberals distrust the liberal media. Their intent, say the neoliberals, is to acknowledge the political correctness of other family values and living styles. For example, if the family's primary purpose is to continue the species, can society abide gay marriages? Or do these relationships wrongly define other types of family living styles? Are these other relationships deliberately intended to change the role of women in the family? Are mothers, now by choice, expected to continue their household duties as caregivers while working outside the home? Within this work-care family, how should parent–child relations be conducted in a two- or three-generational household? In total, these questions about the family are much more significant than liberals' answers might suggest. This, say neoliberals, is the central core of the crisis of the family because without the answers to these questions, free individuals will be destined to live in a liberal society run amok.

It is because of this assumed social impurity that neoliberals decry a liberal media bias and acknowledge their fear of liberalism's multicultural political correctness. These are the destructive linchpins causing society's crisis of the family. It is in this specific situation that liberalism's evils become visible for all to see. In fact, neoliberals sermonize, liberal's libertine America can be touched and smelled. To explain themselves, they refer to inner-city accounts of crime and scarcity, such as those reported by Jonathan Kozol in his studies of New York City poverty during the 1990s.[13] In one study, Kozol reports a conversation with a priest who relates the emotional impact of hymns on poor women with children who are in the midst of experiencing "dangers, toils, and snares" caused by absent husbands.[14] Regardless of the reasons why their husbands left their homes—sent to jail, caught in the snare of drugs and alcohol, died in a drive-by shooting, or simply went away—the women encouraged themselves, developing the inner strength of their own emotions. They transcended the immorality of the majority, exhibited in their lives by government welfare programs, to that creative wealth which allowed them to freely treasure their own experiences.

Reminding us of the Dalai Lama's earlier observations, in another study about nonmaterial wealth Kozol described the sophisticated immaturity of children in the same New York City neighborhood and their reasoned rejection of materialism. Displaying themselves as wealthy, feeling sorry for their moneyed suburban child-colleagues who have nothing other than things to amuse them, these children voice the treasure of hope amid material despair.[15] The children, like their mothers whose husbands have gone, recognize that wealth and riches are not the same thing, say the neoliberals. Riches buy trinkets, but wealth buys freedom. In some ways, neoliberals think Kozol is their representative. He is not, but he understands that "families in crisis" live in many different types of poverty. Existing without jobs and fathers, with illness and crime, children dwell in prison-neighborhoods, cared for by mothers and an unsympathetic government bureaucracy. Kozol's investigations are pictures of children in poverty who are not captured by the tentacles of materialism.

Kozol's children consider themselves spiritually wealthy, free to hope. Still, neoliberals argue that subsisting—like Mitzi earlier—in an immoral world, the lives of these children will be better served when their liberal society matches their morality. Yet, there are scant years for neoliberals to change these dreams to another reality, because by the time they complete elementary school, the children will have either contracted AIDS, gotten pregnant and malnourished, contracted tuberculosis or asthma, learned an out-of-school curriculum to qualify for a life in prison, or lost their lives on the street participating in petty crime to support their habits.

But, the realities of these consequences—what happens to Kozol's children in their neighborhood—are of no concern to neoliberals, for it is better, they intimate, to live a moral life without the benefit of society's sustenance than it is to live within a liberal majority in which all march to the beat of the same drummer. To put the children's problems another way, their problems are the same as the European laborers' who emigrated to the United States because of their governments' refusal to allow them control of their own food production policies. This demonstrates the complexity and immorality of a liberal world, they say. Cynically, they do not use the European laborers as an example to comment on whether the children should emigrate to another land to solve their individual food production policies.

Wayward Fundamentalists

Liberalism's corruption of individuals, families, and society is more pervasive than one would expect, according to neoliberals. Liberalism is now found throughout society and is strategically placed to pervert even Protestant religious thought. Reflecting cultural humanism, churches have become liberal mouthpieces, voicing disregard for the consequences of living in an immoral society. Tolerance of multiculturalism, with its different values and religious traditions, is creating indecision and division within a society that itself is struggling with the inclusion of immigrants. Even evangelical churches, committed to European theologies and social values, are being redirected from their fundamentalist missions. It is this knowledge that is at stake—for without it, neoliberals threaten, this capitalist society will eventually lose its moral and economic leadership in the global free-market economy. And, it will also lose its ability to evangelize its Protestant culture to others in other lands.[16]

Neoliberals believe that liberalism's influence on religion is destructive. Once accepted scholarship is publicly questioned, churchgoers will live in an environment of theological uncertainty. Even the showing respect for other religions causes the religiously immature to question their faith. The obscuring of such fundamental Protestant wisdom as Adam and Eve is disputed by some liberals who characterize them as fictional personalities in ancient stories that were written to help illiterate peoples understand the world's beginnings. Explaining evolution scientifically, while disparaging creationism, liberals are sowing the seeds of social mistrust. Liberals continue to minimize the European value systems by promoting the Bible as one of many books that address values and religious myths. Describing the Bible as a book of history written by unnamed authors, and an unreliable history at that, exposes liberalism's cultural humanism at its most evil, neoliberals declare.

Now we know neoliberal's definition of liberalism. This is why they believe the media are biased and why they fear for Protestantism's decline as a global economic and social force. Neoliberalism is broad in its structure on this issue, embracing conservatives and neoconservatives alike, some of whom are religious fundamentalists and part of the managerial middle class. They agree that neoliberal reform of American schools will not be complete until it replaces liberalism's philosophic bedrock with its own. For neoliberals, that means offering their intellectual alternatives to John Dewey's explanations of *cooperative intelligence*.

Dewey: Authority and Freedom

Centering their reform movement on the elimination of the political *we*, neoliberals concentrate on a problem Dewey foresaw in a 1936 article marking Harvard University's fourth century.[17] Dewey was interested in the relationship of freedom of the individual and the authority of the community—meaning in this case labor unions and corporate management. And, like present-day neoliberals, he too called for reform during a period of global economic and social destabilization.

In his writings, and speaking on several levels to various audiences, Dewey developed the idea of "cooperative intelligence" as a method of solving economic and social problems. At that time, Dewey's views were especially aimed at industrialists who were continuing to demonstrate their intense fear of labor unions. It was not that unionism was misunderstood by capitalists, Dewey thought, as much as it was that they believed labor understood capitalists' hidden intentions all too well. Given an even chance, capitalists thought labor unions would wrest away business management to be administered by "workers' paradises" as in the Soviet Union. Within this complexity, Dewey offered the idea of cooperative intelligence as a problem-solving measure through which industrialists and unions could work together to improve industry so that profits and wages would increase.

Understood from this position, Dewey's thoughts have become lightning rods for neoliberals as he traces post-Reformation European histories of freedom and authority. He questions the conventional wisdom that each sphere (authority and freedom) must resist the other. It is this, Dewey argues, that has caused history to represent freedom within the realm of the individual and to represent authority by government. This need not be so, he states, for when they lose their symmetry, that is, when freedom becomes license and authority becomes regimentation, the spheres are "called upon to restore the balance."[18]

Because of this conventional representation, Dewey states, freedom and authority are viewed as eternal opposites, each determined to master the other. Dewey states that if we thought of freedom and authority not as opposites policing each other, but as a bond that connects one to the other, then it would become clear that each will communicate with and problematize the other. This is obvious, says Dewey, because freedom recognizes that stability is its result, and stability's demand for freedom's questioning is its lifeblood. It is through this cooperative intelligence posture that Dewey notes his philosophy of liberalism. It is also the platform upon which neoliberals voice their disagreement.

THE NEOLIBERAL REFORM

Dewey's discussion of authority and freedom, or of community and the individual, is also the hinge upon which neoliberals discuss their social and economic theory. Uttering different words and using another voice, neoliberals respond to Dewey's thoughts. Unlike Dewey, who explained an active social theory, neoliberals concentrate on a perception of a bewitched past in which consequences are understood even before an action takes place. That is, unlike Dewey, who hypothesized the reality of social change, neoliberals point to the past in which the future is governed by yesterday's truth. That is, they speak of their ideology.

Neoliberal Social Reform: An Exercise in Nostalgia

Perhaps the best examination of nostalgia is Svetlana Boym's *Future of Nostalgia*. It is an investigation of cultural attitudes and personal remembrances of Russian immigrants to the United States at the end of the last century. Her descriptions of how the immigrants viewed themselves within their new American environment while trying to make meaning of their Russian culture is extraordinary. She defines for the reader the reactions to American culture by those who purposely left Russia because they could not control their quality of life. She describes the artifacts the Russian immigrants lovingly displayed in their homes and their spoken memories and reveries for other places and other times. She places her Russian immigrants within a context of poetic and scientific nostalgia in which history began at the moment of emigration.

> Modern nostalgia is a mourning for the impossibility of mythical return, for the loss of an enchanted world with clear borders and values; it could be a secular expression of a spiritual longing, a nostalgia for an absolute, a home that is both physical and spiritual, the edenic unity of time and space before entry into history. The nostalgic is looking for a spiritual addressee. Encountering silence, he looks for memorable signs, desperately misreading them.[19]

Boym's research on European and American histories of nostalgia shows personal feelings of longing were first diagnosed by doctors and philosophers during that period she called "poetic science," that is, that pre-science period when these fields of study were not yet separate. At that time, there was no known cure for the disease.[20] Later, when nostalgia was placed within the social sciences, Boym was able to give it meaning. Nostalgia has, she says, two tendencies: reflective, which is a longing for the past, and restorative, which is the reconstruction of the past's monuments. Boym says these two dispositions mark the flawed process of memory and the construction of mementos and reclaimed or invented traditions.[21]

Boym's examination of her Russian immigrants in the United States is significant in our understanding of neoliberal education reform. It is as if the reflections of her Russian immigrants act as metaphors for neoliberals, struggling to be free from government regulation, to dream of different pasts in familiar places. They remember their feelings in the middle of the past century when the nation's wealthiest capitalists learned of middle-class disgust and disapproval of their actions.[22] That time, when the elite openly flaunted their raw capitalist wealth, sometimes illegally earned, it was judged obscene by workers. They objected to the glitzy, glittery show of conspicuous consumption among the undeserving rich. Eventually, and almost becoming invisible at the end of that period, the capitalist elite lived in golden ghettos dreaming of a time for revenge.

It is this dream for revenge that is the lens through which neoliberals view their reform movement. Their aim is to aggressively recreate a future that satisfies their nostalgia of the time before the middle classes' revulsion of their elitist actions. They want their history to be seamless. Reform means to them to aggressively deconstruct that mid-twentieth-century era of social responsibility they label immoral and liberal. They recognize Dewey as their philosophical archenemy. Neoliberals hunger to reform this society so capitalists may once again roam freely without the threat of government intervention. It is to this the rest of the chapter will attend.

Neoliberal Economic Reform: Schumpeter and the New Modernity

> The fundamental impulse that sets and keeps the capitalist engine in motion comes from new consumers, goods, the new methods of production or transportation, the new markets, the new forms of industrial organization that capitalist enterprise creates.[23]

Joseph Schumpeter defined a world that excludes Dewey. Dewey's world was framed by an industrial modernity where laborers worked together as they performed their tasks. In industries that Dewey knew (automobiles, for example), managers expected laborers to depend on each other in the same way ballet dancers relied on other dancers' talent. Then, expecting a manufactured product, the result of these synchronized steps, investors assumed workers had the knowledge to improve product quality and production efficiency.

Yet, neoliberals contend, this is not the world Schumpeter is talking about. Schumpeter points us to a newer modernity in which information and knowledge are the resources investors hunger for and laborers (who do not exist as Dewey described them) are now the managerial middle class. This difference can be understood by watching the corporation relate to the free-market economy. In industrial modernity, corporations were developed to remain competitive for the long haul. That meant management and labor were expected to manufacture products while operating within the mandates imposed on them by government regulatory agencies. The result of this was that both labor and management produced mediocre products. This is why asking workers and managers to share their knowledge and abilities, regardless of their methods of communicating, is devastating to the corporation and the free-market economy. Bluntly, the purpose of corporations is not to live into perpetuity. It is to compete for their share of the market.

Neoliberal arguments continue. If management's goal is simply to manage the corporation into perpetuity, its style and philosophy will cause the business (and the market) to atrophy. In an information society in which the free-market economy runs unfettered, investors realize corporations will have shorter life spans. Competition from newer, more aggressive corporations will outperform them. Therefore, management's focus is not on the long haul. It is on the development of newer and better products. Its aggressive management style will be more suited to the global economy. Instead of concentrating on government regulatory agencies, management's focus will be on the corporation's continued reinvention of itself. By casting off old and unproductive parts of itself, and developing new production procedures and products, corporations will be able to compete in the free-market economy. This is the essence of creative destruction, say neoliberals. And, in this case, when information and knowledge resources no longer are hampered by each other or forced to rely upon the synchronization of work groups, the corporation will become more versatile. Freed from government oversight, corporations will now be able to respond to the market, forcing management to become more responsive.

But that response to the market was what Dewey was speaking about when he discussed cooperative intelligence. He meant the problem-solving corporate culture was for the betterment of both parties. Neoliberals, on the other hand, defined corporate culture to mean management's core values. It is these core values that management wants to enunciate through decision making and goal development. Unlike Dewey, who thought of corporate culture as the institution's social and economic environment in which cooperative intelligence became the norm, neoliberal corporate culture focuses on its own continual renewal and reinvention within a global economy.

Dewey's cooperative intelligence theory showcased his belief that the fulcrum upon which authority and freedom could cooperate was the scientific method. Using this method—really, the act of thinking—Dewey believed both management and labor could agree on corporate problems, and both could mutually develop hypotheses and working solutions. It was not so much that neoliberals disagreed with Dewey's scientific method. Rather, it was their judgment that both management and labor, using the scientific method, perhaps unable to define problems because of the economic spheres they represented, would remain transfixed, unable to meet market realities. Instead of using laborers, as Dewey suggests in his theory, neoliberals identify management's decision-making partners to be advisors or consultants. They believe those outside the organization, understanding the marketplace from different perspectives, are better able to recognize corporative problems than those who experience them.

Within this rubric, neoliberals identified two types of thinking, each of which relates to or rejoins and relies on the other. One method of thinking is *deconstruction* and the other is *reconstruction*. Deconstructive thinking is the act of creatively questioning inconsistencies, sometimes even the most obvious, thereby exploring the corporation's core beliefs as they relate to its mission. Reconstructive thinking, on the other hand, is the act of evaluating or judging deconstruction's findings. Reconstructionists forge new meanings or new ways of viewing corporate problems after deconstructionists have identified them.[24]

The deconstruction-reconstruction model, neoliberals are quick to point out, is difficult. They say it is intended to be used by those who do not understand the marketplace and corporate core values. The model relies on those (outside consultants) who demonstrate tremendous creative abilities. Often having different, but highly specialized, educational backgrounds, these consultants are able to visualize issues, envision different forms of corporate architecture, and anticipate corporate internal logics (usually voiced by managers). Bluntly, this model of thinking, say neoliberals, belongs to corporate leadership, consultants, and investors. It is intended for those who understand the corporation's relationships with the marketplace, not those who are involved in production.

Most important, neoliberalism's response to Dewey's cooperative intelligence concept may be found in their discussion of his definition of the individual. This, they contend, is the significant issue that separates him from them. They fault Dewey for his voicing a liberal philosophy that defines a political majority to be a democratic good that has the power to regulate individuals. It is from this hotbed that mediocrity springs and is nourished, say the neoliberals. Mediocrity is nursed by collective action in which individuals, losing their freedom to create, are emasculated by the majority. It is Dewey's justification of the corrupt government that gives credence to ideas dramatized in Fogel and Floud's caloric consumption study, discussed earlier in this chapter. While neoliberals stop short of referring to Dewey's ideas as Makarenkian, they are clear in their belief that his explanation voices the old industrial modernity. He conforms his morality to his neighbors, and that is why, say neoliberals, the Deweyan philosophy of cooperative intelligence is designated as liberal.

Through the study of neoliberal objections to cooperative intelligence, we are better able to understand the philosophical gap between them and

Dewey. Dewey's argument about authority and freedom in the final analysis is proven false, in the neoliberals' view, because communities, like industrial modernity's corporations searching for the long haul, become lazy and eventually focus only on their continuation. Unwilling to respond to new environments, and unable to acknowledge creativity, communities become mediocre and thereby contaminate individuals.

All of this means that the core value that sparks creativity in the marketplace, schools, government, religion, and other parts of society is the individual's yearning to rely on himself or herself, say the neoliberals. It is that element, unique in the Euroamerican heritage, that spurs individuals to achieve unlike others in their lifetime.[25] These individuals, neoliberals theorize, are not everywhere. They are those who are free to soar above the mediocre majority. Using Emerson, neoliberals describe the majority as conformists with whom self-reliant individuals are forced to battle.[26] The conflict between the two, in terms of Emerson, is the result of the conspiracy of the many. Or, as neoliberals would have Schumpeter say, the free individual, protected from Dewey's immoral democratic crowd, will creatively destroy the past and construct new futures.

Fixing the Mediocre

Like the Puritans they resemble, neoliberals hunger to reform schools and purify American society. They despise Dewey. His educational theories, they say, have allowed society to become a cesspool. Using measuring sticks that are now referred to as high-stakes testing, they focus their attention on schools. So that we may understand the significance of neoliberals' nostalgic reform efforts, this chapter will close by following the Reverend Paige Patterson and Judge Paul Pressler, two Southern Baptist preachers who, using methods reminiscent of the No Child Left Behind Act, reformed the nation's largest evangelical sect.[27]

To understand Patterson and Pressler's neoliberal theological reform efforts and their importance to school reform, let us first look at Southern Baptist church organization and management. Strong adherents of local control, Southern Baptist churches are organized much like schools. They are independent and take it as their responsibility to employ a pastor (here, read teacher), appoint a deacon body (school board), and tax themselves through a theological dictum called tithing (property taxes). However, local churches join with other independent congregations to form state associations, that in turn join together nationally to become what Southern Baptists call a convention. It is this congregational form of organization and management that has served as Southern Baptists' core values platform.

In most ways, Southern Baptists and neighboring schools share similar social histories. To make the point, from its inception to the 1954 *Brown* v.

Board of Education Supreme Court decision, Southern Baptist teachings mirrored school curricula—both defended segregation. These experiences framed Southern Baptists' contemporary social character, although schools were legally required to obey the law. Like nineteenth-century public school curricula, Southern Baptists built their theological curricula on agrarian scaffolds of Protestantism dominated by males and racial hatred. Analogous to schools at that time, its churches remained provincial and socially tainted because of an unschooled clergy.[28]

Illustrative of this is Southern Baptists' acquiescence to fundamentalism. While some can argue that schools did not follow this path, it must be mentioned they also felt the same pressures of twentieth-century change. Teachers and parents, like churches, felt their futures were threatened by new and different ways of thinking. They did not want their children influenced by old, fuzzy scholars like Einstein, who talked about the relativity of God's time, and teachers could not understand Dewey, who said thinking was based on science, not revelation. Based on this, one can understand the emotions of the *Scopes* trial, its loss, and its twenty-first-century reemergence as a school–church issue.

In this century, with a growing church membership mostly composed of an affluent middle class confused by the new global modernity, they, like their parents and grandparents before them, fear for their future. To them, society has become complicated and without moral compass. They are threatened by globalization, foreign-born workers, job loss, corporate downsizing, and outsourcing. It is upon these social emotions and economic issues that Patterson and Pressler reformed the Southern Baptist Convention.

While the intricacies of the issues and the theological-political battle for the Southern Baptist Convention is outside the scope of this chapter, they are fascinating and represent the rehearsal for the reform of the nation's schools. The single impact these reforms had on Southern Baptists was to hold them accountable (read high-stakes testing) for learning another theological creed (curriculum) of core values. This curriculum teaches church members how to evangelize, that is, how to purify a society they see as liberal. To explain, a Southern Baptist core value is that the family's traditional purpose is sexual and economic. Therefore church members are to abhor gay marriages while evangelizing them for their redemption. Within this core value, fathers are expected to support submissive wives and children. And, mirroring the families' submission, the fathers are expected to look to their preacher-fathers for guidance. Only in this way will society regain its purity.

A high-stakes testing program was developed to monitor the curriculum's acceptance and measure its success. The test was simplicity itself; it had but one question—Do you accept as your personal belief the Southern Baptist curriculum? Those that refused to accept were labeled at risk, that is, they could be expelled from the Convention. Still, the significance of the high-stakes test is obvious. Without it, neoliberal reformers could not control the religious freedom of the church membership.

Together, and most important for Southern Baptists, these neoliberal reforms (high-stakes testing and a single curriculum) are foundational to them and their church. Becoming less diverse in their beliefs and unchallenged with new ideas, they model the outcomes neoliberals have in mind for the nation's schools and their children. In the next chapter, we will investigate the schools' relation to American society, identify neoliberal standards of excellence, and trace neoliberal reform.

NOTES

1. Kevin Phillips contends that there have been four Western or European globalization experiences during the past 500 years, with the American experience being the most recent. Spain, Netherlands, and England represent the other three. His view of their economic rise and fall rests on the concepts of financialization or the retreat from production. Kevin Phillips, *Wealth and Democracy: A Political History of the American Rich* (New York: Broadway Books, 2002).

2. David S. Landes, *Revolution in Time: Clocks and the Making of the Modern World* (New York: Barnes & Noble Books, 1998), 359–60.

3. Robert William Fogel, *The Fourth Great Awakening and the Future of Egalitarianism* (Chicago: University of Chicago Press, 2000), 74–77.

4. The Fogel and Floud study, "A Theory of Multiple Equilibria between Populations and Food Supplies: Nutrition, Mortality, and Economic Growth in France, Britain, and the United States, 1700–1980," was first reported by the University of Chicago's Center for Population Economics as a typescript. See Fogel, *The Fourth Great Awakening*, 76.

5. Progressive, liberal, Social Gospel, and other labels have been used interchangeably by scholars to designate specific groups who were interested in social change during the four or five decades prior to the Franklin Roosevelt administration. In this discussion the author uses the term "progressive" in the general sense.

6. Arthur M. Schlesinger Jr., *The Disuniting of America: Reflections on a Multicultural Society* (New York: W. W. Norton, 1992), 138.

7. Henry Morton Stanley, quoted in Thomas Pakenham, *The Scramble for Africa: White Man's Conquest of the Dark Continent from 1876 to 1912* (New York: Avon Books, 1991), 26. Pakenham's history traces Stanley's search for Livingstone in East Africa during the late decades of the nineteenth century. On the one hand, Stanley admired Livingstone for his beliefs, but on the other, he found it difficult to understand why he had such little use for fame and publicity.

8. Schlesinger, *The Disuniting of America*, 123.

9. Rudyard Kipling, "The White Man's Burden," *McClure's Magazine*, February 12, 1899, verse 1. We should not assume Kipling speaks only with a British imperialist voice, for the poem was written three years after the U.S. Supreme Court (in *Plessy v. Ferguson*) reaffirmed attitudes about their "sullen people."

10. For example, in June 2003, when the U.S. Supreme Court struck down Texas's antisodomy laws (*Lawrence v. Texas*), Justice Antonin Scalia angrily said the 6–3 decision "effectively decrees the end of all morals legislation" (Dave Montgomery, "Supreme Court Strikes Down Texas Sodomy Ban," *Knight Ridder Washington Bureau,* www.realcities.com/mld/krwashington, June 26, 2003).

11. Jeff Cohen, "The Media: Liberal or Libertine?" www2.fwi.com/~total-stranger/media.html, March 25, 2003.

12. Eric Hobsbawm, *The Age of Extremes: A History of the World, 1914–1991* (New York: Pantheon Books, 1994), 322.

13. Jonathan Kozol, *Amazing Grace: The Lives of Children and the Conscience of a Nation* (New York: Crown, 1995).

14. Kozol reports in his study of poverty in New York City a conversation about the hymn "Amazing Grace" with Reverend Groover, a church minister helping the poor. See Kozol, *Amazing Grace,* 225–26.

15. Jonathon Kozol, *Ordinary Resurrections* (New York: Crown, 1995). This text concludes Kozol's study of New York City's children of poverty. The reader follows the twists and turns of Kozol's emotions as he studies the children and women in poverty. At the end, we become aware he has changed his worldview. Now, he glories in the richness of the children and marvels at their dignity.

16. This is a significant concern of Protestants who export their theological and cultural explanations of Christianity. They recognize their truths are forced to compete equally on the Internet and television around the world. Even the internationalization of religions in this country is menacing to them. To illustrate, many Americans who have not had an indoctrinating Christian experience may not exhibit deep emotional stress when they (or others they know) become faithholders in a non-Christian religion. But, it is the faithholders who have been indoctrinated that create traumatic experiences for the churchgoers they no longer accept. Even so, for those who want to become converts, they are preparing to leave part of their personal histories behind so they can live as an "Other" in America. See, for example, Satguru Sivaya Subramuniyaswami, *How to Become a (Better) Hindu,* 2nd ed. (Kapaa, HI: Himalayan Academy, 2000), available at www.himalayanacademy.com/resources/books/hbh/hbh_table_of_contents.html.

17. John Dewey, "Authority and Freedom," *Survey Graphic* 25, no. 11 (November 1936): 603ff., available at newdeal.feri.org/survey/36603.htm.

18. Ibid.

19. Svetlana Boym, *The Future of Nostalgia* (New York: Basic Books, 2001), 42.

20. Boym points out that one cure for nostalgia was found during the eighteenth century. Generals who informed their troops that soldiers experiencing nostalgia prior to battle would be shot had fewer cases of nostalgia than those who did not so inform their troops.

21. Boym, *The Future of Nostalgia,* 41.

22. Phillips notes a period, generally from the end of World War II until perhaps into the second Eisenhower administration, when the gap between America's super-wealthy and the middle class lessened. It was that time when some social commentators referred to the rich as "inconspicuous consumers." See Phillips, *Wealth and Democracy,* 76–79.

23. Joseph A. Schumpeter, *Capitalism, Socialism and Democracy*, 3rd ed. (New York: Harper, 1950), 82. First published in 1942, Schumpeter developed his theories during the 1930s. A contemporary of John Dewey and Anton Makarenko, Schumpeter believed industry was continually in a state of revolution. His ideas were discarded in favor of John Maynard Keynes, but reemerged in the mid-twentieth century.

24. These thoughts are greatly expanded in Richard Foster and Sarah Kaplan's *Creative Destruction: Why Companies That Are Built to Last Underperform the Market, and How to Successfully Transform Them* (New York: Currency, 2001). Foster and Kaplan believe managers who want to remain viable in the free-market economy should follow neoliberal creative destruction theories of balancing long-term goals with short-term reactions to the free-market economy.

25. Bryan Caplan, who is sympathetic to Schumpeter's theories, presents an understandable explanation of neoliberalism's individualism and the economic consequences of the free-market economy in "Self-Reliance and Creative Destruction," his submission to the 1996 Davis Essay Contest sponsored by George Mason University's Center for World Capitalism (available at www.gmu.edu/departments/economics/bcaplan/davis2.htm). While he is interested in the individual, Caplan seems uninterested in the democratic process.

26. Emerson's transcendentalism was overpowering. An environmentalist, he understood the depths of the human environment. He would be appalled with neoliberalism. See, for example, Ralph Waldo Emerson, *"Self-Reliance" and Other Essays*, unabridged ed. (New York: Dover Publications, 1993).

27. Rob James and Gary Leazer, eds., *The Takeover in the Southern Baptist Convention: A Brief History* (Decatur, GA: Baptists Today, 1994). James and Leazer tell us Patterson and Pressler devised their 1979 hostile takeover of the Southern Baptist Convention over coffee and beignets at the Café du Monde, a popular restaurant and tourist attraction in New Orleans' French Quarter, several years earlier. Patterson was then president of Criswell College in Dallas (as of this writing, he is president of Southwestern Baptist Seminary in Fort Worth), and Pressler was a Texas state appeals court judge (he is since retired) in Houston. Both believed the Southern Baptist Convention was too liberal in its relations with society and biblical interpretations. They challenged the functionality of the Convention and its emphases on doctrine.

28. Southern Baptists, like Methodists, copied school district organization during that time when teachers "traveled round" to schools. Both teachers and preachers stayed with parents or church members when they taught or sermonized. In *Southern Cross: The Beginnings of the Bible Belt* (New York: Alfred A. Knopf, 1997), Christine Leigh Heyrman traces the social agreements made among husbands, wives, and preachers in which preachers agreed to recognize master–slave relations if the husbands were willing to pay the preacher a living wage.

8

Neoliberal Reformers: The American Educational Experience

Thus far, we were made aware that globalization's impact on dominant nations, such as the United States, is just as significant to them as is its intrusion into indigenous societies. While we have been mindful of that intrusion in other chapters, viewing globalization's impact on indigenous economic and social institutions, we have learned these societies' attempts to reform their schools to produce human capital are but immediate, knee-jerk reactions to neoliberal demands placed on them. That is, as indigenous reformers grappled with globalization's insistence on school change to facilitate its acquisition of resources and labor, they learned as they acquiesced that they were destroying their traditional societies. Even so, within this destruction, these reformers also learned their countries could no longer remain economically independent. Instead, their new societies, responding to the free-market economy, are now merely economic units that compete with other units that also want to sell their resources and labor to international corporations. Indigenous reformers discovered that the free-market economy is not designed to perform equally for all. That is, the resources and labor they sell to international corporations are purchased cheaply with their profits.

It is for these reasons indigenous societies developed European or, as we have called them, formal schools. They hoped their younger generations, experiencing the same dominant education as Americans and Europeans, could then live and work successfully in a borderless economic world. In fact, and only learned by experience, these formal schools, as we have seen in previous chapters, became the visible reminders of indigenous societies' capitulation to the free-market economy.

Within this neoliberal setting, we also understand globalization's potency on dominant societies such as the United States. Chapter 7 confirms that this nation, too, is part of an interconnected world in which raw capitalism transforms all. What reforms are neoliberals demanding of the United States? Those we found in chapter 7 are massive, unique, and threatening to its pluralist society. We discovered that, as indigenous nations are Westernizing their societies to participate in the free-market economy, American neoliberal reformers are nostalgically restoring theirs to another time-space. Yet, these dissimilarities do not mean the United States and indigenous societies are unlike in their reactions to globalization. Rather, in some important ways they are similar. Both are cultural and social importers—as one imports the social consequences of the free-market economy, the other is nostalgically restoring social monuments from a dreamed-of moral yesterday they believe was sympathetic to raw capitalism.

We learned in chapter 7 that neoliberal reformers believe today's society is liberal and ipso facto immoral. Using that term rather than "licentious," which defines their immorality, it is based, they say, on the social and educational theories espoused by such philosophers as John Dewey. Dewey, they declare, advocated a cooperative society in which people solved problems by working together. But the issue Dewey created, neoliberals assert, is that this developing pluralist majority, reflecting all types of non-Western cultures, personal histories, theologies, and values, has collectively lowered the nation's social and educational standards. This mediocrity is immoral because its anticapitalistic attitude disregards individuals, each of whom, although politically free, is inhibited in demonstrating her or his creativity within the context of the free-market economy.

The neoliberals' conclusion is that mediocrity's voice can be heard in media, government, family, church, and schools. The consequence of this is that American society has forsaken individualism and replaced it with the majority's libertine, collective values. This is the liberal society Dewey championed, neoliberals accuse, and that is why we watched in the previous chapter as neoliberal theologians coerced the Southern Baptist Convention's fundamentalist confederacy to accept a curriculum policed by a high-stakes testing program. The illustration serves a useful purpose in our understanding of neoliberal aggressive nostalgia. It introduces us to the same standards neoliberals are now expressing about schools, except their vocabulary is that of the school and not of evangelical fundamentalism. This chapter will focus on the neoliberal educational reform experience.

NEOLIBERAL REFORM: THE DEMOGRAPHY OF MERITOCRACY

First, let us look at schools through the nostalgic eyes of neoliberals so we can picture the meritocracy that prompts them to aggressively reform schools. In other words, who are the neoliberals specifically referring to when they talk about the mediocre majority?

Part One: Black Children in White Schools

> Before Hopewell, Virginia, got its floating bordello, which made it the wildest place north of Hell, it was so boring that you wished for a fire. That's how Barbara Wyche remembers her hometown. Then came school desegregation, splitting her childhood along a great divide: on one side, the protective cocoon of blackness, where children were taught deference to adults and were gently steered away from racial frictions; on the other, a colder world where teachers didn't seem to care.[1]

David Shipler's description of the impact of desegregation on both Barbara Wyche and her hometown of Hopewell is telling. Before school desegregation, Shipler reminds us, race relations were wrapped in a cloak of social protocol. He describes how that cloak affected one young black teenager. It was best illustrated by Hopewell's geography and where she lived. Barbara's home was separated from her white neighbors only by a street. And, even though it was narrow and dusty, it was as if it was an insurmountable wall imprisoning and separating her from Hopewell's dominant society.

Barbara was taught by her parents not to cross the street. They also told her there were specific stores and parts of Hopewell she should not frequent. It wasn't so much that Hopewell's dominant culture told her what to do as it was the social education she received at home. But, she also learned from her school friends. Shipler describes Barbara talking about her feelings of living on her side of the street and attending an all-black school in her separate community. Her teachers, she says, were warm, inviting, and caring. They wanted students to learn. And, like her parents, teachers encouraged, guided, and taught her the social ballet of race relations.

It was not until Hopewell's schools were integrated that Barbara understood the significance of that ballet. In many ways Barbara thought her experiences in Hopewell's white high school were academically disappointing. She learned the white teachers did not care for students the same way black teachers cared for her. Like black students at that time and place, Barbara assumed the quality of her education would improve.[2] But she quickly discovered that her white teachers seemed less interested in her and the other students' personal and social success. They exuded cold professionalism, concentrating on making sure students understood what was taught them. All this seemed so different from the black teachers' professionalism Barbara had experienced in her segregated school. They challenged her to learn more than what the curriculum demanded. She noticed, too, that her white teachers were not as well educated as her black high school teachers; there had been Ph.D.'s among the teachers at the segregated school, but there were none on the faculty of Barbara's white high school.

Compounding her academic problems were racial issues that festered among students. Barbara, like others in her circumstances, quickly learned that white students believed they owned the school and saw black students as intruders. Shipler tells us that Barbara's feelings about not being accepted were continually reaffirmed by white students' treatment of her. They insulted and belittled Barbara and other black students on their way to school, in the cafeteria, and other places where the races mixed. In fact, in Barbara's case, her parents were so upset with the racial slurs she experienced daily that they would not allow her to walk to the white high school. They sent her in a taxi.

Shipler recalls in his research that one black high school refused to integrate unless its students could take with them the awards they and the students before them had won through the years in interschool sports, music, and academic competitions. This visible history of their school community, which the students wanted to acknowledge and remember, were disregarded and misplaced by the white high school teachers, administrators, and students.

Part Two: Immigrant Children in White Schools

Shipler's investigation of Barbara's experience in becoming part of the dominant culture's school is also reflected by immigrant children's classroom experience. Cristina Igoa, in her book *The Inner World of the Immigrant Child*, exposes the inner turmoil immigrant children undergo in their new American classrooms.[3] Regardless of their previous cultural histories, Igoa states, immigrant children suffer culture shock. In fact, she says, the culture shock they experience in school is sometimes greater than what their parents may feel at work. Lacking social experiences and reflecting the cultural concerns of their parents, immigrant children have fewer mechanisms to shield them from the frustrations resulting from learning different social cues.

It is this lack of normalcy immigrant students sense that leaves them without cultural or social meanings. Culture shock, Igoa tells us, is recognized in the classroom when immigrant students become silent, the physical and emotional reaction to their inability to communicate with others in the classroom. It is during this period, sometimes lasting for years, that immigrant students are forced to come to terms with their new culture and their place in it.

In many cases, Igoa claims, immigrant students are able to leave this stage when they are counseled into socially accepting classroom environments that do not threaten their attempts to communicate and understand another culture. It is here, as they grapple with their culturally uprooting experiences, that immigrant students come to terms with their new life history. Yet, Igoa admits, immigrant students may come to different conclusions about their place in their new world. In some instances, they may find it difficult to have strong, positive self-images because of the visibility of their own racial and cultural characteristics. In other instances, they may conclude from the reactions of others in the dominant culture that they have little in common with their new culture and retreat from it.

A major reason for the culture shock immigrant students experience in school is based on their sense of family and community. They discover their personal histories are exhaustively different than the formal, capitalist, Euroamerican society that rewards individual risk management. It is quite the opposite of their individual backgrounds in which they, as valued family members, were expected to participate in a community. It is this clash between the *we* of their previous life and the *I* of a competitive, capitalist society that immigrant students must now resolve.

Yet, immigrant students' school experiences are little different from those Barbara endured during Hopewell's school integration period. She also lived a life of the *we* in Hopewell. Learning the ballet of racial relations gave her a sense of community, shielding her from the competitive individuality of the *I*'s expressed in the dominant white high school culture. In her reflections, Barbara saw herself as an immigrant. She had emigrated from one culture to another—without ever leaving her hometown.

THREE CASES FOR NEOLIBERAL REFORM: MOYNIHAN, BOURNE, DEWEY

We now grasp the importance of culture shock as it played havoc in the lives of African-American and immigrant children during their uprooting into white schools. But their uprooting was not complicated, nor can it be explained away, by a school that simply reflected capitalism and competition. It was more than that. The school mirrored a European society in which whiteness was valued. It was this European, Protestant social consensus about the purpose of schools that created the scaffolding upon which nonwhite and non-Protestant culture shock was based. And, of equal importance, we now understand that social consensus was also the scaffolding upon which neoliberal aggressive nostalgia is situated.

While these students experienced culture shock, so too did schools. In this case, the shock occurred as schools became more aware of African-American and immigrant students' personal histories. The children were living examples of a plethora of different languages, family styles, theologies, and values, much of which contradicted the Protestant curriculum schools were teaching. Simply put, before the inclusion of these cultures into the nation's classrooms, the school existed, in the main, for white, middle-class, Protestant children. Of course, this is not the school white, middle-class parents see when they look in their children's classrooms. It is the breakdown of this social consensus (educating white, middle-class, Protestant students), neoliberals argue, that has polluted schools. But, the pollution must be understood within a larger, more startling context than that which they mention. The collective culture shock immigrant and African-American students experienced in white classrooms have created stumbling blocks for neoliberals. At the same time, white, middle-class, Protestant children are learning other, and in many cases, non-Protestant ways of viewing the world.

Schools, forced to include in their classrooms students who symbolize realities other than capitalist ideologies, are at risk of losing their traditional Protestant focus, counsel the neoliberals. These schools are emblematic of an old industrial modernity that Dewey advocated, they say, and they are not accountable to the free-market economy. It is this liberal school that forces individuals to forsake their creativity and drown themselves in the mediocrity of the multicultural majority. Diverted from educating students to become middle managers in a global society, schools are compelled to remediate African-American and immigrant students in a curriculum that itself is being remediated to represent them. It is this liberal-values-laden cultural and racial decolonization that neoliberals believe has made schooling ineffective. Complicating this are teacher demands for increased salaries and decreased school responsibilities. The classroom teacher, conceivably beyond neoliberal influence and protected by unions and tenure, causes neoliberals to demand educational reform.

Knowing that liberal societies undergird their strength from social diversity, neoliberals argue that school curricula be standardized as in England, France, and other European countries. They want all students to learn the same European curriculum at the same time. Further, with the use of technology, curricula should be marketed, as if there existed an academic marketplace.[4] This is the platform upon which neoliberals argue that schools be competitive; only the best should survive. In this Protestant, capitalist setting, all students, regardless of their personal histories, are free to compete for their future.

With this, let us explore in greater depth neoliberal concerns about the social forces championing liberal schools.

Moynihan: Ethnicity

There is an alternative. [Reinhold] Niebuhr warns of collective egotism, [W. H.] Auden of collective egoism; however termed, it readily enough becomes destructive. But, there is nothing wrong . . . with an intelligent, responsible self-respect, even self-regard. The challenge is to make the world safe for and from ethnicity, safe for just those differences which large assemblies, democratic or otherwise, will typically attempt to suppress.[5]

Senator Daniel Patrick Moynihan's comments are focused on the international impact ethnicities have on American and European societies. He tells us that traditional twentieth-century dominant society style of dealings with ethnicities, some newly released from Cold War Soviet containment and others unreported in the international media, will no longer work. If some policies had worked previously, he says, it was not that they were better understood by dominant societies. Just as Soviet domination and containment of Eastern European ethnicities delayed their moment of rebellion (after the Soviet collapse), American domination and containment of African Americans and other ethnicities have been equally unsuccessful. Regardless of government policies used to administer ethnic relations, Moynihan tells us, it is still possible to think of ethnic relations differently. In fact, he says, ethnicity defined as collective egotism or collective egoism can be destructive. But, it might simply be a group (no matter how they define themselves) that is interested in expressing its self-respect or self-regard. Of course, says Moynihan, the secret of mature societies is their ability to understand the differences between collective egoism/egotism and self-respect/regard.

These perceptions—collective egoism/egotism and self-respect/regard—are the curriculum issues to be resolved in a global society, say neoliberals. This is the crux of the argument between the multicultural curriculum beloved by the old industrial modernity and the raw capitalist neoliberal curriculum of knowledge management. Moynihan's argument is reflective of the old modernity, neoliberals say, because he insists the terms *collective egoism/egotism* and *self-respect/regard* express different viewpoints about governments' interactions with ethnic groups. In fact, say neoliberals, it is the way governments view ethnicities (as groups rather than as individuals) that demonstrates the terms are, in themselves, not different but irrelevant. The terms, regardless of how they are viewed by Moynihan, do not reflect a world committed to the free-market economy, say neoliberals. That is, both terms, labels perhaps, reflect a dying modernity in which political units are discrete, knowledge is less relevant to daily life, and economic interactions are limited to national boundaries.

Placing Moynihan's considerations within the same liberal camp as Dewey, neoliberals argue that ethnicity should be recognized for what it is—the histories of individuals' relationships with other individuals, not with groups (using Moynihan's definition). In the case of schooling, this is the liberal pollution neoliberals see.

To make the point clear, Arthur Schlesinger Jr. tells us ethnic assimilation in the United States is workable. In *The Disuniting of America*, he points to the historic development of democratic definitions that matured because of the genius of many individuals who represented different cultures in the United States.[6] In fact, he points to the advances ethnicity has shone on the nation simply by bringing to light the patriotism and determination of individual women, Native Americans, Asians, Hispanics, African Americans, and representatives of other historically marginalized peoples. Schlesinger is implying to us that because Moynihan only thinks of ethnicity within the context of a group, rather than individuals, he assumes the issue of multiculturalism to be more complex than it is.

Relying on this argument, Schlesinger cautions us about ethnicity's ugly side. Defining relationships with other groups using a tribal psychology, ethnicities foster social dislikes and distrust. This is dangerous, says Schlesinger, because it affects the quality of society. To illustrate, he points to needless arguments about unimportant issues (such as language) he believes are raised by self-styled multiculturalists or ethnocentric separatists. He refers to these "hypersensitive" speakers as purposely disruptive in their clamor to create ethnic groups they can then represent.

These are the reasons why schools should educate children regardless of their ethnicity, Schlesinger says. Schools bring individuals, regardless of their heritage, to the same social and economic table in which all are able to partake of the same Euroamerican menu. To complete the metaphor, Schlesinger reaffirms that "the American identity will never be fixed," yet "the bonds of cohesion in our society are sufficiently fragile . . . that it makes no sense [for multiculturalists] to strain them by encouraging and exalting cultural and linguistic apartheid."[7] In sum, Schlesinger's worry is that multiculturalism's threat to the United States is not the cultural heritage of individuals as much as it is ethnicities' choice to define themselves in the context of tribes.

It is this description of ethnicity to which neoliberals respond. One reason schools must be reformed, they say, is because the liberal school's inclusion of diversity teaches a curriculum of unrelated facts that are distinct and separate from each other. That is, they refuse to acknowledge a core curriculum composed of European knowledge. Because the liberal curriculum is qualitative and lacking accountability standards, neoliberals contend, ethnic groups and apologists such as Moynihan have promoted multiculturalism as an artificial school issue rather than an issue of teaching diverse students a common European core.

Finally, neoliberals contend, the ethnicity issue can be viewed as a metaphor in which schools, reflecting the old modernity, produce students who are unsuccessful in the free-market economy because they are unprepared to become capitalism's human capital. It is within this context, neoliberals argue, that they want to aggressively reform the school.

Bourne: Ethnicity and Society

Disregarded by or unknown to neoliberals, multiculturalism has developed its own intellectual history. In fact, this history has typically framed curriculum considerations about education in a democracy. For example, at the turn of the last century, Randolph Bourne, a student of Dewey's, argued that America was simply "modern." He assumed immigrants, as they joined American society, would not be expected to give up their birth culture. Rather, he believed, immigrants would become bicultural—blending their birth culture with that which they adopted. Bourne believed persons coming from other cultures would actively accept the new ideas, institutions, and beliefs of the new country. Yet, that did not mean new citizens were expected to give up every part of their birth culture. Part of that would always remain, said Bourne. It was not the act of assimilation that was significant so much as it was the process of the nation continually redefining itself. This he called "transnationalism." It is the social duality of cultural identifications of all who live in the nation. It was this blending of the birth culture with the new culture that made America unique.[8]

However, Bourne also expressed major concerns about the duality he describes. He is afraid that immigrants, as they become more involved with their adopted culture, will become nostalgic for the culture of their birth. It is not, he says, they will want to return to their birth culture so much as it is they will develop and identify artifacts of their previous lives and will restore those to their living present. Much like Svetlana Boym, writing about Russian immigrants more than eighty-five years later, Bourne cautions us immigrants may become caught within a time and place frame in which life stops. How terrible it would be, he says, if immigrants' nostalgia caused them to preserve cultural artifacts that their birth cultures had long since rejected.[9] Obviously, he argues this would cause society to stagnate.

Dewey: Curriculum and Society

It is left to John Dewey to place the purpose of curriculum in perspective and explain its impact on students in a multicultural society. In an article entitled "Creative Democracy: The Task before Us," written as England entered World War II (1939), Dewey wrote about what democracy should mean to Americans.[10] He wrote about human democracy, morality, and personal faith. Even though the topics of his essay seem to be disjointed for the times, he, like others, recognized the European war was the beginning of a global conflagration. And, he thought, if Americans were to understand this violent future in which they were to live, basic tenets must be understood. It is in this spirit the article was written.

Like Bourne, Dewey recognized that American society was the continuing consequence of immigration, and therefore, in place of the term *diversity*, he purposely used the label "Common Man." He implies to us that every person in this society, regardless of class, gender, race, and economic advantage, celebrates a common joining with others who possess different personal histories. Each of us represents the Common Man. Even so, it is this joining, he says, that creates human democracy. Human democracy is a faith, says Dewey, which those who decry Nazi intolerance, cultural hatred, and cruelty must recognize within themselves when they meet others who are different. Unlike Schlesinger, who cautioned the reader against straining a fragile society, Dewey says this human democracy, joining the common life histories of immigrants—that is, the Common Man—is this society's strength.

Dewey describes for us the consequences to a nation in which its citizens learn about democracy but do not understand the significance of an interactive human democracy. In this meaningless education, he says, people believe that democracy operates automatically in state capitals and Washington, DC. Voting (or not voting) is the only high-stakes test people acknowledge as a measure of their good citizenship.

What Dewey is telling neoliberals in this century is that a curriculum whose only visible purpose is to help students pass high-stakes tests is not dedicated to their future or personal welfare. The education it represents is meaningless. Although not using the term *accountability* (Dewey used the term *passive education*), Dewey presents the argument that high-stakes testing, even witnessed by others, is still meaningless and misrepresents their education. Says Dewey, the curriculum must be personally meaningful; otherwise, students will not choose to incorporate it into their daily lives. Said simply, curriculum is accountable to students, not the reverse. This is what he meant when he gave credence to those who present different views on subjects that are of interest to the community. The act of the Common Man, he says, is to learn about unknowns rather than to react as if the community was threatened.

Using the American geographic frontier as a metaphor to describe the moment from which he spoke, Dewey equates human democracy to the moral frontier each person possesses. In that frontier, Dewey challenges us to consider our thoughts about what transpires when students judge a curriculum to be significant to their lives. He says the ultimate test of a curriculum is predicated on how it influences a person's faith. In his article, Dewey expands on this thought by arguing that democracy must be more than an external process of institutional interaction. It is a faith persons accept so they can make meaning of their lives.

What is meaning? For Dewey, meaning is that tentative answer that results when people, regardless of their personal histories and ethnicities, discuss significant social and personal issues with others who are different. This democratic interaction by the Common Man is the result, or unity, persons experience as they learn about the inconsistencies in their own lives. He says this human democracy, now exhibited as a faith, helps people assess their own actions by letting them judge themselves according to standards they have themselves constructed or accepted. For example, it would be inconsistent if a person argued for the civil rights of ethnicities but was not willing to accept them into his or her own life.

It is this development of a personal faith Dewey is referring to when he writes about experiences in this and other articles and texts. Experiences are much more to him than the passive actions of viewing, looking, and observing. And while some may equate experience with the sensation of a personal activity or relationship, such as enjoying a fine dinner with good friends, Dewey defines experience in a much more comprehensive realm. Superficially, experience is the interaction of a person with and in an environment, but it involves much more than the internal passive *me* and *mine* of the individual. It is the whole person's active physical, emotional, intellectual, and spiritual participation in and about a dreamed future. At its ideal, experiences culminate in an individual's sense of understanding. That sense of understanding may be for a period of time or until other experiences cause the individual to reflect on his or her value system. And, while these dreamed futures or culminations are not always part of a person's life—that is, we may be forced to live with inconsistencies—it is that unity we desire. Its lack becomes our opportunity to explore and experience a changing, seemingly elusive future.

Really, Dewey is telling neoliberals that students' private high-stakes tests or accountability programs are composed of problems (inconsistencies) they experience in their private lives. Students want to know if the curriculum will help them solve inconsistencies that act as impediments to their sense of unity. Recognizing inconsistencies and testing for unity is the act of thinking, Dewey says, and should not be considered unique. This is the scientific method. Now that we know what a problem (an inconsistency) is, the process of testing it will contribute to students' life histories. In fact, says Dewey, experience may be more important to people than the results they might garner from solving problems.

These are the elements of a liberal school, according to Dewey. Its curriculum is composed of experiences in which students learn how to solve problems (inconsistencies). Curriculum is internal and personal. Accountability is within the province of students whose high-stakes tests are focused on unity, the results of their dreaming, thinking, hypothesizing, and problem solving. All of these are interrelated, Dewey believes. They are part of the pluralist society Bourne describes and are reflective of a complex, pluralistic, democratic society of the Common Man.

NEOLIBERAL REFORM: PREPARING FOR ACADEMIC CAPITALISM

Writing during the late 1980s, a period when globalization's glimmer was first seen beyond the confines of international trade, Phillip Schlechty draws our attention to the role schools have played in American educational history.

> The factory system depended on routinization, standardization, and centralization as the primary means of organizing human action. It was this system that enabled America's economy to outstrip those of the other nations of the world. Decisions to change the system are not easily taken. Business leaders have made such decisions not because they want democracy in the workplace. Rather, they have begun to find that . . . those who have knowledge must be in a position to apply what they know.[11]

Schlechty tells us that schools, while giving lip service to Dewey's theories, have, in the main, disregarded him and responded to capitalist philosophers instead. To state the idea more clearly, as Dewey defined children to be individuals living and learning in communities, Schlechty tells us schools have traditionally classified students as human capital. Because of this, he says, the true story of the American school is found in its constant response to capitalists' demands that it create a continuing supply of loyal, docile workers for American investors.

To illustrate, during the industrial era, beginning in the middle decades of the nineteenth century, schools broadened their curricula in answer to capitalists' insistence that schools teach children to tolerate the boredom and drudgery of the factory floor. In this case, schools developed curricula, both formal and informal, to give students classroom experiences that taught them to obey orders, work by themselves or in small groups, and respond respectfully to the authority of the capitalist class.

Schlechty's description of American education is not uniquely his, however. He is supported by other scholars, including Alan J. DeYoung, who wrote of the educational theories of Adam Smith, Karl Marx, John Stuart Mill, and other economists who have theorized school curricula.[12]

Schlechty goes on to caution that globalization has revolutionized the marketplace, making the capitalists' need for factory workers no longer urgent. Schools that continue to reflect the factory floor are therefore out of date and are teaching students to live in a past modernity. Schlechty quickly tells us today's schools must be reformed (he focuses his arguments on school administrator leadership) so they can produce workers who manage information in a global economy. Never mentioning him by name, Schlechty acknowledges Schumpeter's creative destruction theory and the school's place within this new modernity of aggressive and creative knowledge workers.

Educational reform will not become a reality, says Schlechty, as long as schools respond to economic theories from assigned positions on the periphery of the global economy. He espies an immediate future in which knowledge itself will become a marketable commodity, bought and sold in a free-market academic economy. Not yet recognizing neoliberal nostalgic visions of the school, Schlechty says, "I leave to others to imagine ways whereby the play life of schools can be made richer and more rewarding— rewarding not only to students but to adults as well."[13]

But Schlechty (and we) did not have long to wait to learn of neoliberals' vision of a richer and more rewarding school. Neoliberalism's federal legislation, the No Child Left Behind Act, will, they say, restore schools to be the social monument they nostalgically recall from an earlier time and place.

Let us look at that legislation so we can understand its influence on American schools.

No Child Left Behind Act (2002)

Analogous to the theo-political maneuvers that resulted in the neoliberal takeover of the Southern Baptist Convention, the No Child Left Behind Act (NCLB) is predicated on the same twin standards of excellence espoused by Patterson and Pressler. That is to say, education's neoliberals, using the NCLB as their template, are reforming education by identifying a single Euroamerican curriculum (creed) to which schools are held accountable (high-stakes testing).[14]

First, let us look at accountability's high-stakes testing.[15] It is through the NCLB that neoliberals imagine schools to be academic enterprises competing in a global free-market academic economy. It is as if schools, in neoliberals' minds, were corporations employing teachers they regard as knowledge managers, whose task is to produce students they liken to products or human capital. Competing in the free-market academic economy through high-stakes testing, academic enterprises are held accountable for the knowledge their students display. Failure in this free-market academic economy is reflective of the consequences of those churches that failed the Southern Baptist Convention's high-stakes tests discussed in the previous chapter. In this case, schools also suffer by being labeled "at risk." They lose students to profiting schools that produce students who score higher on high-stakes tests, while mulling the options of either improving their products' test performance or closing their doors. Accountability—that is, high-stakes testing— is significant for neoliberals because it identifies those creative individuals who, they insist, are being overshadowed by the mediocrity imposed on them by the multicultural liberal school. Said another way, accountability forces teachers to be answerable for the meritocracy of their students.

But, accountability by itself is of little use to neoliberals who are intent on restoring this social monument. Missing, waiting to be restored, is an educational creed, a single (perhaps, national) Euroamerican curriculum to be learned by all, so accountability's tools can identify creative individuals lost within the milieu of multiculturalism and mediocrity. This is the reason neoliberals assert that the present curriculum—that confederacy of core values, influenced by local idiosyncrasies and multicultural issues—must be replaced. Otherwise, they warn, Dewey's curriculum of human democracy will continue to produce mediocre students.

Knowing this, let us look at the neoliberals' second standard of excellence, the core (single) Euroamerican curriculum. Just as theological neoliberals developed a creed to replace a confederacy of Southern Baptist core values, education neoliberals, using the NCLB, have developed a Euroamerican core curriculum embracing mathematics and reading performance. These two subjects are reflective of a past basic curriculum nostalgically referred to as the "three R's" (reading, writing, and 'rithmetic). Legitimated by accountability's high-stakes testing, this core curriculum is placed within a multicultural liberal curriculum neoliberals judge to be mostly a confederacy of untestable subjects.

Neoliberals think it is important that we understand the impact of holding teachers accountable for this nostalgic core curriculum. Regardless of discussions about the curriculum's narrowness or its perceived influence on other nontestable areas, its intent rests singly on its ability to identify creative students. It solves problems, "perhaps the biggest . . . [being] that we have passed children from grade to grade, year after year, and those child[ren] haven't learned the basics of reading and math."[16] Unlike those who fail, accountability encourages these students to continue their studies in the school's other subjects: languages, literature, science, and the arts. The knowledges these represent, although not subjected to accountability's scrutiny, are broad and important in the education of the nation's developing middle-manager class.

For those who fail, who seem to be uncreative and not destined to become part of the middle-manager class, a second curriculum concentrating on literacy is offered. Told of their inability to continue their education with those who passed the high-stakes tests, these students are encouraged to improve their reading proficiency, forsake learning other subjects because of their difficulty, and accept the widening academic, social, and economic gulf between them and their former classroom colleagues. Creating a second worker class within the free-market economy, these students, usually those whose personal histories represent non-European cultures, become part of an economic flotsam, working in the private service sector, graduating into a class called the working poor. They are destined to become the continuing examples of an underclass, unseen and unheard in the capitalist economy.

But, this need not be the case, neoliberals say. The NCLB gives those who fail high-stakes tests unexpected opportunities to succeed. Not a reward for failure, the act's opportunities are those by which students may elect to rise above the multicultural mediocrity of their individual classrooms by choosing private or other public schools that have a reputation of accountability. In fact, this competition in which students and their parents interpret information as products, teachers as knowledge managers, and schools as corporations, neoliberals quickly mention, is the consumer lens through which students and their parents may choose the education they want. As consumers, students and their parents are actively involved in the free-market academic economy. Said another way, the NCLB allows students and their parents to shop for their education in the same manner as they shop for jeans, checking for size, color, and fit. As in retail stores, the quality of the jeans students and their parents purchase is dependent on the amount of money (in this case, vouchers, tax credits, or family wealth) they possess.

In sum, neoliberal reformers picture schools as private academic corporations that compete for profit in the free-market academic economy. Successful schools are those that are accountable, use vouchers as academic currency, and sell to students and parents their product (curriculum) and delivery systems. As students successfully prove their knowledge through high-stakes tests, they advance step by step to their economic goal of becoming middle managers, while those who fail are deprived of important tools for success. This is the school, committed to the privatization and curriculum standardization described in the NCLB, that neoliberals hungrily await. Its human capital, composed of free individuals creating wealth while living in gated communities and separating themselves from the economically disadvantaged, will be evidence of their restored social monument.

Academic Capitalism: Privatization

Milton Friedman, a neoliberal economist, believes schools should not be operated by governments. He says public agencies, even those that are friendly to corporations and the ideals of capitalism, will over time develop social responsibility orientations that are totally unrelated to the free-market economy.

> Any institution will tend to express its own values and its own ideas. Our public education system is a socialist institution. A socialist institution will teach socialist values, not the principles of private enterprise.[17]

Friedman says he believes even corporate managers who are committed to capitalist theories sometimes are persuaded to become socially responsible. They divert their attention from creating profits for their investors to financially supporting public or private single-agenda agencies. This is the same ideology, he says, schools believe. That is, they must be socially responsible to accommodate a Deweyist curriculum aggrandizing the mediocre majority rather than that which elevates the creative individual. But, this is not just his worry, Friedman says. Increasingly, the American public is becoming aware that the government response to social responsibility issues has not solved social problems, but simply created larger bureaucracies.

It is this supposition of socialism and ineffective bureaucracies Friedman speaks about that undergirds neoliberals' desire to reform and privatize schools. At its simplest, Friedman argues, privatization must occur so schools will discontinue teaching curricula venerating social responsibility. To hasten privatization, Friedman chastises private enterprises that express social responsibility by supporting public schools with their wealth and expertise. It simply delays the time, he admonishes, when children and their parents— that is, the schools' customers—can make choices about which school and quality of education they want to purchase.[18] These customers, says Friedman, buying their education with vouchers, the schools' new currency, will be part of private schools' financial profit platform.

Does Friedman want private schools to teach values that are opposite to those of the public schools? At first blush, this appears to be the case. But understanding Friedman's discussion about the harm corporations inflict on themselves by responding to social responsibility issues shows his thoughts are much more complex. Obviously a disciple of Adam Smith, but interested in corporate ethics, Friedman describes school privatization. A school, to him, is an academic corporation that competes openly and honestly with other academic corporations in the free-market academic economy. Financed by investors who are interested in gaining a profit from schools, the corporation offers a curriculum and delivery system to potential customers who compare it and its price with those of the competition. Profits are earned, says Friedman, because of customer satisfaction with the quality of the product offered in relation to its cost. Is the purpose of privatization to teach students the value of capitalism and the free marketplace? Of course, says Friedman. In fact, students and their families will even experience a capitalist relationship with the school. Mostly, the corporation, purposefully dressed in value-laden clothes, will teach students how to wear them when they become middle managers in an economic democracy.

But there is more to privatization than the economic relationships among schools, teachers, students, and their parents. Privatization is also the seedbed from which schools, beyond what investors and managers assume are their purposes, can become capitalists in their own right. That is, like Schlechty, Friedman argues that schools are capable of creating, packaging, and selling knowledge. But retailing knowledge is not the corporation's only responsibility. Schools must be willing entrepreneurs in the free academic marketplace.

Academic Capitalism: Marketing

Undoubtedly, Friedman's privatization theories are attractive to neoliberals because they are based on the premise that vouchers and private investment, perhaps even tax credits and federal and state funds, will become the accepted forms of academic currency. Upon these and other revenues, the financial scaffolding of academic enterprises will be constructed for its investors to garner profits. This form of neoliberalism, or academic capitalism, is described for us by Les Levidow:

> Recent tendencies have been called "academic capitalism." Although university staff are still largely state-funded, they are increasingly driven into entrepreneurial competition for external funds. Under such pressure, staff devise . . . "efforts to secure external monies."[19]

Levidow forces us to think of public schools as private corporations structuring themselves as they develop their own revenue pools to finance their for-profit missions. Explaining these revenue pools and for-profit missions, he presents us a fascinating explanation of neoliberalism in which the market forces of supply and demand enter the academic arena. While concentrating on higher education in Europe and the United States, Levidow postulates that governments, in their rush to disencumber themselves of their bureaucracies so they might appear leaner, have forced universities (and school districts) to become profit-driven enterprises. (This is the evidence of national and local divestiture, he implies, that supports Friedman's contention of the public's negative response to governments' involvement with social responsibility issues.) Continuing, Levidow tells us schools are now faced with the dilemma of educating larger numbers of students while subsisting on smaller budgets.

It is this public education dilemma that Levidow speaks about that neoliberals insist privatization is able to solve. Now, designed to compete in the free-market academic economy, schools—using standard business management practices such as cost analysis and efficiency studies—will focus on lowering educational costs by standardizing curricula and introducing technology-based delivery systems. Just as cost analyses will help academic capitalists control curriculum quality and delivery, market analyses will generate additional revenues through research that creates positive public images of the corporation as an educational enterprise. That is, marketing campaigns will advertise images of academic corporations to which customers will positively respond. Beyond the goal of increasing its market visibility, market analyses will also identify specific student clienteles that will best succeed in its classrooms within specific cost structures. Focusing on market niches such as suburbs and identifying students by class, economic advantage, gender, and personal learning

histories, marketing will develop customer profiles or models most recep-
tive to the school's advertised product—its curriculum.

In sum, marketing is the crux of school privatization. Just as marketing
creates a customer base on which educational enterprises will focus, it also
creates the corporate agenda students and parents will espouse in their business dealings with the academic enterprise. No longer focusing on students
as the center of conversation, academic enterprises will define their relations
with parents and students within a business framework. Parents, now customers, equating curriculum to a commodity they purchased, will focus their
attention on how well their children are learning and what their level of success will be when measured by high-stakes tests. In the same vein,
student–teacher relationships will change. The teacher, no longer seen as a
partner in the child's learning, is now pictured by the parent-customer as a
knowledge manager who, using technology, teaches a standard curriculum.
The student, now an information gatherer, responds as a knowledge product, demonstrating through high-stakes testing the quality of the academic
enterprise's product and delivery system.

THE NEOLIBERALS' CHALLENGE: EDUCATING A THREE-LEGGED STOOL

> But looking at education as an industry is profoundly unnatural for profes-
> sional educators—and for the great bulk of the journalists covering educa-
> tion, who have a marked and distressing tendency to go native.[20]

In this statement, Peter Brimelow acknowledges a fundamental point that
neoliberals will not prevail in their quest for school reform until the last de-
fenders of mediocrity have been neutralized. Unlike their theological neoliberal colleagues we discussed in the previous chapter, who did not encounter entrenched professionals in their hostile takeover of the Southern
Baptist Convention, education neoliberals have been confronted with three:
professional teacher organizations, schools and colleges of education, and
teacher education accrediting associations. It is upon this three-legged stool
of professional legitimacy the neoliberal reform of public schools is being
fought.[21]

Looking closer at the three-legged stool is the neoliberal argument
about what constitutes teaching and the economic role of teachers in the
free-market academic economy. Should teachers become workers employed by privatized schools to produce profits for investors, as neoliberals contend? Or are teachers professionals responding to their own intrin-
sic rewards their teacher associations and education professors say is their
career? Simply stated, neoliberals argue that teachers, taught in schools and

colleges of education to call themselves professionals, only join teacher organizations to protect themselves from competing in the free-market academic economy.

None of this should be a surprise to teachers and their academic and or-
ganizational allies, say neoliberals; even doctors and attorneys who sell their
unique knowledge to the public do not compete totally in the free-market
academic economy. They are subject to their own professional associations'
codes of discipline, which isolate them from the marketplace. Still, teachers
are different. They do not sell their unique knowledge like doctors and attorneys. Employed by the government to perform specific, legislative mandates, teachers reside outside the free-market academic economy. For this
reason, neoliberals think teachers, without the need to account for their actions, mistakenly believe they can positively compare their unique knowledge of the classroom with the surgeon's unique knowledge of the operating room.[22]

Nonetheless, neoliberal reformers view teachers as information or
knowledge workers. The work of teachers is to deliver information to students in various settings, including classrooms and those created by technology. Understanding this, the unique knowledge teachers learn in schools
and colleges of education, including social foundations, curriculum, teaching methodologies, testing, and educational psychology, is irrelevant to their
jobs, say neoliberals. Their work is to dispense information, not to enter into
the private lives of students. Like workers in other industries, teachers should
be held accountable to the free-market academic economy, not as capitalists
but laborers. That is, teachers should be expected to produce quality products at the lowest possible cost.

To paint a face on the low esteem in which neoliberals hold teachers and
the act of teaching, Brimelow ridicules how they walk: "wobble and waddle
. . . with thighs like tree trunks, bellies billowing, jowls jiggling."[23] Although
Brimelow does not mention it, this is the physical stereotype of docile workers who labor in the information field described by Schlechty and expected
by neoliberals. With this understood, how do neoliberals view the professional three-legged stool upon which teachers sit?

Teachers' Associations

Remembering the economic and social histories of labor and capitalist
tensions in the previous century, teachers' associations, say neoliberals, are
but masquerades intended by teachers to gain public acceptance of their
self-touted importance. Teachers' associations are nothing more than labor
unions, they say. And teachers' unions are the inherent foes of investors,
even taxpayers, who presently employ teachers in "government schools."[24]
To support their claim, neoliberals insist teachers' unions are more interested

in expanding the quality of teacher benefits and welfare than providing quality classroom labor for the taxpayer.

In fact, education reform is an economic issue, say neoliberals, between
capitalists and a worker class that wants society to view it differently than what
it really is. To illustrate, while teachers do not like the word "union," they have
nevertheless purposely followed traditional labor union practices of discouraging competition in the workplace. Teachers' associations have historically
lobbied for state mandates that recognize only graduates of schools and colleges of education as qualified teachers in the nation's classrooms. It is for this
reason neoliberals urge state legislators to develop alternative teacher certifi-
cation programs that allow others, who are not education graduates, to become classroom teachers. Thinking of alternative education as a form of "scab
labor," neoliberals advance this process as a form of "union busting."

Unionism is part of American economic history, according to neoliberals. Teachers' associations led by the National Education Association (NEA)
and the American Federation of Teachers (AFT) are in the same league as
those labor unions that preached socialism in the twentieth century. Believing collective bargaining to be an unfair socialist practice in which teachers
band together to negotiate salaries and welfare benefits, neoliberals such as
Brimelow contend this is calculated to protect mediocre teachers. Good
teachers, like celebrities, he says, should have the freedom to become their
own agents, opting out of the collective bargaining process if they believe
they can better negotiate with a school system. At the same time, Brimelow
and others argue for repeal of collective bargaining legislation at the state
level. Perhaps recognizing that many states have discouraged teacher strikes
and walkouts, Brimelow continues to focus on these elements to do away
with teachers' associations.[25]

Perhaps, the most significant feature Brimelow and other neoliberals
question is the NEA's Code of Ethics and the AFT's Bill of Rights and Responsibilities. These are seen as blatant tools teachers use to defend their
supposed professionalism. Furthermore, these two declarations are self-
serving because they simply argue that the job of teachers is to make classrooms "closed shops."

The National Education Association's Code of Ethics

The NEA's Code of Ethics, composed of a preamble and two general
principles, focuses on teacher commitment to students and the profession.
While the code speaks about freedom to learn and teach in the classroom, it
is their ethical behavior and conduct that are teachers' highest responsibilities. It is because of this that teachers are expected to enter into a professional relationship with students, encouraging them to develop attitudes of
inquiry and knowledge-gathering while identifying important life goals. In

the same vein, the Code of Ethics encourages teachers to improve the profession by working together to raise their professional standards while discouraging unqualified persons from teaching.

These principles, say neoliberals, are the antithesis of capitalism and an economic democracy. They are the NEA's acknowledgment that teachers, voicing platitudes about social responsibility, are in fact closing classroom doors to quality instruction. Masking themselves as professionals, neoliberals argue, teachers' associations are encouraging their members to think they are beyond the competitive world in which teaching is considered more important than mediocrity's protection.

The American Federation of Teachers' Bill of Rights and Responsibilities

Like the NEA, the AFT assumes its members are professionals. Yet, accepting its historic role, first birthed as a union, then joining the American Federation of Labor (AFL) and the Congress of Industrial Organizations (CIO), the AFT has acted as a support organization for both classroom teachers and school support personnel.[26] From its early days in Chicago, the AFT pictured its existence as part of classroom teachers' struggle to exist in a capitalist world uninterested in children other than their role as human capital. These are the reasons neoliberals give to show that the AFT's Bill of Rights and Responsibilities is nothing but a labor union's traditional tool to force investors (in this case, taxpayers) to bargain with workers.

Rejecting this interpretation, the AFT says professionalism is based on a compact, or an agreement, between the school and its students and teachers. This compact, the Bill of Rights and Responsibilities, is the school's acknowledgment that teachers and students are equal and should be treated equally by school boards. That is, students and teachers cannot achieve their educational goals without the school's cooperation in maintaining high standards of conduct and rigorous academic standards in its programs. Specifically, the declaration claims that the acts of teaching and learning cannot take place in schools that do not promote safe environments, encourage student perceptions of academic excellence, develop academic programs that assist students of various needs, or support teachers who encourage rigorous academic standards.

Schools and Colleges of Education

Coupled with neoliberal criticisms of teachers' associations is their complaint of academic mediocrity sponsored by schools and colleges of education. Brimelow notes:

> In the career selection process that takes place during college, the groups of students who choose teaching as a career, taken as a whole, are not as high achieving as their college peers with respect to SAT scores.[27]

Brimelow's argument is that a major reason classrooms remain citadels of mediocrity is because schools and colleges of education attract mediocre students. Implied, of course, is that schools and colleges of education are, by extension, part of the mediocrity citadel. This is the reason, he suggests, why education professors are held in such low esteem by their colleagues in the learned professions.

Without research histories and settling for training grants focusing on classroom methodologies, Brimelow postulates, professors of education have developed a special vocabulary (he calls it "Ed-speak") to protect themselves from their colleagues' criticisms. That is, Brimelow argues, professors of education want to make their curriculum appear more complicated and sophisticated than it really is.

Teacher Education Accrediting Agencies

It is left, however, to the schools and colleges of educations' accrediting agencies to argue the professional role of teachers in schools and society. Developing alliances with state and other professional education accrediting agencies, neoliberals recognize these combined organizations control teacher education and, thereby, the nation's classrooms.

The most powerful of the accrediting associations is the National Council for Accreditation of Teacher Education (NCATE). Represented throughout the United States, its power lies in its ability to bestow national recognition on schools and colleges of education that promote a single agenda of social responsibility and professionalism. Within that rubric, unspoken yet understood, is the council's power to *withdraw* recognition from education programs, thereby sentencing them to near-death status. Using accrediting teams composed of professors of education and their sympathizers, say neoliberals, the NCATE evaluates teacher education programs against national standards. Included in their ever changing list are issues that deal with education faculty quality, curriculum, physical facilities, budgets, and others that affect those who believe teaching is a profession.

Another national association, little known to neoliberals, is the Holmes Group. Composed of deans of schools and colleges of education, this agency's purpose is to influence the direction of teacher education programs. The group, concerned that traditional teacher education programs are open to neoliberal criticism, is encouraging higher education institutions to develop five-year teacher preparation programs, in which the first four years are dedicated to academics and the fifth year to professional courses. This should, the group believes, result in schools and colleges of education withstanding neoliberal opposition.

In fact, say neoliberals, neither the NCATE nor the Holmes Group understands its reform intentions. It is not the extent of teacher training or the quality of teacher work in the classroom they wish to reform. Rather, the issue is the economic role of the teacher-laborer dispensing information in privatized schools to student customers, who, passing high-stakes tests, eagerly await the time when they will become middle managers in an economic democracy.

It is this perceived unfairness neoliberals hearken to, voicing their judgments in opposition to schools' mediocrity. At the same time, teachers are privileged, they say. They protect themselves by lobbying for federal and state legislation supportive of their members. They encourage themselves to teach students their values of social responsibility in which the wealthy are morally responsible to support the working poor. They campaign for economic assistance from those they criticize. It is within this context, neoliberals argue, they want to aggressively reform schools into those social monuments they nostalgically recall.

The neoliberal reform movement raises serious questions about the construction of their educational social monument. In the next chapter, we will identify that time and place neoliberals nostalgically long for and describe the school modeled in their minds as exemplary. Finally, the next chapter will spawn questions about the future of this nation's democracy and the questions neoliberals do not want us to ask.

NOTES

1. David K. Shipler, *A Country of Strangers: Blacks and Whites in America* (New York: Alfred A. Knopf, 1997), 94–95. Shipler, a Pulitzer Prize winner, offers an important perspective of race relations. Generally, he states, before *Brown v. Board of Education* (1954), racial separation was institutionalized though legislation. After that, racial separation was institutionalized through individual relations.

2. Cathi Cornelius, in her study of mid-twentieth-century Oklahoma City's school integration plan, found that many African-American community leaders believed no price was too great to pay for their children's education in all-white schools. Cathi L. Cornelius, "Village Perspectives: A Case Study Investigating the Perspectives Concerning the Oklahoma City Public Schools Neighborhood Schools Plan/Student Reassignment Plan," Ed.D. diss., Oklahoma State University, 1999.

3. Christina Igoa, *The Inner World of the Immigrant Child* (New York: St. Martin's Press, 1995).

4. This is an interesting argument. Although both presidents George H. W. Bush and Ronald Reagan spoke in favor of national curricula, the Constitution has been forceful about state and local control. National curricula in the United States may not be the reality neoliberals envision, although the No Child Left Behind Act (2002) approaches this goal through economic reward.

5. Daniel Patrick Moynihan, *Pandaemonium: Ethnicity in International Politics* (London: Oxford University Press, 1993), 173. The text, an expansion of the 1991 Cyril Foster Lecture at Oxford, discusses the problems of ethnicity in a global society.

Moynihan is referring to Reinhold Niebuhr, "Law, Conscience, and Grace," in *Justice and Mercy* (San Francisco: Harper & Row, 1974), and W. H. Auden's introduction to Constantine Cavafy, *The Complete Poems of Cavafy*, trans. Rae Dalven (New York: Harcourt Brace Jovanovich, 1976), xiii.

6. Arthur M. Schlesinger Jr., *The Disuniting of America: Reflections on a Multicultural Society* (New York: W. W. Norton, 1992), esp. 19, 40–41, 134–35.

7. Schlesinger, *The Disuniting of America.*

8. Bourne is a student of Dewey, Randolph Beard, and Charles Woodbridge. For a discussion of Bourne and his relationship with other philosophers in post–World War I America, see Louis Menand, *The Metaphysical Club: A Story of Ideas in America* (New York: Farrar, Straus and Giroux, 2001).

9. Boym refers to this as "restorative nostalgia." She noted in her research of Russian immigrants in the United States that they displayed artifacts in their homes to remind them of their birth culture. See Svetlana Boym, *The Future of Nostalgia* (New York: Basic Books, 2001).

10. John Dewey, "Creative Democracy: The Task before Us," in *John Dewey and the Promise of America*, Progressive Education Booklet No. 14 (Columbus, Ohio: American Education Press, 1939), available at www.beloit.edu/~pbk/dewey.html. Dewey's article is written as if it were a letter of encouragement to the American people. He mentions his age (he is eighty years old) and reflects on the happenings in America during that time. The article was read by philosopher Horace M. Kallen at an occasion to honor Dewey in New York City on October 20, 1939, six weeks after the beginning of World War II.

11. Phillip C. Schlechty, *Schools for the Twenty-First Century: Leadership Imperatives for Educational Reform* (San Francisco: Jossey-Bass, 1990), xv–xvi.

12. DeYoung says schools became important economic entities when industrialization required educated workers. Because of that, educational philosophy was best explained by economists, beginning as early as Smith. Of course, he argues educational philosophies directing today's schools are just glossed-over economic theories. See Alan J. DeYoung, *Economics and American Education: A Historical and Critical Overview of the Impact of Economic Theories on Schooling in the United States* (New York: Longman, 1989).

13. Schlechty, *Schools for the Twenty-First Century*, 153–54.

14. See David Marshak, "No Child Left Behind: A Foolish Race into the Past," *Phi Delta Kappan* 85, no. 3 (November 2003): 229–31. I agree with Marshak that the No Child Left Behind Act is an exercise in neoliberal restorative nostalgia, yet I am less certain of the time period he identified. Regardless, I do not dispute his scholarly intent or historical interpretation, although it is probable that neoliberals are more interested in the Victorian period. Marshak is correct about raw capitalism's charm beginning to wear poorly.

15. Specifically, the NCLB defines accountability through state-created math, science, and reading standards. It mandates the nation's schools report test scores that chart student learning. Test scores appear publicly so parents can decide if they want their children to continue their education at those schools. Of course, schools that continue to perform poorly will be held accountable. For details on the act, see the U.S. Department of Education's Website "No Child Left Behind," www.ed.gov/nclb/landing.jhtml.

16. President George W. Bush, speaking at the White House about the NCLB on its second anniversary, January 8, 2003.

17. Milton Friedman, "The Business Community's Suicidal Impulse," *Cato Policy Report* 21, no. 2 (March/April 1999): 6–7, available at www.cato.org/pubs/policy_report/v21n2/friedman.html.

18. "School choice" is an emotional term. The wealthy interpret it as a code word for sending their children to private schools. John Chubb and Terry Moe argue that reform cannot take place when the school is itself the problem. To understand their position more fully, see John E. Chubb and Terry M. Moe, *Politics, Markets, and America's Schools* (Washington, DC: Brookings Institution, 1990).

19. Les Levidow, "Marketizing Higher Education: Neoliberal Strategies and Counter-Strategies," *Cultural Logic* 4, no. 1 (Fall 2000), para. 3, available at eserver.org/clogic/4-1/levidow.html (Levidow is quoting from S. Slaughter and L. L. Leslie, *Academic Capitalism: Politics, Policies and the Entrepreneurial University* [Baltimore, MD: Johns Hopkins University Press, 1997]). Levidow discusses higher education survival from the viewpoint of knowledge marketing or academic capitalism.

20. Peter Brimelow, *The Worm in the Apple: How the Teacher Unions Are Destroying American Education* (New York: HarperCollins, 2003), xviii.

21. Anna Wilson and I have defined professionals as those who exhibit unique knowledge, agree to a code of ethics, and join an organization with policing powers. By this definition, priests and pastors, for example, are not professionals; they refer to their vocation as "called of God." See William E. Segall and Anna V. Wilson, *Introduction to Education: Teaching in a Diverse Society*, 2nd ed. (Lanham, MD: Rowman and Littlefield, 2005), 29–48.

22. Wilson and I do not claim teachers and nurses are professionals in the same sense as attorneys and medical doctors. We consider them semiprofessional because teachers' organizations have yet to develop policies to enforce their codes of ethics. Segall and Wilson, *Introduction to Education*, 32.

23. Brimelow is describing his observations at the 1999 National Education Association national convention in Orange County, California. Reminiscent of white Southern legislators describing the debating styles of newly elected ex-slaves, Brimelow refers to teacher debates as "human hot-air balloons" (*The Worm in the Apple*, 1).

24. Neoliberals refer to public schools as "government" schools. They allude that public schools are agencies of the federal government like the post office.

25. Brimelow (*The Worm in the Apple*, 211–15) refers to the Fuller Supreme Court in the early years of the last century. In regard to worker contracts, the Supreme Court (in *Lochner v. New York*) set aside a sixty-hour workweek contract because it violated workers' and employers' liberty to a binding contract. The Fuller Court is an excellent legal example of neoliberal worker freedom.

26. John Dewey was one of the AFT's first members.

27. Brimelow says teacher education students are mediocre. Citing data from a study by Drew Gitomer and colleagues, Brimelow says teacher education graduates' average combined SAT score (1029) is significantly lower than that for all college graduates (1085). See Drew H. Gitomer, Andre S. Latham, and Robert Ziomek, *The Academic Quality of Prospective Teachers: The Impact of Admissions and Licensure Testing* (Princeton, NJ: Educational Testing Service, 1999), 20.

9

Victorian Classism: Capitalism or Liberty?

In chapter 8, we looked at globalization's impact on American schools. While they underwent little of the cross-cultural trauma indigenous schools experienced as they adopted capitalist curricula, American schools were aghast when neoliberals held them accountable for teaching that same value-laden curriculum to students whose personal histories represented an ever expanding global culture.

Understanding this, in chapter 8, we centered our attention on neoliberals' plan to reform American schools, identifying demographic problems they believe plague the nation's classrooms—meaning cultural inclusivity gained by integration and immigration. These, along with other social ills, are the prime causes of education's mediocrity in the minds of neoliberals. Unappreciative of racial and cultural intermixing, neoliberals foresee the time when they believe European values and theologies will become minority expressions in the nation's classrooms. This is neoliberals' consummate fear—the economic, theological, and cultural contamination of their children's education as schools retreat from Protestant values.

Chapter 8 also highlighted neoliberal abhorrence of scholars who approve of school's racial intermix. These liberals, they believe, are dangerously wrong, as if they are committing a sin when they voice their multicultural philosophies spawning a stronger democracy. Even Daniel Patrick Moynihan's discussion of cultural diversity in a global community is the antithesis of individualism, they say. And Randolph Bourne's discussion of the term's definition belies the unchanging core values upon which American life is based. In the same fashion, but with an articulated dislike for John Dewey, neoliberals find his ideas of the Common Man repulsive.

They denounce his contention that today's immigrants, many voicing their life histories, are the ingredient of a vibrant democracy.

Believing Dewey has rejected religion, neoliberals judge his utterances to be liberalism's call for wresting school control from its capitalist heritage. They believe liberals want the United States to become a welfare society that embraces multicultural core values. Dewey raising his idea of democratic human interactions to the level of a faith is ample proof of his irreligiosity, say neoliberals. They are appalled when he says we should look first within and evaluate our own personal experiences before we search for reasons to raise others' standards of moral conduct. This faith—Dewey's theory of the Common Man, bringing order to each person's life—they say is now taught in schools. These are the types of issues that undergird the neoliberal No Child Left Behind Act and give credence to Milton Friedman's philosophy of academic capitalism.

Yet, it is beyond legislation and academic capitalism that neoliberals have experienced their greatest challenge. As chapter 8 pointed out, ordinary classroom teachers, their university professors, and the organizations to which they belong are the stumbling blocks to neoliberal school reform. It is this confrontation, voiced through opposing definitions of the term *professional*, that fires the clash about curriculum and high-stakes testing. Unlike the Southern Baptist preachers we discussed in chapter 7 who do not consider themselves professionals, teachers, and their allies, recalling a past time in which they were labeled as mere workers, are now protective of their professional status. Threatened by neoliberals' philosophy (in which they will again be labeled workers), they envision themselves vulnerable to those same outside forces who once orchestrated their careers through economic and social power.

This chapter will concentrate on describing neoliberalism's nostalgic time past and the schools they want to reform. Then, we will consider their reform movement's influence on American education.

NEOLIBERAL PSYCHOLOGY: FINDING VICTORIAN SCHOOLS

New centuries have often been stress points in the psychology, if not the immediate fortunes, of the world's leading economic powers. Like its predecessors, the United States found its uncertainties rising sharply as the calendar turned.[1]

Kevin Phillips's comments are startling in their description of the psychological environment in which neoliberals find themselves. He tells us that at some specific point (Phillips uses centuries' ends as his example) dominant societies, in this case the United States, are spurred to review their immediate past and measure their worth against an ominous, unseen future. His comments echo those of the Dalai Lama and Bill Rowley in chapter 1, who spoke of schisms and the social impact of technological revolutions.

This explains part of the neoliberals' need to reform schools. They are nostalgic about living in an earlier, (they believe) stress-free time. Because they abhor the mediocrity of their present and immediate past, they are motivated to construct a bridge joining their future with an imagined past in which purity was the norm. To be clear, it is the imagined past in which capitalism roamed free and social pluralism was either illegal or marginalized. Nor is neoliberal nostalgia the same as that expressed by the Russian immigrants Boym studied in chapter 7. As we learned in that chapter, Boym's immigrants used reflective nostalgia to help them survive their exile experience by decorating their homes with artifacts. The point is that Boym's Russian immigrants quickly learned that reflective nostalgia allowed them to be resilient. That is, their exile experience forced them to be outward looking, authorizing them to construct their own values and benchmarks upon which their future failures and successes could be evaluated.[2]

Now, placing Boym's theory of nostalgia within this setting, let us turn our attention to the aggressive nostalgia epitomized by neoliberals. Unlike Boym's reflective, outward-looking Russian immigrants, neoliberals are the reverse. Their nostalgia is aggressive and they look within. While Boym's exiles are experiencing new lives in new cultural and social environments, neoliberals are not. In fact, they consider themselves the protectors of their Protestant heritage now polluted by the diversity created by immigration and integration. This is why neoliberals are unyielding in their judgment of others. They are compelled to use their ideology to measure the correctness of each and every new socially damaging reality. Judging their environment against inward, absolute values with high-stakes tests, they condemn liberal society and its polluted school.

VICTORIAN PSYCHOLOGY: CAPITALISM

Robert William Fogel has reported to us the dream upon which neoliberalism's time past rests.[3] It describes the Victorian age, the joining decades of the nineteenth and twentieth centuries, when robber barons ruled. It was a period of absolutes, a time in which science was looked upon as the Devil's henchman, urban problems and labor unions were symptoms of communism, and gender and social diversity did not exist—or was ignored. In this white Protestant world, Victorian America hailed raw capitalism as natural, in which the strong won and the weak perished. Social and economic power was masculine. It was based in the white church (family in which the preacher was a demanding father) and supported by the white school (family in which the teacher was a nurturing mother). It was a period of racism, nativism, and colonialism, but mostly classism.[4]

In some ways, it has fallen to Fogel, a University of Chicago professor and Nobel Prize winner in economics, to explain neoliberalism's aggressive quest to recreate this Victorian past. While others, including Friedman, reached into the fields of economics and corporate management for theoretic scaffolds to explain raw capitalist educational reform, Fogel integrates these specialties into an understandable whole. Fogel chooses to do this by shedding some of his economic robes to speak to us as a social and theological historian. It is through the understandings of institutional (government, economics, and church) histories of leadership and followership, he says, that we grasp the essence of the American experience.

Fogel explains contemporary America's quandary.

> At the dawn of the new millennium, the critical issues are no longer whether we can manage business cycles or whether the economy is likely to continue to grow at a satisfactory rate. . . . Although the consolidation of past gains cannot be ignored, the future of egalitarianism in America turns on the nation's ability to combine continued economic growth with an entirely new set of egalitarian reforms that address the urgent spiritual needs of our age, secular as well as sacred. Spiritual (or immaterial) inequality is now as great a problem as material inequity, perhaps even greater.[5]

Fogel says that, in each of the three previous Great Awakenings, at least one institution (government, economics, or church), but usually church and government, has taken the leadership roles in constructing a homogeneity between the reactionary forces of society and technological innovation.[6] To illustrate, says Fogel, the nation's first Great Awakening centered on Protestant theological issues prompted by capitalism's growth. This, in turn, says Fogel, was thrashed out in the late eighteenth-century political scene culminating in the American Revolution and crowned by the U.S. Constitution. Other Great Awakenings, says he, have also occurred in American history. For example, in the mid-nineteenth century, churches partnered again with government to abolish slavery, an agrarian labor resource disguised as a social institution that capitalists no longer needed.

But, it is the last century's Great Awakening he points to that aroused neoliberals to return to Victorianism. Fogel describes this Great Awakening in the mid-twentieth century when America's economic cornucopia, the result of capitalism's ever advancing industrial age, spewed material possessions on larger and larger segments of the American population. This government-instigated distribution of capitalism's material things and riches (Fogel calls this the "welfare state") brought with it changing social values. Perhaps the most radical change in social values, he implies, was that the members of the burgeoning middle class expected, as if it was their birthright, to participate as equals in the nation's increasing prosperity.

This Great Awakening culminated in the civil rights movement. These were intense decades, Fogel admits, in which the previously disenfranchised classes and genders (blacks, for example, and women) demanded to be treated by capitalists as if they were the middle class. They wanted a share of capitalism's riches. Foremost in this was blacks' demand that they share in the social and economic benefits only education could bring. What Fogel is telling us is that contemporary neoliberalism is hungering for a return to a nostalgic Victorian time past so that raw capitalism, unencumbered by bureaucracy and legislative mandates, can once again employ docile workers to make their dreams of uncontrolled profit come true.

Accepting his conclusion as descriptive of Victorianism, it is clear, even though he does not use the term, that Fogel is a neoliberal. He believes raw capitalism, morally free in a competitive world, spurning the mediocrity of others, is charged with reforming schools and society to mirror its own image.

VICTORIAN PSYCHOLOGY: INDIVIDUALISM

Fogel explains why neoliberals are motivated to reform schools in this problematic society. Dubbing it a "welfare state," it is as if individual expectations are lowered. He implies students are taught in their schools to become mediocre and await the benefits capitalists have created. This is the modern, liberal school—reflecting a welfare society, expecting students to graduate from grade to grade regardless of their efforts—that neoliberals criticize.

But neoliberals claim to think of their Victorian society in much broader terms than do liberals—as a society in which competing individuals replace or take upon themselves the functions of social institutions. Individuals, no longer mediocre or expecting rewards for work not done, become competitors in a society committed to the free-market economy. Just the opposite of the welfare state, Victorian society is rambunctious and combative. It is elitist and exclusive. Those who are not able, or cannot compete, give way to the truly free, creative individuals. In short, the free-market economy is the Victorian society. Its standard, drawn from its Protestant heritage, is economic. Victorianism is the capitalist creation of wealth. The creative life, for the Victorian, is service to profit and riches.

VICTORIAN LIFE: CHURCHILL AND BLUM

Sir Winston Churchill and Jerome Blum are important to us because they describe their conflicting impressions of the Victorian period. As they viewed that age, they considered classism, especially of the aristocracy, from different points of view.

Churchill, born in 1876 and having experienced its lived history, described Victorianism as commanding and global.

> The nineteenth century was a period of purposeful, progressive, enlightened, tolerant civilization. The stir in the world arising from the French Revolution, added to the Industrial Revolution unleashed by the steam-engine.
> . . . The aristocracy, who had guided for centuries the advance of Britain, was merged in the rising mass of the nation. . . . The United States . . . which knew no class distinctions, preserved the structure of society during the economic development of the American continent.[7]

Churchill understood that age because of his military experience in British colonies and political responsibilities in international affairs. It was natural for him to acknowledge the continuing evolution of England's elite simply because, as a member, he accepted its history. It is from that position he viewed the United States as a classless society, for he saw no landed gentry or educated elite. What he saw was a half-continent of limitless space, not the inequality of commoners.

Blum, on the other hand, examined Victorian classism from a much later period. To him, Victorianism, especially the American elite and English aristocracy, was not evolving within a social democracy as Churchill saw. It was only practicing the fine art of conserving the existing class structure.

> The elegance, the domination of political life, the deference shown by the rest of society, and above all, the supreme self-confidence of the English landed elite, made it the envy and the model for the nobility in the rest of Europe. They emulated the manners, dress, country mansions, gardens and deer parks of the English elite. The attachment of the English to tradition held a special appeal for the elites of other lands. No other people seemed to hold on to its past by so many ties.[8]

Born at the end of the Victorian era, the year before World War I erupted (1913), Blum pictured the Victorian elite as social parasites. They were evil and self-serving. The war and its aftermath of failed peace efforts confirmed for him the odious nature of that genteel class.

Yet, there are commonalities between Churchill and Blum. Both wrote about (and experienced, in the case of Churchill) the murky underside of classism. Each understood the intricate social ballet classism practiced with others as well as with those inside their social circle. Writing at different moments, they fathomed the intricacies of class boundaries between elitism and wealth. They knew Victorian classism could exist even in a minor way without wealth, but that wealth by itself could not be construed as an immediate entrée into the upper classes. Class manifestations in that era were seen by Churchill and Blum, including the public modeling of "civilized society," as a curriculum learned in British public schools. While the elite willingly sustained classism, even as they became irrelevant, what is important in our study of educational reform is for us to understand that neoliberals believe they are the new elite and are impervious to class irrelevance.

VICTORIAN CLASSISM AND THE SCHOLARSHIP OF MOB RULE

In his text *The Metaphysical Club: A Story of Ideas in America,* Louis Menand cites a time in this country, beginning with Oliver Wendell Holmes's Civil War experiences and ending nearly a century later with the death of Dewey, when new ideas and social realities threatened a dying Victorian ideology. This story, as he calls it, devotes its attention to Holmes and Dewey, along with William James and Charles S. Peirce. These four intellectual giants, each grappling with the emerging colossus called "science" and the social consequences of the Civil War, recognized that these dizzying changes created public bewilderment. In this work, Menand shows the reader how the four intellectuals developed new ways of thinking, brought about by science, so the public could understand their lives and social environment better. He does this by showing the reader the new ideas they forged in such disparate disciplines as jurisprudence, crowned by Holmes's theory of the "reasonable man," Dewey's premise of culture's impact on schools and curriculum, James's foundational ideas in psychology, and Peirce's founding of semiotics.

All of the ideas and events these scholars experienced in the twilight of the Victorian period Menand encapsulates in their sectarian veneration of democracy. Democracy meant something different to the four intellectuals than to their Victorian predecessors, who suspected it was just much ado about mob rule. Victorian society was like Peter Gay's description in which the staid bourgeois or "middling classes" acquiesced to social direction by the aristocratic authorities.[9] Unlike classism, either seen in Queen Victoria's image or as explained by Gay, democracy for the intellectuals in Menand's text was an ongoing process in which everyone, regardless of class, participated.

And Democracy, as they understood it, isn't just about letting the right people have their say; it's also about letting the wrong people have their say. It is about giving space to minority and dissenting views so that, at the end of the day, the interests of the majority may prevail. Democracy means that everyone is equally in the game, but it also means that no one can opt out.[10]

In fact, democracy was not a result of deliberations for these men; it was a platform upon which ideas were discussed and weighed. Simply, democracy for Holmes, Dewey, James, and Peirce was that it existed.

Yet, democracy could not rest on inclusivity's stage alone, for all citizens must share the responsibility to act. That is, Menand says, democracy is not just the responsibility of the *right kind* to speak; it is the responsibility of the *wrong kind* to speak as well. This is what James meant about democracy. Democracy is a marketplace of ideas that, regardless of their origin, must be debated. Simply said, democracy for Menand's heroes centered on the idea of leveling out society's playing fields so all could exercise their responsibility. For them, democracy was the antithesis of classism and ideology.

But democracy must be more than inclusivity's informal process. Democracy portrays society as a parliament in which everyone, including minorities, has opportunities to speak and trade ideas. Said another way, inclusivity's parliament is the arena in which the majority listens before it speaks. Even though the interests of the majority may prevail, says Menand, it is much more than that—it is that majority interest that emerges because of minority support. In this parliament, it is the majority that manages with the consent of the "loyal opposition."

This is what Menand means when he speaks of responsibility. Democracy is not a game among social classes in which only a few play, nor is it a capitalist reward for winners who want to remain in the game. Even though democracy cannot, regardless of social construction, exclude any, it must give all participants identical rules to guide them in the exercise of their responsibilities. Democracy is not about class, race, gender, sexual orientation, economic advantage, or any other artificial barrier intended to disenfranchise "others" from society's parliament.

Victorian Model, Part One: Playing on Classism's Playing Field

Imagining themselves to be Victorians, neoliberals are loath to interact with others outside their class. They idolize the exclusiveness of privacy in the Victorian sense in which individuals and families are respected. Their heroes are not those who create the pandemonium of classless disharmony. Their male hero is that individual who controls his own life and family and creates his own success. In the neoliberal mind, heroines are those who mirror the Victorian wife Gay talks about. She is married to the hero and sets her life course casting about for both his and her success. She supports and encourages her husband and has domestic responsibilities. They become, as it were, using Southern Baptist terminology, a union in which she is submissive.

Democracy, as described by Holmes and Dewey, is antithetical to their class society. It is the family, living in private as they did in Victorian times, say neoliberals, not the liberal parliament hosting minorities, that is society's core. In fact, the family is the neoliberal vehicle upon which classism and social exclusion exists. It is the family, living in gated communities, in houses architecturally bespeaking Victorian curb appeal, that is important. Shopping in upscale malls, attending neighborhood mega-churches, and sending their children to private schools (of which we will speak next), all separate them from the lower classes, just as it did for their Victorian models a century ago.

Democracy is an awkward social structure for neoliberals. To them, it is based on cooperation, not individualism or classism. Its insistence on blurring social division and glorifying multiculturalism permeates American society. It is, they say, almost socialistic and certainly irreligious in its values. Democracy propagates the welfare state. It supports the mediocre who are interested in living off the earnings of others. Simply, neoliberalism is antagonistic to a democracy that does not require social separation between the individualism of the few and the mediocrity of the many.

Does this mean neoliberals want to withdraw from this democratic society? Not really. Neoliberals are more interested in reforming present-day democracy to reflect their classism. They want the multicultural "others" to learn which class in their capitalist society will be their permanent home. Just as the theological neoliberals we discussed in chapter 7 proclaimed their mission to improve society for the coming of their God, so capitalist neoliberals proclaim their mission to reform education to welcome Victorian classism.

Victorian Model, Part Two: Schools for Boys

These are the reasons neoliberals want to reform public education. While present-day public schools are grounded on citizenship—that is, citizens participating in a community—neoliberal schools are predicated on classism and social separation. As neoliberals campaign for educational reforms, this is the model they see in their mind's eye. They are intellectually and socially comfortable with Victorian education because it focused its broad purposes on Protestant moralism, religious instruction, and classical Greek (today, meaning academic) education. Plainly, the Victorian school exemplified European values, morals, and academic rigor, which the Victorians would consider the hallmarks upon which reasoning is based, and neoliberals would agree.

But Victorian schools did not treat all students equally. Even within social classes there was separation, so curriculum purposes differed. For Victorians, what you learned was based not so much on who you were but on what you were. Not surprisingly, their schools shunned nonwhites and were segregated by gender.

Victorian schools for boys were harsh and academic. Focusing on European classics (subjects we would today refer to as literature, grammar, history, science, mathematics, foreign languages, physical education, and science), school curricula concentrated on Protestant morality. Studying (and memorizing) verses and books of the Bible was the first essential in young students' academic lives. They pored over New Testament books that taught the Protestant theology of meekness (meaning classism, depending on the school in which the student was enrolled). In the United States, but also in England, students learned to respect the important theological hatreds between Protestants and Catholics.[11]

School curricula, as Gay mentions, were heavily gendered—that is, they were masculine. Boys, especially those who represented the upper reaches of society, quickly learned that the fundamental difference between boys and girls was they were decision makers and girls were not. Even grown women, including their mothers, they quickly learned, approached life and their social environment in a childlike, "feather-headed" fashion. To solve this social problematic, Victorian schools taught boys that, as men, their social role was to help women in the same way they would help younger children. In some schools, for example, male students learned how to make genteel conversation with girls, dance, and maintain a tightlipped courtesy. Novels written by then popular authors such as Sir Walter Scott were avidly read by students, Gay points out, as they learned more about chivalry and gallantry. Students learned morals from popular textbooks such as *McGuffy's Reader*. This elementary school text, suffering through enumerable printings, helped boys and, in some cases girls, learn what was moral and right-minded social behavior. This was realized through stories, pictures, and poems, in many ways a literary first in interactive learning.

The curriculum was masculine in another way. Pupils became acquainted with "great man" theories. They learned about masculinity through history, literature, mathematics, and the sciences. In England, for example, the curriculum highlighted literary figures such as Shakespeare; in the United States, the political correctness of Washington. In both countries, Victorian schools accomplished their missions—students learned about elite males and assumed others such as laborers did not exist, even though they were expected to be economically ever present. Expectedly, Victorian education's success was demonstrated when students knew more about great men than those others who worked in their homes, factories, and farms.

Victorian school culture, especially that reserved for boys, was based on physical and mental abuse. Boys were stereotyped by their teachers as physical and lazy and therefore were routinely beaten and whipped into submission. What good Victorian teacher did not know that students, fearing the strap, cane, or whip, would be motivated to behave properly if punishment was irregular, erratic, and unpredictable? Defensive and ever on their guard, students continually worried how their actions would be interpreted by the teacher. Yet, parents and their children accepted this abuse. To them it was normal for teachers to make children cry and, worse, hurt. Victorian teachers were expected to spank small boys, cane them in middle grades, and whip them in secondary schools.

Let us picture what spanking was like in Victorian classrooms so we are more able to understand neoliberal criticisms about lack of discipline in present-day schools.[12] Churchill's letters to his mother from boarding school unwittingly described the almost sexual gratification his teachers exhibited as they caned him for lisping, a speech disorder he never overcame. Teachers, including Churchill's, "walked the aisles," fondling their switches, paddles, canes, and leather straps as if they were military batons.[13]

Victorian abuse, disguised as discipline, not only formalized children's relations with teachers but also created social separation from their parents. Losing day-to-day connections with them, children treated their mothers and fathers as respected adults deserving of admiration. Even so, social separation was handled differently depending on the social class and country in which students lived. In England, and in some other European countries, social separation was accomplished through the boarding school system. Separation of boys from their mothers and fathers (mostly mothers) was touted as the essential first step in education. Removed from the culture and confines of the home and now able to concentrate on their studies, some learned how to be self-reliant, that is, to become masculine. Even if schooling meant an education outside the boarding school system, as sometimes was the case in the United States, separation for some children meant they had fewer opportunities of protecting themselves from abusive teachers and older students—they had no one to talk to.

Victorian schools were private. Parents assumed they would purchase their children's schooling. Given these choices, parents competed with their neighbors for their children's placement in the school of their choice. Lord Randolph Churchill, Winston's father, never once thinking of sending his son to a publicly supported school, wrote how he was plagued with Winston's limited academic ability as he was expelled from one school after another.[14] Yet, Victorian schools gave boys understandings of social class. Undoubtedly, many as they grew to adulthood thought of their school experience as a rite of passage. It became a benchmark upon which life's later experiences could be measured.

Victorian Model, Part Three: Schools for Girls

Although Victorian schools were masculine, that did not mean Victorian girls were without educational experiences. But recalling those days, it is easy, even now, to grasp the classism and gender those schools and classrooms represented. It is that curriculum of division and separation today's neoliberals are anxious to reinstate in present-day schools. The segmentation of society, to them—regardless of whether it is based on race, economics, gender, religion, or any other combination—gives individuals greater opportunities to live apart from others they claim are different.

Accordingly, the issue of Victorian women's education did not rest on whether they should be taught the same curriculum as their brothers. Instead, it was whether girls' education should focus on the same social aims. Did this mean that men's education was poor? No. In fact, their education was much the opposite. It taught boys the operational processes of classism, created in them attitudes of masculine leadership, and organized their thinking abilities based on a classic Greek curriculum. In some instances, the education of boys and girls in that neoliberal time past had the same goals. Broadly, schools' aims were to produce the same quality representatives of both genders. That is, just as boys' education was intended to create masculine leadership, girls' was intended to create female followership.

For girls, then, learning in their schools was not masked in violence, and teachers were less likely to "walk the aisles" carrying straps and canes as symbols of authority. Even so, their education was not sedate. Attending private schools, usually owned and operated by women, or less expensive publicly supported elementary schools, girls quickly came to terms with society's expectations of their gender.

Their curriculum was not a repeat of their brothers. However, it was expected they know their three R's. Beyond this, girls were taught the genteel art of womanhood. In elite private schools, girls learned how to be social ornaments, that is, to be childlike and inconspicuous. They were taught to be unobtrusive in their married lives and to be their husbands' helpmates. They even learned how to entertain their husbands' guests. For example, what wife would want to embarrass her husband in front of his friends by setting a poor table, being a poor housekeeper, or being unable to take part, in a minor way, in the male-dominated conversation? Aside from this they were taught to be demanding enough to take on the business of home management—that is, the enterprise of hiring, firing, and training servants. Indeed, for many girls, this curriculum taught them to respect homemaking.[15]

While the aim of Victorian women's schooling was to "please themselves as they pleased others," it is important for us to realize their schooling was much more responsive to the marketplace than the men's. While women, especially those in the laboring classes, found themselves trapped in home-bound activities, including midwifery, they found newly organized public elementary schools responsive to their out-of-home needs. These schools, especially in the United States, were the material results of hurried capitalist responses to economic problems caused by changing labor needs and increasingly competitive markets. Bluntly, the American factory system, like that in Europe, was becoming more complex as manufacturing became more complicated.

We must remember that it was not the capitalists who were altruistic in wanting to support women's education. Rather, factory owners stereotyped women in somewhat the same manner as they classified the ever increasing numbers of immigrant children flooding the city's slums: Both—the women and children—were ignorant and worked for cheap wages. In fact, it was of little concern to capitalists if the new publicly funded schools educated both lower-class boys and girls together. Of course, lower-class men, not women, would be hired first for factory floor positions. But girls would be hired by factory owners for specialty jobs such as seamstresses. These jobs required small, delicate hands, something laboring class men did not possess, capitalists thought.

As the Industrial Revolution continued in the last decades of the nineteenth century, it became apparent that men, in their quest for greater employment opportunities, would eventually capture many traditional economic roles reserved for women. Even so, there was still room for women in the labor force. For those with elementary schooling and a willingness to work outside the home, male stereotyping permitted them to compete for some semiskilled factory positions, such as cigar and cigarette making. In fact, these particular occupations were considered acceptable, or even attractive, by Victorian society.[16] But semiskilled jobs such as these were also economic interims. As soon as technology created cigar- and cigarette-making machines, the women lost their jobs.

There were other jobs, too, newly created by the Industrial Revolution, that attracted the educated young woman. With the growth of department stores, with its bolts of cloth and ready-made clothes and home appliances, women found clerical positions within the retail trade. At the same time, it was the loss of family roles such as medicine and midwifery that symbolized women's continued followership role. Once the dispenser of her family's medical needs, women nurses became assistants to male doctors, who supplied much the same treatment to families—except, this time, outside the home. Capitalists themselves created some new jobs for women. With the invention of the typewriter, women assumed traditional masculine business roles such as secretaries, stenographers, and clerks. Preparing themselves in private vocational programs run by other women or some public schools, girls entered business offices knowledgeable in the Dvorak typewriting method and Gregg shorthand.[17]

I do not want to create the impression that all Victorian women, regardless of social class, were interested in leaving home for work in capitalist offices and factories. That was not the case, perhaps mostly because the home still required its own laborious upkeep, even to the extent of employing other young women to take on the supplemental chores performed by chambermaids and nannies. However, many wives, in all but the lower classes, found it difficult to accept their husbands' stereotyping, especially if they knew they were the more intelligent of the two. At any rate, domestic labor was still thought of as a female activity. Gay, for example, mentions that some married men, even those who had lost their jobs, continued to express stereotypes that their wives' role should be in the home. He points out that they believed these gender codes so strongly, they were unwilling to allow their wives and daughters to join the job market even if the wages they earned could save the family from financial ruin.[18] Notwithstanding these male stereotypes, it is the relationship between women's schooling and labor that belies neoliberal nostalgic placement of Victorian women solely within the confines of the home.

The out-of-home role, and its attendant education, that befitted women the most during this nostalgic period was the job of teacher. The majority of teachers in the United States continued to be men until the national economy made them too expensive for school districts to employ. At the same time, responding to factory owners' demand that laborers have an expanded education, many public schools increased the number of school days in their academic calendar.[19] Unable to increase teacher salaries, districts began employing more women, who were willing to work the extra days without additional financial compensation.[20]

To the Victorian masculine mind, women were ideal teachers. They were, as they were expected to be in this class society, delicate and noncreative. Like lower-class laborers, women teachers were supposed to be docile and submit to male supervision. In fact, as described in the previous chapter, industrialists—like today's neoliberals—viewed them as workers laboring in the academic factory. It is this type of training neoliberals want teachers to have.

Teachers were trained in schools sometimes called "normal schools."[21] They were really nothing more than extensions of the primary or elementary curricula taught to young male and female students.[22] The goal of the normal school's mostly male instructors, many of whom had both classroom and administrative experience, was to teach the rudiments of "teacher work." For example, concentrating on the attributes of good teachers, Grace Faxon, in her text *Practical Selections*, described good teachers as those who know they should not ask for their supervisors' approval for teaching good students, for they learn by themselves.[23] It is those less able to learn, she says, on whom teachers should concentrate. How is this done? Faxon is clear.

Teachers must demonstrate a moral force in the classroom. Their carriage should create among the students that feeling she and they are on a great mission. Students should witness her "moral power of leadership" and accept the teacher's demand that school work be done. Faxon says the results of moral leadership are seen in parental acceptance of the teacher in the classroom and student submission to her classroom management style. Good teachers, says Faxon, are those who learn to control themselves first before they control others.

Nonetheless, it was the "practice school" that offered "practice teachers," that is, normal school graduates, the real teacher work.[24] Teachers' work was much different than that which normal school students learned from their instructors. Controlling students only a few years younger than she, using different teaching methods than Faxon's text discussed, and learning subjects she had not taken in primary school so she could teach the lesson the next day helped a teacher understand the complexity of the classroom. All the while the practicing teacher knew her supervisors were evaluating her on her writing and printing skills, the neatness of her lesson and plan books, the accuracy of her attendance register, and classroom cleanliness. She knew she would be evaluated as doing a poor job if her students did not sit upright in their desks and did not remain busy and silent. Her classroom climate was expected to be strict, unbending, and absolute. These were the important issues beginning teachers learned because this was how they demonstrated their willingness to be exact, neat, and docile. Teaching was hard work.

Victorian Model, Part Four: Schools for Capitalists

Now that we have examined some types of Victorian schools, the question remains: what did neoliberals find so wanting in mid-twentieth-century America that they were willing to overlook their schools in favor of Victorian education? Of course, as we have mentioned earlier, the Victorian period represents to them the last time when American society came to terms with unregulated capitalism as an economic and political reality.[25] Because of this, it is impossible for neoliberals to have allowed themselves to search for schools in more recent times. Certainly, that could not happen in the last century when capitalism and individualism, they believed, were lost to what they called "welfarism" and "multiculturalism." These are the polluted years, unacceptable to neoliberals, in which schools fostered mediocrity in a licentious, liberal society.

The Victorian era is a capstone period for neoliberals. This is the time, they contend, the debates between capitalism and society were resolved. Broadly, these debates centered around economics, education, and classism or the individual's place in the community. In 1776, the same year the Declaration of Independence was signed, Adam Smith postulated in his text *The*

Wealth of Nations that national wealth no longer could be dependent on government agricultural policies.[26] Now, he said, anticipating the Industrial Revolution, wealth must be created in the private sector.

In rudimentary language, what Smith meant by "wealth creation" was that economic intercourse called "supply and demand." That is, the secret to his proposition rested on the fulcrum of production cost versus the product's perceived worth. In a capitalist society, thought Smith, the price (agreed on by the buyer and seller) could also be resolved by manufacturers, who would compete for the greatest market share by maintaining the lowest possible production costs. While economists even in the Victorian period agreed with Smith, many felt capitalism could exist only in a utopia. For example, Thomas Malthus feared uncontrolled population expansion would forever doom the poor from appreciating capitalism's promise of prosperity. David Ricardo, on the other hand, believed capitalism would cause extraordinary social upheavals especially aimed at the landed gentry.

Smith, Malthus, and Ricardo, among others, all agreed that schools were of critical importance in a capitalist society (although none discussed a curriculum in any detail). It is Smith who argued best for education. Said he, the problem with factory work is that laborers will find it tedious. Over time, he said, laborers will become sluggish and mentally dull. Of course, labor tasks can be taught to workers by factory owners, he said, but schools should teach them citizenship. In this case, Smith's citizenship curriculum was an education that would stretch workers' imaginations and challenge their intellectual abilities. They should, he thought, have something to think about while they work. This is the positive relationship between schools and factories, says Smith. It potentially improves production at no cost to the factory owner.

Karl Marx was suspicious of capitalists who touted social benefits for laborers. Writing in the mid-nineteenth century, aware of European worker revolutions on the Continent, Marx wrote against the tumultuous backdrop of classism, capitalism, and rising middle-class managerialism. Focusing on capitalist–worker relations and production costs, Marx expressed a deeply held worry that factory owners were purposely creating conditions in which laborers would eventually be forced to compete with each other for lower-paying jobs. Using the term *specialization*, Marx pointed out that capitalists were restructuring production work into a series of small menial tasks, allowing them to employ cheaper workers and more unskilled labor (children and women) than skilled. It was these management techniques, Marx said, that focused on classism, forcing workers to accept lower wages, even as they grudgingly competed with their coworkers for needed jobs. From this, Marx concluded that classism was the platform capitalism required, not worker education, if it was to succeed. Classism was the capitalists' whip, gaining them their riches from the sweat of labor's brow.

It is somewhat surprising to some today that Marx and Smith were in broad agreement on schools' purposes, although they came to those conclusions from opposite positions. As we mentioned, Smith theorized schooling was a welcome activity for laborers to counter the factory floor's dulling effect; that is, he was thoughtful about the relationship of production to education. Marx, almost a century later, accepted Smith's thoughts about the dulling effect of factory work but viewed education as part of people's private domain, trusting their lives would improve. Marx did not care if the schools helped the factory owners; he was more interested that workers' lives improve.

But Marx was more cynical about schools than Smith. Smith's original thoughts, voiced in the late eighteenth century, were that public funding for schools would logically increase, reflecting capitalism's prosperity. Not so, said Marx. Capitalists' penchant to compete among themselves in the marketplace would dull their interest in schools. Beyond all this, Marx claimed, job specialization would always keep laborers poor. Undoubtedly, the young Victorian women we watched become teachers in the last section would not have judged Marx's presentation as cynical, even though their schooling had not taught them his name.

It is this argument, which Marx lost, that so pleases today's neoliberals. Regardless of Smith's hopes that publicly funded schools would teach laborers, what cheers the neoliberals is that Marx's fear of laborers always remaining poor proved to be true. Now we learn the last reason why neoliberals want to recreate Victorian schools: Their schools separate society not only by class and gender but also by wealth.

NEOLIBERALISM'S CLASSISM AND DEMOCRACY'S LIBERTY

John Winthrop, the appointed governor of the Massachusetts Bay Colony, gave perhaps one of the greatest speeches in American history, of less than two minutes' length, to his fellow colonists aboard the *Arbella* sometime after their March 1630 departure for Salem, Massachusetts. Even though his speech was heavily laced with obligatory Protestant theological terms common to the seventeenth century, it was clear the governor was expressing his deeply held religious convictions. Yet, he spoke of the society, a utopia, he wanted built.

> . . . that men shall say of succeeding plantations: "the lord make it like that of New England." For wee must Consider that wee shall be as a Citty upon a Hill. The eies of all people are uppon us. . . . Wee shall be made a story and a by-word through the world.[27]

To make his dream come true, Winthrop admonished his listeners to bond into a community. He said to them, "Wee must be knitt together in this worke as one man," and fearing they might drift from the community in off-hours, he told them, "Wee must entertaine each other in brotherly Affection."

What Winthrop was telling his shipmates was their lives were to ever be tied together into a community as if they had become a single person. To make his point, Winthrop continued his admonitions, telling them they would learn to rejoice, mourn, labor, and suffer as a community, not as individuals. No one should think he or she will be independent of the community, he told them, for its success had to be the creation of all of them. So complete was his thinking in this, even referring to the rudimentary colonial economics he expected of his colony, that he asked the membership to "abridge ourselves of our superfluities, for the supply of others necessities."

Winthrop gives us another picture of Protestantism not promoted by neoliberals. It is not an articulation of Martin Luther's theology, they say. Winthrop voices a Protestantism of shared community participation. Obviously arrogant and captured in his own classism, Winthrop sees beyond this as he voices his dream he called a "Citty upon a Hill." But, we must not be fooled into thinking he voiced those views because of the absence of capitalist economic philosophy, which was then developing but would blossom in the next century. We know he understood the relationship of government, investment, and profit, for the colony he was founding was part of that. Importantly, what we understand most from Winthrop was he had a clear idea of freedom—that is what he meant when he used the word "liberty."

Yet, liberty, or freedom, is an ambiguous concept. It was another fifteen years before Winthrop explicitly defined it. In 1645, now deputy-governor of Massachusetts and acquitted in his impeachment for interfering in the colony's judicial system, Winthrop spoke his mind about liberty best in his "little speech."[28] In his address, Winthrop quickly notes that the definition of freedom is not universal. He alludes to two types for freedoms: one he called "natural," and a second he called "civil" or "federal." Natural liberty, he said, is that freedom which allows people to do evil. It is unrestrained freedom, in which individuals are free to connive, to do as they choose to whomever they wish. It is that liberty, Winthrop says, that allows people to do immoral and shameful acts. It is what we today might call "licentious." This is the type of liberty that runs rampant through society, Winthrop says, because society has not developed authorities to curtail it. Evil liberty is the enemy of truth and peace.

The second form of liberty, says Winthrop, is good. It is that moral liberty that exists in society through political covenants and social agreements. In fact, says Winthrop, moral freedom is the base upon which authority exists and society cannot live without.

Anticipating Dewey's concept of the Common Man centuries later, Winthrop goes on to discuss democracy. Pointing to the election of public officials (magistrates), Winthrop asserts that these authorities should be chosen from the people they represent so that when they make mistakes or exhibit their own personal peccadilloes, they will be understood by those who understand their own innermost feelings. This is the agreement between government and the governed, intimates Winthrop. The electorate is to exercise tolerance and the elected are to remain faithful to them.

Classism and Liberties, Part One: Winthrop and Dewey

Dewey had undoubtedly read Winthrop's little speech. It is as if both of them, never knowing neoliberalism's words and speaking centuries apart to different audiences for different reasons, were like attorneys-at-law, partnered in prosecuting evil. They anticipated neoliberalism's fateful flaws. It was not so much about democracy they spoke, for Winthrop lived only for his utopia—their mutual interest remained liberty's prosecution of neoliberalism. They said in their different ways that liberty or freedom cannot be experienced by those living beyond the bounds of community. Liberty is not the experience of the prisoner living in a cell, for its absence is the vacuum that represents the lost treasure of freedom. Using Winthrop's concept, good liberty is the community's wealth. Good liberty exists through its shared experience.

But it is the other liberty that neoliberals possess, the evil liberty that Winthrop spoke about in his speech. Evil liberty is that unrestrained relationship individuals have with each other—the result of their uncontrolled, unregulated power over others. Evil liberty is, in a much broader sense, that license coveted by dictatorial social classes empowering them to seize others' freedom. Neoliberals' evil freedom is based on their exclusion of others they label mediocre. But, evil liberty's seizure and exclusiveness should not be competition's product. Competition is a community experience in which all, regardless of their personal histories, participate freely and openly. Competition is not the raw economics of a free-market economy; it is the marketing of ideas in the social marketplace, as Holmes said. It is the business of life in which individuals construct covenants with each other. These agreements, as Winthrop mentioned in his 1645 speech, are but demonstrations of good liberty that civil societies experience. Good liberty is federal in its conduct with elected officials, Winthrop reminds us. It is not the dictatorship of one in a society of one. Liberty is tolerance.

Classism and Liberties, Part Two: Schools and Tolerance

Even though Winthrop and Dewey were products of their own times, viewing schools and education through different social prisms, they widely agreed on schools' overarching purpose of permitting older generations to communicate with the younger. The act of learning was different for each, however. For Winthrop, learning was almost oral—memorizing, reciting, and repeating. Dewey considered these learning styles archaic. He wanted his students to learn the scientific method, the process of asking questions and searching for answers. Winthrop and Dewey were also different in what should be taught in their schools. While Dewey wanted students to learn how to learn, Winthrop wanted his students to learn his Protestant Bible's utopian truths. But, most important, they agreed that experience was the critical part of the students' education. They wanted them to understand, and perhaps even create, their own life experiences so their lived existence would become more meaningful.

It was liberty, society's linchpin, they heralded as their shared faith. Winthrop's faith, absorbed in his utopia, thought good liberty—that relationship between the elected and the electors—was fragile and had to be experienced by students. Otherwise, he thought evil liberty would destroy his utopia. Confirming Winthrop, Dewey authenticated his faith, admonishing those who judge to look first into themselves. With this, he states his faith in the Common Man, that generalization in which individuals, representing society's cultural milieu, become the nucleus of a strong democracy. Said simply, liberty for Winthrop and Dewey was the platform upon which peoples practice tolerance.

It is Winthrop's and Dewey's utopian and scholarly faiths, their declaration of tolerance, that addresses education reform, neoliberalism's Achilles' heel. Nostalgic for the social and economic advantages only Victorian exclusiveness can bring, neoliberals unhesitatingly embrace classism, with its twin demands of social fundamentalism and raw capitalism. It is this motivation neoliberals attend to when they aggressively attempt to reform schools to mirror those Victorian monuments.

Yet, Dewey and Winthrop speak of other times neoliberals hesitate to recall. These are the times when peoples fought for freedom and when elite classes, in their efforts to maintain their own economic power, found liberalism's refreshing winds menacing. In America, and later in Europe, it was that period when classism was forced to experience its own stilted sameness. In part, it was these revolutions that gave birth to and later abandoned Victorian classism. This is what Dewey was talking about when he reflected on the passive education he received in his youth and the "new education" he proposed.

During these reforms and revolutions, the term *liberalism* meant "tolerance," the practiced gestalt different classes experienced as they joined together in communities of their own choosing. Neoliberals also recall the dissonance of those periods. It was when schools stopped mimicking classism in favor of the tolerance mirrored in Dewey's democracy and of which Winthrop spoke.

In the final chapter, we will investigate the future of educational reform in a global context as neoliberal ideologies confront new realities.

NOTES

1. Kevin Phillips, *Wealth and Democracy: A Political History of the American Rich* (New York: Broadway Books, 2002), 405.

2. Boym mentions that true exiles blame only themselves for their failures. See Svetlana Boym, *The Future of Nostalgia* (New York: Basic Books, 2001), 337–44.

3. Robert William Fogel, *The Fourth Great Awakening and the Future of Egalitarianism* (Chicago: University of Chicago Press, 2000).

4. This is the period of the Supreme Court's *Plessy v. Ferguson* (1896) decision that reaffirmed segregation. *Plessy v. Ferguson* was overturned on May 17, 1954. In this case, the question revolved around the constitutional issue of black and white students attending the same schools.

5. Fogel, *The Fourth Great Awakening*, 1.

6. Fogel's thoughts center on Protestantism and evangelism (he refers to these as "enthusiastic"). He also implies that other religious belief systems such as Judaism played little or no role in social reconstruction.

7. Winston S. Churchill, *A History of the English-Speaking Peoples* (New York: Dodd, Mead, 1958), 4:viii.

8. Jerome Blum, *In the Beginning: The Advent of the Modern Age; Europe in the 1840s* (New York: Charles Scribner's Sons, 1994), 173.

9. Peter Gay, *Schnitzler's Century: The Making of Middle-Class Culture, 1815–1914* (New York: Norton, 2002). Gay follows the life of Arthur Schnitzler, a Viennese playwright (1862–1931) whose life ran the gamut in that city's aristocratic and petty bourgeois social circles. Gay is quick to point out that even though this group of Victorians appeared very diverse, they recognized they lived in a class society and wanted to better themselves in it. Changing the system did not seem to be their priority.

10. Louis Menand, *The Metaphysical Club: A Story of Ideas in America* (New York: Farrar, Straus and Giroux, 2001), 440–41.

11. In the United States, for example, anti-Catholicism was so well ingrained in the Protestant curriculum that Catholics were forced to develop their own private school system. Protestants built theirs at public expense, using tax monies contributed by all, including Catholics.

12. Spanking is outlawed in some states in the United States. In others, especially in the South, spanking is still considered an appropriate form of discipline; however, legislation in many states discourage its use. At the time of this writing, corporal punishment in school is still considered legal by the Supreme Court.

13. As noted in chapter 3, many formal school teachers in developing countries mimic this disciplinary tactic. They assume European discipline, unlike the traditional discipline of the village, must be harsh so that children will learn the culture of the factory floor.

14. Churchill's school days, as he described them in his letters home, paint a horrible picture. Although we want to think our classrooms are more humane in this

century, Winston's life, like some students' lives today, was focused on pleading for parental help. No one, not even his mother, whom he dearly loved, understood his difference was because of his extraordinary capacities. His teachers found him an impossible dullard and not the genius he was. Winston Churchill, *My Early Life: 1874–1904* (New York: Scribner, 1996).

15. Some of the most impressive women educators in the United States during that period were Emma Willard and Catharine Beecher, Henry Ward Beecher's sister. Beecher is remembered for her founding of a "Female Seminary" at Hartford, Connecticut, in 1828, but it was left to Mary Lyons to found Mount Holyoke at South Hadley, Massachusetts, a seminary that she said would rival Harvard. It does.

16. For example, Georges Bizet's female lead Carmen, in the opera of the same name, portrays a sensual woman who exhibits all the masculine characteristics attributed to Victorian men. In contrast, Don José, her lover, is portrayed as weaker even though he is a matador. Jacob Riis, by contrast, in his *How the Other Half Lives: Studies among the Tenements of New York* (New York: Charles Scribner's Sons, 1890) showed women cigarette makers' vulnerabilities in New York City.

17. These courses became the bulwark of new secondary school vocational programs in the United States. They taught young women the elements of office administration: typewriting, shorthand, and bookkeeping.

18. Gay, *Schnitzler's Century*, 206.

19. The number of days that constituted the school year in this period ranged from 140 to 160. Its variability was based on such factors as the school district's financial health, the community's economic base, geography, and teacher supply. Eventually, states settled on 175 days in a school year—a standard most states continue to use in the twenty-first century.

20. The public school year, especially in the United States, was structured to meet the needs of an agricultural society. Agrarian societies traditionally did not allow women to work outside the home—and inside house cleaning was not considered work—unless the household had servants, and then it was accepted. As the United States and Europe industrialized, women were allowed out of the home to be secretaries, nurses, teachers, and so forth, but their pay in those jobs was very low. In those positions, if a married woman became pregnant, she was fired. With the influx of women teachers, men who were teachers moved from the elementary schools to high school—which required some higher education. Today, 87 percent of all teachers are women (whose pay is extraordinarily low). Men fill most administrator positions, whose pay is greater (for example, in Oklahoma a beginning teacher's salary is approximately $29,000, while a superintendent's salary in a middle-income community is about $50,000–$80,000).

21. "Normal school" meant a school that taught students to reach a particular academic standard (norm).

22. Normal schools traditionally accepted both boys and girls. They had to have a primary education, and girls were expected to be 16 years old and boys 17 years old when they applied. See Adolphe E. Meyer, *An Educational History of the American People*, 2nd ed. (New York: McGraw-Hill, 1967), 378–79. While he gives no reason for the age differential, Meyer is clear in his research that boys traditionally dropped out of teaching in the early months of instruction, while girls usually remained.

23. Grace B. Faxon, *Practical Selections from Twenty Years of Normal Instructor and Primary Plans* (Dansville, NY: F. A. Owen, 1912), 11, 13, 15–16, 20.

24. "Practice schools" were usually publicly funded monitorial schools. Practice students taught with the supervision of a classroom teacher and supervised by the principal. Eventually, normal schools opened their own practice schools so their instructors could supervise their students. Dewey used this idea to test some of his educational theories while at the University of Chicago in the early years of the twentieth century. He called his school a "laboratory."

25. Gay (*Schnitzler's Century*, 253–79) implies that the Victorian social controversy about privacy was as much discussed as individualism is discussed today. He tells us that privacy is the mark from which people saw themselves less as members of a community and more as individuals, an important element in neoliberal discussions of contemporary American society.

26. Adam Smith, *An Inquiry into the Nature and Causes of the Wealth of Nations*, 3 vols. (Dublin: Whitestone, 1776). Smith's text is a classic. Writing with passion, he believed he lived at a critical time in history. There are many reprints and secondary sources available; however, readers may enjoy Smith's original.

27. John Winthrop, "A Modell of Christian Charity," sermon written aboard the ship *Arbella* en route from England to New England, March 1630. Available at history.hanover.edu/texts/winthmod.html.

28. John Winthrop, "On Liberty," 1645. Better known as Winthrop's "little speech," it was twice as long as his "City upon a Hill" sermon delivered aboard the *Arbella*. In some ways, this speech is his most famous, for in it he speaks directly in defense of liberty. Available at www.constitution.org/bcp/winthlib.htm.

10

Consequences and Quagmires: Combating Neoliberalism's Reform of America's Schools

The previous chapters illustrated neoliberals' complex relationship with schools in this country and elsewhere and how that relationship fueled their motivation for educational reform. Almost psychotic about the tenor of contemporary society, and unable to construct a vision of a future world without a free-market economy, neoliberals searched for a tension-free time past. We identified their nirvana in chapter 9 as being the Victorian period. But because of this embrace of Adam Smith's capitalism, neoliberals faced a dilemma. Smith's fundamentalist theories rested as much on contemporary educational philosophy as on economics. As a consequence, neoliberals relied on and advanced Victorian philosophies of classism, gender, and education to reform contemporary schools.

Stepping further into the quagmire, neoliberals also discovered that their model Victorian schools were different from contemporary American and indigenous schools. While Victorian schools had overt relations with churches and tentative relations with economics—that is, lower-class men and women's education was labor sensitive—their relations with government remained inconsequential until factories needed an educated workforce. That is, their relationship with government was based on economic, not social, priorities. To remedy this, neoliberals chose to advance capitalist principles in the late twentieth century, supporting school privatization in Europe and America while advancing formalistic curricula extolling labor in developing nations. Together, these views fit well within neoliberals' sweeping school reform efforts. Globally, they want to reform schools to comply with their ideologies rather than societies' realities. That is, the indigenous youths we discussed in chapters 5 and 6 were educated to be part of a competitive global labor force.

Meanwhile, in dominant countries, especially the United States, those same indigenous people, now referred to as "undesirables" or the "mediocre," were forced into social underclasses and confined in economic ghettos. The consequence of these capitalist policies resulted, some neoliberals thought, in totally new and different social and economic relations between dominant and indigenous societies. In truth, it was nothing more than neoliberalism's re-creation of a Victorian world in which their economic philosophies ruled. It was part of globalization's scaffolding.

For many neoliberals, Victorianism, with its mantra of free trade, was a perfect stage upon which to build a free-market economy. Colonialism's managerial experiences, as we pointed out in chapter 2, gave Victorians experiences with different cultural and social organizations and economic philosophies and enterprises. But, it was in the Victorians' management of indigenous societies that neoliberals saw schools as enterprises that could partner with investors to create profits. They even witnessed the power of the Protestant missionary schools teaching indigenous students how to be good workers and helping them to disengage from their birth culture. This curriculum of deculturalization, later to be applied to those students they labeled mediocre in the United States, was instituted through formalistic teaching methods that culminated in high-stakes testing.

Nevertheless, neoliberalism's worry was socialism—or at least that is what they called it, when it was really only Karl Marx's plea for workers to protect themselves from Victorian capitalist labor policies. Disagreeing with Adam Smith, especially about education, Marx believed his trickle-down economic theories would not work as public school funding policies. Even though both were interested in schools, as mentioned in the previous chapter, education was to be the sole property of labor, according to Marx, not a taxpayer-paid extension of capitalism's labor quality control policies.

But, as we know, Marx would not win this argument. Others—that is, the undesirables and the mediocre—couched their educational philosophies in noneconomic terms. Even so, neoliberals were fearful these ideas would run counter to Victorian classism and the free-market economy. For example, in the new Soviet Union, Anatoli Lunacharsky's approval of John Dewey's explanation of the scientific method, followed by Anton Makarenko's "Soviet Man" frightened neoliberals. They saw these philosophies supporting labor, not capitalism.

Still, it was Dewey in the United States they dreaded most. Neoliberals believed his thoughts could spark a class war between capitalists and labor, with schools as the battleground. The last century's emotional panic, now seen as socially destructive even by neoliberals, included attacks against the educational philosophies of such respected international figures as Tanzania's Julius Nyerere. The neoliberals believed Nyerere's "rural socialism" was his hidden economic agenda to enhance indigenous labor. So too did capitalists view Mahatma Gandhi's *Satyagraha*. His effort to combat Victorian classism was couched in the curriculum of literacy. Learning about dead white heroes was not a person's end-all, Gandhi said. Capitalists were appalled. Gandhi's philosophy called for schools to teach eternity's unconditional love rather than factories' rules of work.

Neoliberal interpretations of these and other failed attempts to develop indigenous schools were significant for another reason. Including the Soviet case, these attempts, neoliberals believed, were indigenous societies' expressions of ingratitude for the cultural benefits bestowed upon them by capitalists during colonialism. In essence, neoliberals hated these educational expressions of classless education. They were nothing, they stated, but veiled attempts by socialist leaders to attack capitalism and glorify undesirables.

Neoliberal wrath was reserved for Dewey, however. Like the others we met in earlier chapters, Dewey was not alive to participate in a continuing conversation with neoliberal educational reformers. But that was unimportant to neoliberals as their thoughts angrily converged on his educational philosophies and his personal faith in democracy. Convinced these demonstrated his socialist leanings and irreligiosity, and fearing the high international esteem in which he was held, neoliberals were positive his ideas were threatening. To them, he was subversive, even though they discovered his ideas were still vibrant and debated by others at the millennium's turn. Frankly, the neoliberals resented John Dewey. Their archenemy of educational reform was a ghost, and it was awkward for them to explain why he threatened them so.

With this as the educational debate between neoliberal reformers and those they call liberal, we see them direct their arguments about whose purposes schools should serve. Should schools produce human capital, the free-market economy's laborers? Or should schools fritter away their energies on a diverse society? To appreciate the depth of this debate, let us first place it in a global context.

NEOLIBERALISM'S GLOBAL CONSEQUENCE

Charles Kimball, in his book *When Religion Becomes Evil*, gives his readers a rare opportunity to search for meanings created by a single, violent encounter between two global cultures.

> If God is omnipotent, why didn't God prevent the airplanes from striking the World Trade Center towers? Or, as some religious leaders suggested, did God actively participate in the events of September 11? Osama bin Laden

and Jerry Falwell seemed to agree on this point: bin Laden interpreted the destruction of the towers and the crash in the Pentagon as a sign of God's support for his struggle against evil; Falwell suggested these horrifying events were God's way of telling us of his displeasure with abortionists, pagans, feminists, the ACLU, People for the American Way, and gays and lesbians.[1]

While Kimball leaves the reader to his or her own emotional descriptions of that calamitous event, it is for us an intriguing exercise of learning about global social and educational dissonance. Even though bin Laden and Falwell undoubtedly differ on the starkness and human cost of the happening, these two icons of disagreeable extremes agree its cause was evil.

Some of Falwell's representations of evil are those Kimball mentions: abortionists, pagans, feminists, the American Civil Liberty Union, People for the American Way, and gays and lesbians. These and other evils, forcing their contamination on a once-pure Protestant society, are now its bane, Falwell believes. Fascinatingly, bin Laden despises these selfsame evils represented by Falwell's satanic multicultural society. Its depraved education, exported around the world, is polluting Muslims wherever they live. Its books, movies, dress, television, and music are fixated on curricula of cultural devaluation and economic pillage. This education is the filth of degenerate infidel capitalists who steal the resources of the world's poor so they can become even more wealthy. Together, it is this horror of the perceived evil bin Laden and Falwell see that prompts each to yearn for a time, a nirvana, when wickedness was nonexistent.

Impure Futures

We now glimpse the diversity of global reactions to neoliberal education reform. This time, neoliberal consequences are detected among indigenous societies that are inextricably caught up in the capitalist web, which depends less on community deliberation than on raw economics and competitive advantage. Owning only natural resources whose economic worth is measured by the free-market economy, indigenous societies are now forced to educate their younger generations to become laborers so they can at least qualify as human capital in the global economy. Educated in formal schools, taught in languages not spoken by their parents, students learn curricula that entice them to devalue their birth culture. At the same time, their leaders, observing the old way's disappearance, are mindful of the depletion of their natural resources. They are fearful of the time when capitalists will no longer profit from their assets. Because of this, they too become wistful for a tension-free past—their own nirvanas—those times when globalization and its formal schools did not exist. It was that time, they believe, before they were forced to participate in economic rapes that were explained away by capitalist formal schools and Protestant values. Nirvana is that time when indigenous societies controlled their own social and economic structures, just like neoliberals expect of theirs.

Bernard Lewis, in *What Went Wrong*, details his sophisticated investigations of Muslims' centuries-long retreat to their present dependence on those they call "infidels."[2] His study is significant in part because of the time of its publication. By coincidence, Lewis's text was in the final preparation stages for publication at the time of the September 11, 2001, terrorist attacks on the Pentagon and the World Trade Center. His conclusions, not being despoiled by that day's events and subsequent emotions, have a greater standing of impartiality than if the book had been published later. They cut to the elemental questions about the consequence of Middle East reactions to globalization. Lewis describes the growing feeling in the Muslim world that, "attributing all evil to the abandonment of the divine heritage of Islam advocates a return to a real or imagined past. That is the way of the Iranian Revolution and the so-called fundamentalist movements and regimes in other Muslim countries."[3]

In fact, to make his point clear, Lewis—unaware of the approaching September 11 tragedy—wrote of the starkness of suicide bombers. He uses them as a metaphor as he queries whether the Middle East can survive if its behaviors were to provoke another period of foreign domination.

We learn from Lewis of Muslim frustrations as this once creative culture experiences continued marginalization by a Europe they identify less by countries than religions. The Muslims' frustrations lie beyond their long subjugation by the Ottoman Empire. It is their late twentieth-century admission that their technical knowledge lags behind that of even some of Europe's oldest Asian colonies that is humiliating. But, Muslims did learn mostly from France and England during the twentieth century, Lewis tells us, that military might, nationalism (including anti-Semitism), and capitalism were potent modern European weapons tooled for economic domination.

Experimenting (and failing) with each of these weapons during the last half of the twentieth century was frustrating and forced them to turn inward. Painting the Middle East in broad strokes, Lewis tells us that Muslims are now compelled to ask themselves two inherent questions: Should Islam be modernized to compete with other societies in a free-market economy? Or, casting away any thoughts of global participation, should Islam nostalgically recreate those vintage years we call antiquity?

Now we know why bin Laden and Falwell recognized the same evil on September 11, 2001, and were not shocked by their nostalgic actions and statements of wanting to live in stress-free nirvanas. They were terror-struck that globalization's consequences will force them to live in an impure future.

Impure Futures and Formal Schools

The Muslim experiences are not so unique as to separate them from those endured by other societies we discussed in previous chapters. In chapter 2, as we learned, indigenous societies, first as colonials and then as economic units in a free-market economy, have also resisted globalization so they can live their histories and social values outside the Protestant Reformation experience. To illustrate, even though indigenous societies also express deep commitments in their covenants between God and worshipers, the defining differences between these theologies and Protestantism, as discussed in chapter 2, are based on what constitutes the individual's role. It is the Protestant context of individualism, schooling, and competition—rather than community, education, and affiliation—that creates the arena in which neoliberal educational reforms are actively debated. It is the prompt from which nirvanas are sought.

These are the consequences neoliberal schools present on a daily basis to adults and children alike. In chapter 5, for example, we recounted the conflicting futures these issues presented to young adults such as Joseph. A young Tanzanian, scarcely fluent in English and with only sufficient formal schooling to cause him to doubt his birth culture, Joseph cast aside his village inheritance and distanced himself from his family. He moved to Tanzania's capital Dar es Salaam to experience the "modern" delights of the European culture he learned about in his formal school. He was excited when he saw that Dar es Salaam was so different from the village of his youth. Earlier, when he lived in the village, Joseph learned about life's values from his parents and other adults. He learned the techniques of clearing and cleaning banana fields while working with other men in the village. Even though Joseph's education was centered on learning the fullness of village life, he felt this curriculum was dull and would not prepare him to live in the new world fast advancing to his village doorstep.

In his new urban life, Joseph learned that working was vastly different than what was expected of him in his village. Before, he learned to work with others depending on the seasons. Now, in Dar es Salaam, he worked every day by himself as a taxi driver. Like other workers in other societies like his, Joseph learned that urban labor meant more than just performing its physical tasks. He was now forced to think about things he had never thought about before—such as the high values capitalists placed on profits. Even so, the connection between the economics of poverty and the social values of self-motivation, laziness, and loitering were still new and not always obvious to him. Now, Joseph's success (or failure) was his alone to bear.

It was apparent to Joseph that his life was now beyond his control. Swayed by the ornaments of Protestant culture—urban living, television,

VCRs, clothes, and music—Joseph's orientation changed. In fact, it forced Joseph, without quite understanding what was happening to him, to re-create himself using only what little formal schooling he possessed. Now, that formal school curriculum extolling Protestant values and capitalism would sever him completely from his life history and cultural heritage. Joseph's decision to move closer to the free-market economy created in him a dim awareness he was simultaneously living in two cultures, but he no longer was able to distinguish one from the other or decide which was better.

Joseph's inability to judge which culture he wanted to live in is striking and commonplace in labor-resource-driven societies. Simply, his life, whether he liked it or not, was now controlled by an economic system of which he had only recently heard. Joseph had become a true capitalist laborer. He was now part of a national economic asset called human capital. He was working for himself but profiting others he would never meet. It is upon this fragile educational history, depending on his ability to cope with the free-market economy, that he will from time to time become nostalgic for his own personal time past. His nostalgia will not be reflective of his early years living with his parents in his village. Nor will it be the self-congratulatory nostalgia reserved for those who succeed. Joseph's nostalgia will be aggressive. He will be motivated to follow others, perhaps demagogues who talk about re-creating a tensionless nirvana, something he has never experienced—but knows must exist.

It is easy for us to understand and even sympathize with Joseph's dilemma. Yet, there is a perplexing question remaining for us about his life and future in Dar es Salaam: Would his life have been happier had he stayed in his village, learning from his parents and other adults? Would he have had a more satisfying life working with friends in banana groves, not weighted with the personal responsibility of competing in the free-market economy? Bluntly, would Joseph's life been better if he had decided not to attend a formal school?

In fact, this was the same question Mitzi asked herself a half a world away in the United States. She had few good experiences in school, and it seemed to her that education had very little meaning. The teachers taught a curriculum that was foreign to her and her life. They even demanded she obey silly classroom rules and act in ways she knew were artificial and outside her personal experiences. So, like so many others living in her neighborhood, she decided not to attend formal school—she became a dropout.

In chapter 6, we were also introduced to her as a soon-to-be young mother. Although she had never heard of Tanzania and did not know Joseph, Mitzi, an African American, would have recognized her life to be much like his had they met. Even though she lived among the embellishments of great wealth, others more powerful than she and her family had situated her into a fixed economic underclass. But, it was more than an underclass in which poverty was the currency, Mitzi learned her neighborhood was reserved for them by others. It even had its own history of dependence. It is upon this scaffolding Mitzi learned that if she wanted to succeed, it would never be within the confines of her neighborhood. Yet, the dominant European society's idea of success was not hers either. Its success was lined and balanced with Protestant values praised in capitalist schools. This is what Mitzi meant when she called her education "white."

While Mitzi's decision to remain in the inner city with her newborn baby may have been uppermost in her mind when we met her, she quickly learned that the economic and social boundaries between her inner city life and the lives she saw on television were real. And, while wealth's second-hand social ornaments slowly filtered down to her and others in her neighborhood, she saw on television that the ornaments whites had, living outside her colony, were still brighter and better.

Mitzi was discovering the consequences of neoliberal educational reform and what it means to be concealed in a global capitalist society. Not a contributing member of the investor class, Mitzi's neighborhood is judged like all other indigenous societies. It is an economic unit competing globally with other economic units in the free-market economy. Its resources and labor are judged by capitalists for their worth. With few identifiable resources (mostly worthless) and having dropped out of formal school (now judged worthless), her neighborhood has nothing to tender in a free-market economy.

Not understanding the world around her, Mitzi and her neighborhood are economically and socially vulnerable. Now, she and others are experiencing continued economic exclusion as unskilled jobs disappear and retail stores close their doors. In fact, Mitzi acknowledges her vulnerability. She already learned the job she most hungers for is outside her neighborhood. In fact, it is in the center of white wealth that she will earn her minimum wage. And it is here she will learn she cannot afford the ornaments she thinks are essential to her life. Mitzi is undergoing a life change. She has become socially invisible and an economic liability. All she thought would improve her and her unborn child's life were to be seen on television but not hers to use or own.

There were others we have met in earlier chapters who also personify the consequence of neoliberal educational reform. Each is a personification of his or her indigenous society's dance with raw capitalism and the free-market economy. Whether it was young Yuri, a Russian university student studying foreign languages in Moscow, or Jay, a soon-to-be-retired Indian university professor, each was searching for avenues through which he could attune his life with globalization's social and economic realities. Even Hector and Ester, whom we met in chapter 5, found their accommodation in the most personal manners possible, one was quickly incorporated into her immigrant El Paso family, the other returning periodically to Juárez to be culturally refreshed.

It was different with Edwin. While the others we have spoken of were part of the resource labor experience, Edwin was not. From Canada, he was the epitome of formal schools' curricula. Educated to become a university researcher, he craved to be an academic capitalist. Searching and writing proposals for research grants, he knew how to manage resources while he created new knowledge. Edwin had found his profession, family, and home among investors and understood them, while he exercised his talents as a middle manager. Unlike the others, he would not be nostalgic for another time and place because, for him, his present was his nirvana.

It was left to Munyika and Lindani, whom we met in chapter 6, to symbolize the consequences of neoliberal education in indigenous societies. Partners in a bicycle repair shop in Zomba, both believed their opportunities for profit creation were possible. Accepting globalization's promises and believing in the power of investment rather than resources and labor, both placed their hopes, wealth, and talents on a local franchise of an international bicycle firm—only to discover that the capitalist system they thought they knew was purposely using them as financial conduits. Their role in the free-market economy, they learned, was to transfer their hard-earned profits to larger pools of wealth in other countries. Munyika and Lindani's practical education in globalization, originally highlighting financial opportunities they had not seen in a resource labor society, was disastrous. What both learned from neoliberal education's final exam was not that they had failed the curriculum but that the curriculum had cheated them. Now, looking for a purer future rather than the profits propagandized by neoliberals, we see them considering Islamic education more seriously.

NEOLIBERALISM'S GLOBAL QUAGMIRE: EDUCATION REFORM

We have learned that the global consequences of neoliberalism are based on more than the complexities of raw capitalism and the free-market economy. Just as neoliberals identified Victorian times as their nirvana to realize their economic dreams, so too are indigenous societies identifying their own nirvanas—except in their cases, their nirvanas are reactions to neoliberalism, as is the case of Muslims' experimentation with theological societies such as the Islamic Republic of Iran.

Unilateralism

These are the consequences of neoliberal education reform hidden in globalization's complexity. Globalization is not just the intercourse of national economies, nor is it the static colonial parliamentary relationship between governors and the governed. Globalization is both more and less than that. Even though its international discourse is consigned to the free-market economy in which wealth dominates, it is also the venue through which societies are being schooled to fit the class society for which neoliberals hunger. Pointedly, just as education reform exemplified neoliberal aggressive nostalgia, culminating in a recreation of their Victorian class society, its unilateralism is experienced as the sparked reactions of indigenous societies who are also nostalgic to return to less stressful periods. These periods, perhaps only identified by some, such as in the Middle East, are the antithesis of globalization's concept of one world in which cultures and societies relate to each other through competition and profit.

Globalization's unilateral logic is built on economics. It is disinterested in the compatibility and order fostered by community, which neoliberals believe is the hothouse that breeds mediocrity. Therefore, neoliberal education reform is unable to, and does not want to, express consensus. Its education makes sense of its world only through the capitalist curriculum. Neoliberal education does not teach about the relationship between the powerful and the weak as did schools during the ages of empire and colonization. Its unilateral curriculum purposely disregards the cultural history of society. Unlike schools in the age of empire, which forced the indigenous to judge themselves according to foreign standards, neoliberal education teaches the process of profit creation, saddling the indigenous with poverty while the wealthy remain as they are.

Neoliberal education reform takes on the many forms of globalization in which everyone is educated to compete in the free-market economy. Its relations encompass the state and engulf international treaties. It is aggressively equal to unequal powers expressed through economic policies developed by self-sustaining, exclusive international agencies and corporations that refuse the traditional trappings of a national heritage. Globalization is not just economic domination. It is the naked teaching of unilateralism.

Multilateralism

> It wasn't a matter of deciding when to go to college. It was a given. There were eight of us and we all went to college. I have a brother who got his Ph.D. when he was twenty-four. We were blessed that we had ability . . . my parents emphasized the importance of using it and giving something back.[4]

Iola Taylor, now a retired teacher in Texas, recalled her experiences living in a segregated neighborhood during her youth, giving a word picture of her early life and talking about the respect and love she, her siblings, and parents showed each other. Undoubtedly, her parents' education level was less than that of the rest of the family, yet she voiced her admiration of them, likening their parental advice to that of her brother's academic success. She spoke as a member of a family that celebrated each other's lives as shared experiences.

It is in Iola's recollection of family—coupled with the community and school remembrances of Barbara Wyche in Hopewell, Virginia, described in chapter 8—that we see the joining links among these social institutions. It is even more clear to us as we recall Barbara's comparison of her white schooling experiences with those she remembered from her segregated school. In essence, Iola and Barbara recalled their families, communities, and school lives as interconnected and interrelated personal experiences. These remembrances were more significant to them than if they had experienced each separately. It is the same for most of those we met earlier in this book and again in this chapter—these memories cannot be stated in the plural. To them, their memories are singular, just like the universe, remaining in their minds, living and breathing.

Both Iola Taylor and Barbara Wyche picture for us what education in segregated America was like for students. For them, their schools, teachers, and fellow students were simply extensions of their immediate families. Iola and Barbara had the same life experiences in their own communities: Both lived within walking distance of their schools. Each grew up playing in neighborhood parks with children who later would be their classmates. They knew their friends' families. They knew their teachers personally before entering their classrooms as students. And, because teachers were members of their communities in that segregated society, their parents were acquainted with them and were aware of their teaching reputations.

Iola and Barbara's teachers mirrored the same community attitudes as their parents. Like them, they were also lifelong members of the community, many times with personal histories from the same schools in which they now taught. In fact, it would not have been altogether uncommon for a student's teacher and parents to have shared academic experiences in the same classrooms in which they were now receiving their education. And, while it was these experiences that cast teachers into roles as community leaders, it was the quality of their higher education that shaped them into educational models, many having earned Ph.D.'s.

Disciples of Dewey, teachers like those mentioned by Iola and Barbara used his educational philosophy to teach students in the academic community called the classroom. Thinking of themselves as teachers' partners, parents supported their children, celebrated their academic accomplishments, and encouraged them to learn. It was the binding of this community triad (teachers, students, and parents), in which each was supportive and responsible to the others, that became the platform upon which education was based. That is, as students experienced schooling and its social aspects within this setting, they learned who they were. It was the ultimate education!

Let us now look at this type of education from the vantage point of globalization.

Wise parents, Joseph Nye Jr. tells us, those who have displayed their love and respect for their children by modeling the right beliefs and values, will be rewarded in due course with their admiration.

> Soft power rests on the ability to set the political agenda in a way that shapes the preferences of others. At the personal level, wise parents know that if they have brought up their children with the right beliefs and values, their power will be greater and will last longer than if they have relied on spankings, cutting off allowances, or taking away the car keys.[5]

It was like that for Iola Taylor, voicing her admiration for her parents for passing on to her and her siblings their appreciation for education. It was because they rejoiced in their children's lives, she said. In later life as a social studies teacher, Taylor incorporated her family experiences into her teaching philosophy. Demonstrated as a teaching technique, she modeled her love and respect for her students by encouraging them with positive opportunities to learn and succeed. Taylor was an excellent teacher. She helped her charges become responsible for their own education.

But, we learn from Nye that he is not a classroom teacher, nor is he recounting for us his parental experiences. Instead, he is a U.S. diplomat and is speaking about global diplomatic power. He is telling his readers that in rare periods during the last half-millennium three nations (Spain, Netherlands, and England) enjoyed unchallenged diplomatic authority as single global superpowers. In that position, each used its economic strength and military might to intimidate its neighbors. Calling these strengths "hard powers," Nye tells us that (with the possible exception of England at the beginning of the twentieth century) this was the only effective political technique they believed would advance their international agendas.

This is not the case of the United States, Nye's designated fourth single global superpower. Enjoying the same international status and possessing the same *hard powers* as Spain, Netherlands, and England, the United States also has another strength, which he calls *soft power*. "Soft power," says Nye, is elusive and difficult to describe. Yet, it is as strong as American economics and military might. In fact, this power is the reverse of hard power. It has global integrity—the international regard of other nations for American social values and organizations. We experience its integrity when other societies and peoples openly demonstrate their desire to include American social values and organizations into their day-to-day lives. This is what Nye is referring to when he writes about how the United States, leading by example and exemplifying social values such as free universal education, rule of law, freedom of speech, and separation of church and state, can set the global conversation. It is the measure of a nation's international stature to formulate global choices.

Nye has described for us another worldview in which global leadership is not based just on traditional economic and military intimidation. He is asking us to look at the world and its peoples through eyes that do not see others as fitting into competing economic units. He is speaking of a three-dimensional world in which nations' diplomatic agendas are marshaled into global consensus with American leadership. This, says Nye, is *multilateralism*—nations working together for agreed-upon aims. Multilateralism is the process Nye wants governments to understand. It is democratic leadership. And, for us and our purposes, it is what Taylor admired about her parents.

Taylor would have also recognized Nye's theory of multilateralism as a diplomatic explanation of her educational philosophy. It was the essence of what she taught her Austin social studies students. And, it was the essence of what Barbara Wyche learned in her segregated school in Virginia. It is that which motivates students to learn about others' dreams so they can build better communities for themselves and others.

Although multilateralism is a political term, it is also the essence of liberal educational philosophy. It is suggestive of Randolph Bourne's discussion in chapter 8 of multiculturalism in the early years of the past century in which he argued that immigrants to these shores should not be expected to give up their birth culture. Rather, they should become bicultural. He termed this ongoing process of national redefinition "transnationalism."

Dewey addressed Bourne's thoughts. He simply said that Bourne is correct, yet cultural diversity should be society's strength—its human democracy. It is this faith, according to Dewey, that rejects superficial differences of class, gender, race, and economic advantage in favor of joining with others to become the Common Man. In sum, both Dewey and Bourne recognize Nye's concept of multilateralism for what it is: the democratic process built on the strength of global diversity.

NEOLIBERAL EDUCATION REFORM: A REPRISE

We have devoted our attention in this text to neoliberalism's educational reform while directly confronting only some of globalization's complexities. Though significant economic and social theories of Smith, Marx, Friedman, Fogel, and others have been discussed, they have been placed on the edge of this investigation, except where they had a direct bearing on neoliberal education reform. It is not that globalization and its philosophers are irrelevant—in fact, as in this chapter and others, they have continued to remind us of their significance. Globalization is somewhat like the proverbial elephant in the living room—always there but spoken about only in whispers. Now, this elephant, to continue the metaphor, has continually obliged us to look at neoliberal educational reform from a multiplicity of perspectives, enriching our understanding.

Educational reform in the United States is not the recent phenomenon that some neoliberals believe. In fact, many teachers talk about educational reform as if it were an ongoing process that continuously molds and refits classrooms to new and different ideas or local community needs. It is understandable why teachers believe as they do, watching them attend their local universities or independent seminars in their off-hours, learning new curricula and different teaching methodologies. Yet, their responses are only partly correct because significant economic (and political) demands on schools can easily be explained away as community needs. But, that does not mean economic demands and community needs are the same thing. Trite as it must sound, economic power predominates. In fact, scholars, including Alan DeYoung, are prompt to voice their thoughts that economics has been the prime motivation for American educational reform in the last several centuries.[6]

To illustrate DeYoung's point, the mid-twentieth-century civil rights school reform efforts were important to the economy because of the increased educational opportunities for millions of African Americans. These translated into untold billions of dollars to build a stronger Cold War consumer economy. The Cold War was also significant for the nation's economy in other ways. It created a higher education research base that met the immediate needs of the arms race, spawning new and different industries that created and sold new products and technologies to the military and civilian society alike. In many ways, university research programs still feel the Cold War's vibrations and its reordering of military and economic priorities. We are also reminded of Dewey's "new education." As noted earlier in this text, he was concerned with complicated late Victorian economic philosophies that centered partly on the education of laborers' children.

Compared with these reform movements, however, the present neoliberal school reform efforts stand out because of their differences. To illustrate, educational reform has traditionally consisted of diverse voices, each of which has spoken on behalf of different national audiences. While the process was noisy and complicated, the discussions dealt with people's opportunities to participate in and partake of the American dream. On the other hand, neoliberal educational reform was designed by powerful capitalist interests whose goals were to create school curricula taught and tested by schools for their own financial benefit and not the education of children.

We are quick to point out that the neoliberal reform movement is more complex than simply hungering for financial profit. It is a result of many motivations, some of which are psychological, theological, and political. Undoubtedly, capitalists' greed for profits during the late Victorian period was handsomely paid back to them by a disgusted public during the Depression and post–World War II years.[7] And, today's neoliberals remember and resent the increased federal and state taxation policies that required capitalists to return to the people much of their ill-gotten gain.[8] In many ways, this, along with the psychological concerns of a new millennium, explains neoliberalism's nostalgia for those Victorian days when the untaxed wealthy safely lived far from immigrant laborers and others like them.[9]

Dewey was correct in his description of capitalist education. Writing in the early twentieth century, he spoke about his public school education in the late Victorian period in Vermont. It was his first duty as a student to maintain the classroom's decorum. Dewey was like most young students in the United States and Europe during that time: he sat quietly working at his desk. He was graded by his teachers on his ability to work in silence until his teachers told him to do otherwise. He answered teachers' questions when they asked him, seldom volunteering additional information or engaging them in conversation. While Dewey, as a child, probably did not think of his education as complicated, he did know what he knew was what his teachers wanted him to know.

Later, when he talked about his school life, he mentioned that his education had caused him to become intellectually and socially passive—a ready receiver of information. As he wrote about an education that engaged students, we can still feel his sense of liberation. This is the conflict between Dewey and the neoliberals. As long as he was passive, he was in an acceptance mode necessary to work as a factory laborer. Once he became an active learner, neoliberals knew that he would never take orders on the factory floor. For capitalists, Dewey was then useless.

COMBATING NEOLIBERALISM'S REFORM OF AMERICAN EDUCATION

Lord Robert Cecil, later Lord Salisbury, a major political and intellectual figure in Victorian England, commented on the U.S. Civil War's influence on English and American society. He wrote in 1862 about the contradictions between democracy and classism (aristocracy), observing that democracies are nothing but illusions whose leaders are elected to office pandering to the public's sentiments of equality.

> [Democracy] is not merely a folly. It is a chimera. It is idle to discuss whether it ought to exist; for, as a matter of fact, it never does. Whatever may be the written text of a Constitution, the multitude always will have leaders among them, and those leaders [are] not selected by themselves.[10]

Societies' great leaders, according to Cecil, are those who are perhaps, but not always, born to high social standing and are marked as intellectuals who understand power and culture. Good leaders are those who are summoned, not elected, he says.

We should not characterize the thoughts of Lord Salisbury (who was prime minister most of the period 1885–1902) as politically unsophisticated or naive. They are reflective of classic Greek philosophy that influenced English and American social and political views at that time.[11] Lord Salisbury speaks volumes to neoliberals today. His words act as bugles calling reveille for the dawn of a new day, setting neoliberals free from the mediocrity of a multicultural society. Can the aristocracy of leadership be democracy's product? Of course not, reply neoliberals—today's democracy is polluted by its *licentious* social evils. Democracy was not honed on the anvils of classism and competition.

But, to assume Lord Salisbury's comments about leadership are correct, that good leaders can only exist in the rarefied air of Victorian classism, is but to beg the question. His major point is that democracy is but a mist. It cannot exist and cannot educate the multitude to any significant level of responsibility—and certainly not to become leaders. Of course, he means the Victorian elite and bourgeois education.[12] Lord Salisbury is the personification of neoliberal education reform, preparing us to understand that leadership is not dependent on mediocrity but is the product of a rigorous neoliberal education.

In fact, Lord Salisbury's point is well taken. He and today's neoliberals assume that leadership is the sum of that education, resulting in economic advancement. Basically, their argument is that just as factory workers in Victorian times were required to have a modicum of reading, writing, and arithmetic to complement their arduous physical work on the factory floor, globalization requires lower and middle managers to develop strong mental muscles to accomplish their corporate tasks. Said another way, the neoliberals' assumption, which would be supported by Lord Salisbury, is that economic development (capitalism) is the direct result of leaders who have a Euroamerican education.

However, we must not assume, as do neoliberals, that there is an absolute and direct relationship between economic development and a Euroamerican education. Their premise, that schools are capitalist subcontractors of corporations, is not true—there are differences between schools' purposes and economics. While capitalism is concerned with the economic interplay among investment, labor, and resources, all aimed at profiting from an ever increasing standard of global affluence, schools are concerned about the issues that affect human beings.

We are not referring to schools such as those Milton Friedman and Peter Brimelow propose. Their schools, products of vouchers and tax credits, are modeled after retail stores at the mall, selling information like overpriced athletic shoes to teenage shoppers. The schools we refer to are those written about by Gandhi, Dewey, and Nyerere and practiced in classrooms by Taylor and experienced by Wyche. Their multilateral curriculum of community, teachers, parents, and students is the soft power of which Nye speaks in international diplomacy. It is this curriculum that creates discourses with others, husbanding social diversity so it can be seen in students. It creates opportunities for students to learn about physical, social, emotional, and personal environments, mentoring them so they experience global relationships and diverse cultures. They become Dewey's model of democracy—the Common Man.

This multilateral curriculum gives students opportunities to cooperate and participate in community building so they can experience multilateral responsibilities—that participatory leadership Nye refers to. Said simply, this curriculum is that leadership that is formed into cooperative problem-solving communities. It is that education in which ethics is centermost, of which the Dalai Lama spoke in chapter 1. It is the active compassion drawn from others who convey the respect and understanding they themselves want.

These are the basic educational opportunities students expect of schools in a global society. They want to learn with others around the world about issues of war and peace, poverty and affluence, authoritarianism and political justice, globalization and communities of culture, and other endeavors that touch lives. Unlike neoliberalism, which uses high-stakes testing to assess what students know, this multilateral curriculum gives students opportunities to develop their own codes of ethics and sense of justice so they can bridge racial, gender, religious, and social differences as citizens of the world. They, as Dewey would say, become their own assessors of what they need to know.

Like neoliberal formal schools, this multilateral school also aims at amassing wealth. Rather than the profits of competition for which neoliberals educate, this school's wealth is found in the multilateralism of the global community.[13] It is upon this school that investors will gladly shower their largess when they sense that capitalism can only exist on a globe defined by human dignity.

NOTES

1. Charles Kimball, *When Religion Becomes Evil* (New York: HarperSanFrancisco, 2002), 48.

2. Bernard Lewis, *What Went Wrong: Western Impact and Middle Eastern Response* (New York: Oxford University Press, 2002).

3. Lewis, *What Went Wrong*, 158.

4. Anna Victoria Wilson and William E. Segall, *Oh, Do I Remember! Experiences of Teachers during the Desegregation of Austin's Schools, 1964–1971* (Albany: State University of New York Press, 2001), 41. This interview of Iola Taylor, a retired African-American teacher in Austin, Texas, recalled her family life in Austin during segregation. She expressed her family's warmth as a generational intermix in which adult and sibling successes alike were celebrated as a family. Her brother received a Ph.D. in constitutional law from the University of Indiana and is currently the chairperson of the Department of Political Science at San Diego State University.

5. Joseph S. Nye Jr., *The Paradox of American Power: Why the World's Only Superpower Can't Go It Alone* (New York: Oxford University Press, 2002), 9.

6. Alan J. DeYoung, *Economics and American Education: A Historical and Critical Overview of the Impact of Economic Theories on Schooling in the United States* (New York: Longman, 1989). DeYoung's text is an early overview of this significant topic. Written before neoliberalism was fully mature, he saw the reform movement as an attempt by economics to improve schooling—not replace it.

7. In *Wealth and Democracy: A Political History of the American Rich* (New York: Broadway Books, 2002), Kevin Phillips mentions that the psychology of taxing the poor while giving tax breaks to the wealthy was excusable because they contended this would compensate the wealthy for their economic losses when the feudal system collapsed (p. 219). Of course, what Phillips is referring to are the debates surrounding the Thirteenth Amendment, creating the income tax. He notes that Treasury Secretary Andrew Mellon, even after the wealthy had saved $4 billion a year in 1926 (when the federal budget was $3 billion) was able to remit another $6 billion within a nine-year tenure in office.

The process of tax rebates has continued in the George W. Bush administration. For example, in 2002, the gap between the poor and the wealthy continued to widen. In that year, the top 20 percent of households in the United States accounted for 50 percent of all income (compared to 44 percent in 1973). The bottom 20 percent of households' share of the income fell from 4.2 percent (1973) to 3.5 percent (2002). Beginning in 2002, the middle class and poor were now shouldering half of the tax burden. See Leigh Strope, "Income Gap Widens between Rich, Poor," *Tulsa World*, August 17, 2002.

8. The Roosevelt administration's efforts to reverse the benefits to the wealthy created a feeling of animosity toward him and the Democratic party by the wealthy for generations. Many of the wealthy referred to him as a "traitor to his own class." However, as Phillips points out (*Wealth and Democracy*, 219–21), Roosevelt's economic purity was tempered by politics—Big Oil continued to receive oil depletion tax credits (this was corrected in the windfall profits tax legislation in the 1980s).

9. Eric Hobsbawm (*The Age of Extremes: A History of the World, 1914–1991* [New York: Pantheon Books, 1994], 265–67) notes that technology's impact on global

wealth and poverty was absolute. Becoming more sophisticated in the 1970s, computer technology in one way or another impacted the everyday life of everyone on the globe. Technology's cost of production was prohibitive and required an educational system that created engineers and others to manage its growth. Hobsbawm also says technology is capital intensive. He meant that labor-intensive societies had less chance of participating in technology's wealth production than did capital-intensive societies.

10. Robert Cecil, quoted in A. N. Wilson, *The Victorians* (New York: W. W. Norton, 2003), 252. Lord Robert Cecil (later Lord Salisbury and member of Disraeli's cabinet and prime minister) wrote these comments about democracy in the October 1862 issue of the *Quarterly Review*. While some today would consider his ideas ultraconservative, they were reflective of the Victorian societies in England and the United States. See also Lady Gwendolen Cecil, *Life of Robert, Marquis of Salisbury*. 2 vols.

11. For example, the U.S. Constitution requires the president to meet the same general requirements as the ancient Greek philosopher-king.

12. As prime minister, Lord Salisbury introduced the 1891 Education Act, aimed at giving all children a free elementary education. The reader is reminded that this legislation was intended to give young adults basic skills in reading, arithmetic, and writing so they could become good workers.

13. This echoes His Holiness the Dalai Lama (*Ethics for the New Millennium* [New York: Riverhead Books, 1999]), who speaks about an educational experience that transcends cultural and social differences. He wants all citizens to respect others. To him, good deeds are those that each of us respectfully do when we learn about other's faith traditions.

Epilogue

In chapter 1, we discussed emblems of change and how they created social disruptions in developed and developing nations. The Dalai Lama labels this confounding moment in history a "global schism" and says it divides peoples more profoundly than any of the separations created by political and theological ideologies. The chapter spoke of the fears neoliberals have as they experience these global changes in the United States. Without understanding the interconnected consequences that global change presents, they wish for Victorian times, their nirvana, where purity and security were accepted social norms.

But neoliberals found that creating nirvanas was not easy work. They learned their Victorian nirvana was based on schooling as much as it was on capitalism and classism. Knowing why neoliberals are now interested in reforming schools here and elsewhere, their reform efforts were contextualized, placing them, as they would insist, within their major interests (capitalism and classism). We traced the international rise of capitalism and its influence on schools to its present neoliberal state, first through colonialism, then Victorianism. Presently, we are watching neoliberals separate themselves from American democracy, rejecting it so categorically that Victorian ideologies have become the accepted education conversation.

However, neoliberal's aggressive school reform behavior, built on their terror of what they believe the future holds, has not been fully debated. Neoliberalism is, as we point out, a reiteration of classic Victorian liberal philosophy that breeds classism and unregulated capitalism. Neoliberal schools therefore have become enterprises competing in a *free academic market economy*. They emphasize high-stakes testing and hanker to teach a pluralist society curricula that exclude children's heritage while they learn worker values.

Yet, the word *neoliberalism* is unique. It is used in varying degrees in countries around the world but, for reasons explained earlier, it is not commonly used in the United States. Neoliberalism, as we now know, means classic liberalism. But the term *liberal* has been redefined by neoliberals in the last several decades to mean something other than the original that John Dewey would have recognized. Dewey defined the term to mean the democratic value of tolerance, but neoliberals have taken the definition to its absurd extreme. They picture liberals as Victorians once pictured Oscar Wilde: sickly people who, because they lack morals or values, easily accept others who are different. They enjoy living in a licentious society.

While we know that definition is an expression of neoliberal nostalgia, the term *liberal* in fact had its beginnings in the late 1700s and the early Victorian decades. The word was treated in chapters 8 and 9 in its economic context—to name Adam Smith's theories and others like him with whom Karl Marx had difficulty. But, it had its social definitions as well, as later chapters pointed out. It influenced (one hates to say "developed") the industrial state and nourished a nineteenth-century society that today we call Victorian.

Victorianism was destined to be the outcome of the original liberal capitalistic philosophies. Its social consequences, found in classism, genderism, colonialism, and other "isms," divided and categorized peoples. Its theologies were based on Protestantism for no other reason (beyond Luther's revolutionary thoughts) than that their Sunday church experiences had to reflect their economic and social ongoings during the rest of the week. The original liberals, like their neoliberal inheritors, first thought common education was a waste of public tax monies because there was no guarantee of economic returns. Their eventual acceptance and support of schools came about because they learned that knowledge, even at its most rudimentary, could improve production and profits.

These vibrant Victorian robber baron capitalists whom neoliberals admire, fast paced in their colonization, became experts in managing economic and government enterprises in a Protestantized world, allowing them new ways of viewing themselves. It seemed to them that the then indigenous societies gave them permission to think of themselves in godlike terms. By World War I (1914–1918), however, much of that had passed away. Gone was the task of acting as the globe's police force. Gone, as we noted in chapter 9, was the elite class that Lord Salisbury considered so well educated it could immediately be summoned for social leadership. Victorianism eventually succumbed to history—and it is this that the neoliberals have yet to learn.

Much of the Victorian world passed from existence, not so much because of external forces as from within. It was not because of the poverty the working classes suffered as consequences of technology and urbanization. Nor was it the evils of colonialism, a global war, multicultural societies, Darwin, lurid plays, or sex-filled poetry and photographs. Victorianism passed away because of a plethora of excesses by capitalists who profited from labor the most.

At one extreme, it was capitalists' uncaring attitude about laborers, whose quality of life was so threatened that it decreased factory production and reduced profits. At the other extreme, as even Sir Winston Churchill and others observed, was liberals' boredom with their absolute wealth. The absurdity of economic and class differences struck society in countless ways. It was always the same, even when it was written about by humorist P. G. Wodehouse and performed in plays and sung at the Palladium and Her Majesty's Theatre; few liberals paid attention. But, it was more than just these causes. There were more than can be mentioned. Collectively, they created a feeling and uncertainty that swept society then as it does now. People questioned the meaning of their wealth, power, and military might. Rich and poor thought their lives would not change for the better regardless of what they received from their economy.[1] And they were right.

Victorianism's collapse is best described by Churchill. After expending its military might in colonial rebellions and soon its national wealth in a world war, the prime minister, Lord Salisbury, resigned in 1902. He was the personification of the Victorian era, said Churchill. Like the era he represented, he had "with him an aloofness of spirit, now considered old-fashioned."[2]

This is today's neoliberalism. Supported by their school tools, honed to reform, neoliberals are like the Victorians before them, blind to their world. They cannot see themselves as Churchill saw Victorianism—aloof and old-fashioned. Victorianism's hard powers, its military might and economic wealth, symbolize the neoliberal unilateralism of which Joseph Nye Jr. speaks. Because of that, neoliberals picture schools as economic agents in the pay of corporations. They cannot imagine schools as Nye's soft power, reminding us of the world's high regard for this bastion of American democracy. It is because of this their school reforms will fail.

NOTES

1. A. N. Wilson's text *The Victorians* (New York: W. W. Norton, 2003) discusses this era in wonderful detail. It is impossible to miss his thesis that we are learning about ourselves. See his chapter 26, pp. 409–425, for this specific discussion.

2. Winston S. Churchill, *A History of the English-Speaking Peoples* (1958; reprint, New York: Barnes & Noble Books by arrangement with Dodd, Mead, 1993), 4:384.

Bibliography

Akbar, M. J. *Nehru: The Making of India*. New York: Viking, 1988.

Arnold, Sir Edwin, trans. *Baghavadgita*. Mineola, NY: Dover Publications, 1993.

Blake, Robert, and William Roger Louis, eds. *Churchill: A Major Assessment of His Life in Peace and War*. New York: W. W. Norton, 1993.

Blum, Jerome. *In the Beginning: The Advent of the Modern Age; Europe in the 1840s*. New York: Charles Scribner's Sons, 1994.

Bowen, James. *Soviet Education: Anton Makarenko and the Years of Experiment*. Madison: University of Wisconsin Press, 1962.

Boym, Svetlana. *The Future of Nostalgia*. New York: Basic Books, 2001.

Brimelow, Peter. *The Worm in the Apple: How the Teacher Unions Are Destroying American Education*. New York: HarperCollins, 2003.

Caplan, Bryan. "Self-Reliance and Creative Destruction." Submission to the 1996 Davis Essay Contest sponsored by George Mason University's Center for World Capitalism. Available at http://www.gmu.edu/departments/economics/bcaplan/davis2.htm.

Cecil, Lady Gwendolen. *Life of Robert, Marquis of Salisbury*. 2 vols. London: Hodder and Stoughton, 1921.

Chubb, John E., and Terry M. Moe. *Politics, Markets, and America's Schools*. Washington, DC: Brookings Institution, 1990.

Churchill, Winston S. *A History of the English-Speaking Peoples*, vol. 4 (New York: Dodd, Mead, 1958).

———. *My Early Life: 1874–1904*. New York: Scribner, 1996.

Cohen, Jeff. "The Media: Liberal or Libertine?" www2.fwi.com/~totalstranger/media.html, March 25, 2003.

Cook, Alice Hanson, Val R. Lorwin, and Arlene Kaplan Daniels. *The Most Difficult Revolution: Women and Trade Unions*. New York: Cornell University Press, 1992.

Cornelius, Cathi L. "Village Perspectives: A Case Study Investigating the Perspectives Concerning the Oklahoma City Public Schools Neighborhood Schools Plan/Student Reassignment Plan." Ed.D. diss., Oklahoma State University, 1999.

Dalai Lama, His Holiness, the. *Ethics for the New Millennium*. New York: Riverhead Books, 1999.

de Witte, Ludo. *The Assassination of Lumumba*, trans. Ann Wright and Renée Fenby. London: Verso, 2001.

Dewey, John. "Authority and Freedom." *Survey Graphic* 25, no. 11 (November 1936).

———. "Creative Democracy: The Task before Us." In *John Dewey and the Promise of America*, Progressive Education Booklet No. 14. Columbus, Ohio: American Education Press, 1939. Available at www.beloit.edu/~pbk/dewey.html.

———. *Liberalism and Social Action*. 1935. Reprint, Great Books in Philosophy series. New York: Prometheus Books, 1999.

DeYoung, Alan J. *Economics and American Education: A Historical and Critical Overview of the Impact of Economic Theories on Schooling in the United States*. New York: Longman, 1989.

Du Bois, W. E. B. *The Souls of Black Folk*. 1903. Reprint. New York: Penguin Books USA, 1996.

Ellsworth, Scott. *Death in a Promised Land: The Tulsa Race Riot of 1921*. Baton Rouge: Louisiana State University Press, 1992.

Emerson, Ralph Waldo. *"Self-Reliance" and Other Essays*. Unabridged ed. New York: Dover Publications, 1993.

Erickson, Kai T. *Wayward Puritans: A Study in the Sociology of Deviants*. New York: Allyn & Bacon, 1966.

Fagerlind, Ingemar, and Lawrence J. Saha. *Education and National Development: A Comparative Perspective*. 2nd ed. Oxford, England: Pergamon Press, 1989.

Faxon, Grace B. *Practical Selections from Twenty Years of Normal Instructor and Primary Plans*. Dansville, NY: F. A. Owen, 1912.

Fogel, Robert William. *The Fourth Great Awakening and the Future of Egalitarianism*. Chicago: University of Chicago Press, 2000.

Foster, Richard, and Sarah Kaplan. *Creative Destruction: Why Companies That Are Built to Last Underperform the Market, and How to Successfully Transform Them*. New York: Currency, 2001.

Frank, Andre Gunder. *Lumpenbourgeoisie and Lumpendevelopment: Dependence, Class, and Politics in Latin America*. Trans. from the Spanish by Marion Davis Berdecio. New York: Monthly Review Press, 1972.

Friedman, Milton. "The Business Community's Suicidal Impulse." *Cato Policy Report* 21, no. 2 (March/April 1999): 6–7. Available at www.cato.org/pubs/policy_report/v21n2/friedman.html.

Friedman, Thomas L. *The Lexus and the Olive Tree*. New York: Farrar, Straus and Giroux, 1999.

Fukuyama, Francis. *The Great Disruption: Human Nature and the Reconstitution of Social Order*. New York: Free Press, 1999.

Gaidar, Arkady. *Tale of the Military Secret, Boy Malchish Kibalchish and His Firm Word*. 1935. Trans. from the Russian by George Kittell, Moscow: Novosti Press Agency Publishing House, 1974.

Gay, Peter. *Schnitzler's Century: The Making of Middle-Class Culture, 1815–1914*. New York: Norton, 2002.

Girard, Sundra Kaye. "The Puritan and Soviet Schools: A Comparative Study." Ed.D. diss., Oklahoma State University, 1993.

Gitomer, Drew H., Andre S. Latham, and Robert Ziomek. *The Academic Quality of Prospective Teachers: The Impact of Admissions and Licensure Testing.* Princeton, NJ: Educational Testing Service, 1999.

Grant, Madison. *The Passing of the Great Race; or, The Racial Basis of European History.* New York: C. Scribner, 1916.

Grove, Andrew S. *Only the Paranoid Survive: How to Exploit the Crisis Points That Challenge Every Company and Career.* New York: Bantam Books, 1999.

Heyrman, Christine Leigh. *Southern Cross: The Beginnings of the Bible Belt.* New York: Alfred A. Knopf, 1997.

Hobsbawm, Eric. *The Age of Extremes: A History of the World, 1914–1991.* New York: Pantheon Books, 1994.

Hutchins, Robert M. "The University and the Multiversity: Speech at the 317th Convocation of the University of Chicago." *New Republic* 13, no. 3 (April 1, 1967): 15–17.

Ignas, Edward, and Raymond J. Corsini, eds. *Comparative Educational Systems.* Itasca, IL: F. E. Peacock, 1981,

Igoa, Christina. *The Inner World of the Immigrant Child.* New York: St. Martin's Press, 1995.

Inkeles, Alex, and David Smith. *Becoming Modern.* London: Heinemann Education Books, 1974.

James, Rob, and Gary Leazer, eds. *The Takeover in the Southern Baptist Convention: A Brief History.* Decatur, GA: Baptists Today, 1994.

Kajubi, W. S. Address to seminar on Tanzanian education, in Institute of International Studies, Office of Education, Department of Health, Education, and Welfare, *Education and Culture in Eastern Africa,* 3:1–22. Washington, DC: GPO, 1970.

Kimball, Charles. *When Religion Becomes Evil.* New York: HarperSanFrancisco, 2002.

Kozol, Jonathan. *Amazing Grace: The Lives of Children and the Conscience of a Nation.* New York: Crown, 1995.

———. *Ordinary Resurrections.* New York: Crown, 1995.

Kunnie, Julian. *Is Apartheid Really Dead? Pan Africanist Working Class Cultural Critical Perspectives.* Boulder, CO: Westview Press, 2000.

Lamb, Beatrice Pitney. *The Nehrus of India: Three Generations of Leadership.* New York: Macmillan, 1967.

Landes, David S. *Revolution in Time: Clocks and the Making of the Modern World.* New York: Barnes & Noble Books, 1998.

Levidow, Les. "Marketizing Higher Education: Neoliberal Strategies and Counter-Strategies." *Cultural Logic* 4, no. 1 (Fall 2000). Available at eserver.org/clogic/4-1/levidow.html.

Lewis, Bernard. *What Went Wrong: Western Impact and Middle Eastern Response.* New York: Oxford University Press, 2002.

Lunacharsky, Anatoli. *On Education: Selected Articles and Speeches,* comp. E. Dneprov, trans. Ruth English. Moscow: Progress Publishers, 1981.

Mahoney, William K. *The Artful Universe: An Introduction to the Vedic Religious Imagination.* Albany: State University of New York Press, 1998.

Makarenko, Anton S. *The Collective Family: A Handbook for Russian Parents*. Magnolia, MA: Peter Smith Publishers, 1990.

———. *The Road to Life*. Vol. 3. Moscow: State Foreign Languages Publishing House, 1955.

Marshak, David. "No Child Left Behind: A Foolish Race into the Past." *Phi Delta Kappan* 85, no. 3 (November 2003): 229–31.

Mayer, Frederick. *A History of Educational Thought*. Columbus, OH: Charles E. Merrill Books, 1962.

McLuhan, Marshall. *The Gutenberg Galaxy: The Making of the Typographic Man*. Toronto: University of Toronto Press, 1962.

Mehretu, Assefa. "Regional Integration for Economic Development of Greater East Africa." In Institute of International Studies, Office of Education, Department of Health, Education, and Welfare, *Education and Culture in Eastern Africa*, 1:1–7 (Washington, DC: GPO, 1970).

Menand, Louis. *The Metaphysical Club: A Story of Ideas in America*. New York: Farrar, Straus and Giroux, 2001.

Meyer, Adolphe E. *An Educational History of the American People*. 2nd ed. New York: McGraw-Hill, 1967.

Morison, Samuel Eliot. *Admiral of the Ocean Sea: A Life of Christopher Columbus*. Boston: Little, Brown, 1941.

Morrison, Joan, and Charlotte Fox Zabusky, comps. *American Mosaic: The Immigrant Experience in the Words of Those Who Lived It*. Pittsburgh: University of Pittsburgh Press, 1993.

Moynihan, Daniel Patrick. *Pandaemonium: Ethnicity in International Politics*. London: Oxford University Press, 1993.

Myers, David G. *The American Paradox: Spiritual Hunger in an Age of Plenty*. New Haven, CT: Yale University Press, 2000.

Negussie, Ayele. "The Political Culture of Ethiopia." In Institute of International Studies, Office of Education, Department of Health, Education, and Welfare, *Education and Culture in Eastern Africa*, vol. 1. Washington, DC: GPO, 1970.

Nikandrov, Nikolai. "Education in Modern Russia: Is It Modern?" In Kas Mazurek, Margret A. Winzer, and Czeslaw Majorek, *Education in a Global Society: A Comparative Perspective*, 209–24. Boston: Allyn and Bacon, 2000.

Nye, Joseph S., Jr. *The Paradox of American Power: Why the World's Only Superpower Can't Go It Alone*. New York: Oxford University Press, 2002.

Nyerere, Julius. *Ujamaa: Essays on Socialism*. London: Oxford University Press, 1973.

Onyango, Bernard. "Introduction to Makerere University College." In Institute of International Studies, Office of Education, Department of Health, Education, and Welfare, *Education and Culture in Eastern Africa*, 3:5–6. Washington, DC: GPO, 1970.

Pakenham, Thomas. *The Scramble for Africa: White Man's Conquest of the Dark Continent from 1876 to 1912*. New York: Avon Books, 1991.

Phillips, Kevin. *Wealth and Democracy: A Political History of the American Rich*. New York: Broadway Books, 2002.

Pinkevitch, A. P. *The New Education in the Soviet Republic*, ed. George Counts, trans. Nucia Perlmutter. N.p., 1929.

Polakow, Valerie. *Lives on the Edge: Single Mothers and Their Children in the Other America*. Chicago: University of Chicago Press, 1994.

Prescott, William H. *The Conquest of Mexico*. 1843. Reprint, New York: Bantam Books, 1964.

Riis, Jacob. *How the Other Half Lives: Studies among the Tenements of New York*. New York: Charles Scribner's Sons, 1890. Reprint. New York: Penguin Classics, 1997.

Rousseau, Jean-Jacques. *The Social Contract*. 1763. Reprint, trans. Maurice Cranston. Baltimore: Penguin Books, 1968.

Rowley, Bill. "The Future Is Not What It Used to Be," U.S. Air Force Air University, Air War College, April 1995, www.au.af.mil/au/awc/awcgate/awc-ofut.htm.

Schlechty, Phillip C. *Schools for the Twenty-First Century: Leadership Imperatives for Educational Reform*. San Francisco: Jossey-Bass, 1990.

Schlesinger, Arthur M., Jr. *The Disuniting of America: Reflections on a Multicultural Society*. New York: W. W. Norton, 1992.

Schumpeter, Joseph A. *Capitalism, Socialism, and Democracy*. 3rd ed. New York: Harper, 1950.

Segall, William E., and Anna V. Wilson. *Introduction to Education: Teaching in a Diverse Society*. 2nd ed. Lanham, MD: Rowman & Littlefield, 2004.

Shipler, David K. *A Country of Strangers: Blacks and Whites in America*. New York: Alfred A. Knopf, 1997.

Sierra, Justo. *La Educación Nacional, Obras Completas*. Vol. 8. Mexico City: Universidad Nacional Autónoma de México, 1948.

Smith, Adam. *An Inquiry into the Nature and Causes of the Wealth of Nations*. 3 vols. Dublin: Whitestone, 1776. Reprint. New York: Prometheus Books, 1991.

Sowell, Thomas. *Migrations and Cultures: A World View*. New York: Basic Books, 1996.

Spencer, Herbert. *Social Statics: The conditions essential to human happiness specified, and the first of them developed*. 1851. Reprint. New York: Robert Schalkenbach Foundation, 1995.

Stambach, Amy. *Lessons from Mount Kilimanjaro: Schooling, Community, and Gender in East Africa*. New York: Routledge, 2000.

Subramuniyaswami, Satguru Sivaya. *How to Become a (Better) Hindu*. 2nd ed. Kapaa, HI: Himalayan Academy, 2000, available at http://www.himalayanacademy.com/resources/books/hbh/hbh_table_of_contents.html.

Takaki, Ronald. *Strangers from a Different Shore: A History of Asian Americans*. Boston: Little, Brown, 1989.

Thomas, Hugh. *Rivers of Gold: The Rise of the Spanish Empire, from Columbus to Magellan*. New York: Random House, 2003.

Treaty for the Establishment of the East Africa Community. Organization of African Unity Treaty Registration No. 001/2000; United Nations Treaty Registration No. 37437. Arusha, Tanzania, November 30, 1999.

Weber, David J. *The Spanish Frontier and North America*. New Haven, CT: Yale University Press, 1992.

Weber, Stephan L. *Society in the New Russia*. New York: Palgrave Macmillan, 1999.

Wilson, A. N. *The Victorians*. New York: W. W. Norton, 2003.

Wilson, Anna Victoria, and William E. Segall. *Oh, Do I Remember! Experiences of Teachers during the Desegregation of Austin's Schools, 1964–1971.* Albany: State University of New York Press, 2001.

Woody, Thomas. *New Minds, New Men?* New York: Macmillan, 1932.

Yeager, Roger. *Tanzania: An African Experiment.* 2nd rev. ed. Boulder, CO: Westview Press, 1989.

Zahniser, Steven. *Mexican Migration to the United States: The Role of Migration Networks and Human Capital Accumulation.* New York: Garland Press, 1999.

Index

About the Author

William E. Segall is professor of social foundations in Oklahoma State University's College of Education and a professor in the university's School of International Studies. His graduate seminars in Ethiopian and Soviet educational systems are noted internationally along with his pioneering undergraduate social foundations curricula on the role schools play in understanding international problems. Segall has taught in the United States and Canada and was a principal of a Japanese juku preparing students for European and American university entrance requirements. He is coauthor, with Anna V. Wilson, of *Introduction to Education: Teaching in a Diverse Society* and *Oh! Do I Remember: Experiences of Teachers during the Desegregation of Austin's Schools, 1964–1971.*